SANDSTORM

Dedicated to the memory of my father, who loved books

SANDSTORM

Policy Failure in the Middle East

Leon Hadar

A Cato Institute Book

First published 2005 by
PALGRAVE MACMILLAN™
175 Fifth Avenue, New York, N.Y. 10010 and
Houndmills, Basingstoke, Hampshire, England RG21 6XS.
Companies and representatives throughout the world.

PALGRAVE MACMILLAN is the global academic imprint of the Palgrave
Macmillan division of St. Martin's Press, LLC and of Palgrave Macmillan Ltd.
Macmillan® is a registered trademark in the United States, United Kingdom and
other countries. Palgrave is a registered trademark in the European Union and
other countries.

ISBN 1-4039-6724-5 hardback

Library of Congress Cataloging-in-Publication Data
Hadar, Leon T.
    Sandstorm : policy failure in the Middle East / Leon Hadar.
        p.   cm.
    Includes bibliographical references and index.
    ISBN 1-4039-6724-5
    1. Middle East—Foreign relations—United States.   2. United States—Foreign
relations—Middle East.   3. Europe, Western—Foreign relations—United States.
4. United States—Foreign relations—Europe, Western.   5. United States—
Foreign relations—2001.   6. Iraq War, 2003.   7. Arab-Israeli conflict.   I. Title.
DS63.2.U5H345   2005
327.73056—dc22

                                                                        2004062062

A catalogue record for this book is available from the British Library.

Design by Letra Libre, Inc.

First edition: July 2005

10   9   8   7   6   5   4   3   2   1

Printed in the United States of America

Contents

Preface

"Indeed, there was in the United States, in the days immediately after the military victory in the Persian Gulf, a sense of omnipotence similar to the euphoria that dominated Israel after the Six-Day War in 1967—a feeling that everything was possible in arranging the political cards in the Middle East; that after Saddam Hussein, an Iraqi Thomas Jefferson would come to power in Baghdad, and a window of opportunity would be opened for democracy, stability, and peace in the region."

Sound like the fitting opening remarks of a book analyzing the U.S. military invasion of Iraq in 2003 and the ouster of Saddam Hussein? In fact, those comments were part of my conclusions to *Quagmire: America in the Middle East,* a study of U.S. intervention in that region, that was published in 1992 in the aftermath of the Gulf War and the American military victory in the Middle East that was led by President George H. W. Bush.[1]

That successful military conclusion of the war against Iraq "created unrealistic expectations that were fanned by President Bush's rhetoric,"[2] I wrote ten years ago, suggesting that the "outcome of the Gulf War illustrates the policy dilemmas Washington faces in the Middle East."[3] I argued that the goals that were enunciated in Bush I's war rhetoric about "establishing democracy in the Middle East, forming regional security arrangements, moving toward arms control agreements, and bringing peace between Arabs and Israelis—have only created unfulfilled expectations that are bound to lead to new American commitments and entanglements."[4]

"Americans who thought that it was difficult to bring democracy and free markets to the [former] Soviet Union, that had strong historical ties to the West, will discover that trying to implant those concepts in Middle Eastern systems, that are just emerging from the Middle Ages, is a long and almost impossible mission,"[5] I wrote after the Gulf War, at a time when the Wilsonian rhetoric of Bush I was at its height. I also observed that "neoconservative intellectuals in the United States insist that the global spread of democracy will also produce an increase in pro-American sentiment," but that "that is not the case in the Middle East," where "anti-Americanism pervades the Arab and Moslem worlds and stems . . . from resentment of both the tacit Arab-Israeli alliance and the direct American intervention in the region." Hence, "the chances of making the Middle East safe for democracy, along with Washington's power to move the region's states in that direction, are extremely limited." I contended that "American efforts can create a backlash and produce major political costs for perceived American interests in the area since such efforts are bound to unleash anti-Western authoritarian forces."[6]

At the same time, I expected that "an alliance with the status quo regimes in the Arab World, such as those in Saudi Arabia and Kuwait, will inevitably turn Washington into a symbol of repression in the eyes of democratic and revolutionary factions." And I concluded by arguing that the United States "faces a no-win situation in its relationship with the existing political regimes." Attempting to democratize them would produce political and social instability and create a vacuum that would entice militant and outside forces to act. Trying to secure the power of existing regimes "would create conditions that could lead to the rise of anti-American successor governments."[7]

Indeed, challenging the tenets of U.S. intervention in the Middle East in the post–Cold War era, I warned in 1992 that the Gulf War and the continuing high-profile American diplomatic and military involvement in the region would produce a backlash against U.S. interests. "Washington will ultimately begin to feel the regional political repercussions of the Gulf War," I wrote, noting that "Middle East societies have always exhibited delayed reactions to domestic and regional crises." Hence, the continuing socioeconomic problems in the Arab world, "coupled with growing hostility toward Washington because of its support for Israel and its war against Iraq, could contribute to similar delayed reaction to the Gulf War." Ten years before the terrorist attacks in New York and Washington, I predicted that "we might even see a resurgence of 'Saddamism,' a combination of Arab radicalism and Islamic fundamentalism that might as well outlive Saddam himself." The United States and the conservative Arab regimes would then face "a regional anti-American Intifada that would threaten American citizens as well as pro-American governments in the Middle East."[8]

Moreover, as I pointed out a decade ago, "European resentment over America hegemony" in the Middle East that was already evident during the Gulf War was bound to rise as Washington tried to marginalize the role of France, Germany, and other European Union (EU) members, setting the stage to what I envisaged as "The Coming American-European Struggle over the Middle East," the title of one of the chapters in *Quagmire*.[9] President Bush I, like President Bush II, expected the European allies to support the American policy in the Middle East without having a major say in the overall strategy. But in a chapter subtitled "Confronting the Gulf War Rift" and in a cautionary note that would have sounded very timely in 2003, as it did in 1992, I argued that "the message behind the European reservations about America's moves in the [Persian] Gulf was that Bush could not have his cake and eat it too: he could not continue to call the shots and expect Europe to pay the costs of unilateral U.S. action."[10] I suggested that unless the occupant of the White House recognized that reality, the Euro-American tensions over the Middle East of 1992 would be transformed into a major rift in the transatlantic alliance, as the Europeans reject the American strategy of establishing hegemony in the region.

These and related observations seem to be as relevant today, following the end of the war against Iraq, as they were more than ten years ago. That much of what I had written ten years ago sounds as though it was composed today, after another American triumph in the Middle East led by another President Bush, demonstrates the sustaining potency of the central theses that were advanced in that 1992 study and that will be re-examined in this book—with even greater force. Indeed, I am arguing that the military victory of the United States in Iraq in 2003 should serve as a new opportunity to rethink the decades-old U.S. policy in the Middle East that was fashioned in the crucible of the Cold War or what I identify as America's Middle East Paradigm (MEP). That foreign policy paradigm has been kept in place despite the end of the rivalry with the former Soviet Union. It continued to evolve following the military triumph of the Gulf War and has led eventually to the war against Iraq and its aftermath.

A core argument of this book is that while the costs of American intervention in the Middle East could be justified in the context of Cold War competition with the Soviet Union, there is no reason why the United States should have continued to sustain such costs following the collapse of the Berlin Wall. Instead, the United States should have adopted a policy of gradual disengagement, or what I describe as "constructive disengagement" from the Middle East that would create incentives for the evolution of a regional balance of power system and encourage the EU to play the role of an off-shore balancer or a "balancer of last resort" in its strategic backyard in the Eastern Mediterranean and the Persian Gulf. I suggest that the only realistic alternative to this proposed process of U.S. "constructive disengagement" from the Middle East is a long and costly route of "destructive disengagement." That means that Americans would have to use their military power and economic resources to deal with growing challenges to U.S. hegemony in the Middle East from regional players and global powers.

The group of neoconservative ideologues who were the main driving force behind the U.S. policy in the Middle East following 9/11 assume that the

United States should pay the full military and economic costs involved in preserving the MEP and American primacy in the Middle East through what amounts to the creation of a U.S.-controlled empire in the region that would serve American interests and even reflect and promote its democratic values. Their leading critics in the liberal internationalist and conservative realist wings of the foreign policy establishment contend that we can continue upholding our MEP and retaining our hegemony in the Middle East in a more cost-effective fashion, by working together with our European allies and by backing the regimes that serve our interests in the region. In order to achieve these goals these critics have put forward a strategy that challenges the neoconservative vision. They argue that Washington needs to move more forcefully to resolve the Israel/Palestine conflict, to adopt a less ambitious and more realistic program for political change in the Middle East, and to draw the outlines of a "division of labor" between the United States and its European allies so as to allow the latter to share the military and economic costs of securing Western interests in the region.

As I make clear in this book, this strategy, which has been advanced by foreign policy thinkers like Democrat Zbigniew Brzezinski[11] and Republican Brent Scowcroft[12] could help to reduce the short- and mid-term costs of maintaining the MEP and American primacy in the Middle East. They certainly should be adopted by Washington as part of an effort to replace the neoconservative imperial fantasy with a more realistic multilateralist approach. But I also argue that advancing such a policy would not be a substitute for reassessing the MEP itself and replacing it with a new Middle East paradigm. It will have to be based on recognition that as part of a new post–Cold War multipolar international system, of an Ensemble of Great Powers, Europe should gradually take the place of the United States as the "balancer of last resort" in the Middle East. Americans should encourage such a process because it would serve long-term U.S. geo-strategic and geo-economic interests. Unless we are willing to readjust U.S. foreign policy in the Middle East in that direction, we should expect to see the region becoming a major global arena for political-military competition between the Americans and the Europeans. The central theme in this book is that the war against Iraq and its aftermath have demonstrated that the Americans and the Europeans are already on a collision course in the Middle East that reflects their increasingly divergent interests in the region.

As a political scientist with a traditional realpolitik disposition, I am not very optimistic that a structural readjustment in U.S. policy could take place unless American elites and the public, having to deal with new diplomatic and military crises in the Middle East, and perhaps even take part in another major war there, recognize that the costs of maintaining U.S. hegemony in the Middle East outweigh the benefits to American interests. For better or for worse, our anarchic international system, unlike our domestic politics, lacks legitimate, effective, and peaceful mechanisms for adjustment. As great powers adapt to major changes in the balance of power only in response to systemic pressures from other powers, some form of long-term U.S. "destructive disengagement" from the Middle East is probably more likely than the more benign "constructive" one I advocate.

But we should not regard such Euro-American conflict over the Middle East as a foregone conclusion. Analysts of international politics of the idealist persuasion may be overstating their case against realists by arguing that democracies never go to war against each other; but they are correct in arguing that in democracies, foreign policy decisions are not the exclusive domain of governments and elites, but can be influenced at important critical junctures by mediating opinion makers and the general public. As a proponent of a realpolitik tradition of foreign policy I am not very optimistic that Europe and the United States will be able to cooperate in managing the transition of power in the Middle East; as someone who is an idealist by nature, however, I am still very confident about the power of public opinion in this country to affect government policies. I hope this book will at least help start a debate in the United States over the American approach the Middle East. Perhaps the outcome of such a debate will make it more likely that Washington will take the route of "constructive disengagement" from the Middle East.

In Chapter 1, "Old Paradigms Don't Just Fade Away: Why Are We (Still) in the Middle East?" I introduce the reader to the conceptual and historical background of America's Middle East Paradigm. I outline the geo-strategic and geo-economic rationales for U.S. engagement in the Middle East during the Cold War, explain the reasons for the continuing American intervention in the region in the aftermath of the end of the rivalry between the United States and the former Soviet Union, and propose why the commitment to the costly MEP should be reassessed, taking into consideration current U.S. geo-strategic and geo-economic interests.

In Chapter 2, "Tilting the Middle East Kaleidoscope: The Rising Costs of American Intervention from the Cold War to the Iraq War," I introduce the reader to the Kaleidoscope model that helps to understand the complex relationship between local, regional, and global players in the Middle East. Applying this model, I explain why outside global players, including the United States and the Soviet Union during the Cold War, have found it so costly to advance their interests in the region, and why the costs of U.S. intervention there have risen after the fall of the Berlin Wall, from the Gulf War in 1991 to the war against Iraq in 2003.

In Chapter 3, "Breaking Up Is Hard To Do: America's Fixation with the Middle East's 'Rival Twins,'" I focus on the role performed by domestic political players, in particular those advancing the interests of the "rival twins," Saudi Arabia and Israel, which, despite their conflicting agendas have a common interest in keeping the MEP alive, and I describe the way the neoconservatives have succeeded in re-energizing this paradigm in the post-9/11 period. I also challenge two axioms that the "rival twins" advance: that America is "dependent on Middle Eastern oil" and that America "needs to do something" to resolve the Israel-Palestine Conflict.

In Chapter 4, "It's Interests—Not Culture Stupid! The Euro-American Rift over the Middle East" I argue that geo-strategic and geo-economic interests in the Middle East explain the current rift between the Americans and Europeans over Iraq and Israel/Palestine and challenge the neoconservative attempt to portray it as a clash of cultures. I provide an historical background to the co-operative and competitive Euro-American relationship in the Middle East during the Cold War and its aftermath, and explain how the current American hegemonic policy in the region is igniting a European challenge.

In Chapter 5, "Extracting the 'Suez Revenge'; Can Europe Challenge U.S. Hegemony in the Middle East?" I continue to pursue the issues raised in Chapter 4, and suggest that in the long run, the changing geo-economic and geo-strategic balance of power between the Europeans and the Americans will create an environment in which a Euro-American conflict over the Middle East will become inevitable. In particular, I focus on the way the interaction between the global oil trade and the U.S. dollar and the euro, as well as the debate over the future of the Western military alliance, will affect this Euro-American conflict.

In Chapter 6, "Replacing the Middle East Paradigm: A Pax Americana—or a Northern Alliance?" I conclude the book by proposing that the only way that the United States will succeed in managing its relationship with Europeans in the Middle East is by adopting a new MEP based on pursuing a policy of American "constructive disengagement" from the Middle East as well as encouraging Europeans to become the off-shore balancers in the region. I contend that such an approach should be integrated into a long-term strategy in that the notion of American unipolarism and hegemony in the Middle East is replaced by multipolarism: an ensemble of great powers that will include the United States, Europe, Russia, and eventually China and India to deal with threats to the status quo in the Middle East and its peripheries.

Not many policy research institutions in Washington would be willing to sponsor the work of an analyst who makes such contrarian arguments, challenges the foundations of American foreign policy in the Middle East, and critiques much of what is regarded as conventional wisdom in the administration, Congress, leading think tanks, editorial pages, and broadcast news shows. But the leaders of the Cato Institute, which has served as my intellectual residence for more than a decade, and in particular, Ted Galen Carpenter, the vice president for foreign and defense policy, have encouraged me to pursue and develop my ideas on American foreign policy in general and about U.S. policy in the Middle East in particular, through policy analyses, magazine articles, op-ed pieces, as well as broadcast interviews and presentations in academic and public forums. I want to express thanks to all the staff at the Cato Institute, and in particular to Christopher Preble, director of foreign policy, for encouraging me to re-examine my views on the Middle East after 9/11 and the war in Iraq and for pressing me to write this book. I am also grateful to the Cato Institute for permitting me to rely on and use in this book some of my work that appeared in other publications.

I am also grateful to David Pervin, my editor at Palgrave Macmillan, for his guidance and constructive criticism. Meg Weaver helped transform my original manuscript into a comprehensible and readable document. Amanda Fernández was responsible for the process of turning that document into a real book.

Finally, I want to thank my wife, Alyn, for all her support.

I

OLD PARADIGMS DON'T JUST FADE AWAY

WHY ARE WE (STILL) IN THE MIDDLE EAST?

American troops bogged down in Iraq and Afghanistan, "nation building" resulting in increased likelihood of local warlords fragmenting fragile states, and the worst rift between the United States and its European allies in memory: these developments are the result of the terrorist attack against the United States on September 11, 2001. That attack has been widely seen as a bolt from the blue, an undeserved and unwarranted assault. The American policies that followed took on an air of inevitability, as if they were natural. Of course they were neither; nor was 9/11. Instead, they—including 9/11—were the result of American policies that have set in motion a conflict between the United States and a resolute foe that perceives itself as defending a Muslim world under attack. The mess the United States is in was preordained by a failure of policymakers since the end of the Cold War competition with the Soviet Union to evaluate the extent of American interests in the Middle East.

Imagine if President George H. W. Bush had, in the wake of the demise of the Soviet Union, spoken to the nation and said something along the following lines:

> Now that the Cold War is over, the time has come for the American people and its leaders to re-examine our policies and our diplomatic and military commitments in the Middle East. These were an integral part of a strategy to contain Soviet expansionism and to permit the Western economies access to the oil resources in that part of the world. As those challenges have been transformed, American policies should change. We need to redefine our interests and policies

in that area, including our military partnerships with and our economic assistance to governments there. We should be less pre-occupied with trying to resolve the conflict between Israelis and Palestinians, a localized national dispute that should be resolved by the two sides and other governments that are affected by it, including the neighboring Arab states and the Europeans.

TO DREAM THE IMPOSSIBLE DREAM

Indeed, consider the idea of an American President reassessing the need for U.S. management of the Israeli-Palestinian peace process and for U.S. troops in the Middle East. Farfetched? Even unimaginable? Agreed. But that is the point. Why is it impossible to imagine, even now, Bush I making such a speech, initiating such a revisioning of American policy in the Middle East? The reason does not lie in his famous absence of vision. Whatever else one wants to say about Bush I, his diplomacy as the Cold War ended and the Soviet Union imploded was adroit, helped no doubt by the skills of a team of seasoned advisors. No. The reason it is impossible to imagine Bush making such a speech is that it calls into question basic assumptions of America's place in the world, especially in the Middle East. To suggest that the United States should have then, and must now, reduce its involvement in the Middle East is to call into question both the importance of the region to the United States *and* the importance of the United States to the region. It is to challenge conventional wisdom that not only has the force of inertia, it also has a constituency invested in portraying the Middle East as important in itself, rather than important because of the resources, chiefly oil, it supplies to the rest of the world.

But as Americans are following the news from Iraq and the Middle East these days, two years after the start of the U.S. war against Iraq led by President George W. Bush, they are probably wishing that the older and more experienced President Bush had made that speech stating Washington's readiness to untie its entanglements in the Middle East after the Soviet Union had ceased to be a threat to U.S. interests. The expanding U.S. military intervention in the Middle East, the rising American casualties in Iraq and Afghanistan, the terrorist acts against U.S. targets, the continuing violence in the Holy Land, and the speculations about new U.S. military campaigns against Iran or Syria are all demonstrating the costs of American policies in the Middle East. Americans observe that the costs are increasing each day. But they fail to see that the policy is providing tangible benefits to their security and welfare.

The ending of the Cold War was one of those rare moments in history when there was a real opportunity to reevaluate and rethink basic assumptions underlying policies. Had there been a reassessment of U.S. ties with Saudi Arabia, Egypt, and Israel—a critical analysis of U.S. support for the status quo in the region and the United States' commitment to secure access to the oil resources in the Persian Gulf—it would have been less likely that the United States would feel the need to use its military power to force Saddam Hussein's Iraq out of Kuwait after it invaded that oil-producing state in August 1990. Under a policy of gradual disengagement of the Middle East, the United States, under the leadership of Presidents Bush I and Bill Clinton, would not have pursued a policy of American hegemony in the region. Under such a disengaged policy, the United States would not have maintained military presence in Saudi Arabia and the Persian Gulf while imposing a devastating economic embargo against the Iraqi people. It would not have backed the Saudi theocracy and the Egyptian military regime while isolating Iran. It would not have treated the Israeli occupation of the West Bank and Gaza with benign neglect while trying to resolve the Israel/Palestine conflict. And it probably would have refrained from marginalizing the political role of the Europeans in the Middle East.

But after 1990 the United States did seek to establish hegemony in the Middle East. This goal was perceived to be relatively cost-free during the administrations of Bush I and Clinton. But this goal intertwined with the effect of the "blowback" from another component of U.S. Middle East policy seen as crucial to protect Saudi Arabia—the backing for the Islamic Mujaheddin guerrillas in Soviet-controlled Afghanistan—and helped create the conditions that propelled the rise of radical Islamic terrorism, and specifically the birth of Al Qaeda. The result was the attacks on the American homeland on September 11, 2001, the ensuing war on terrorism, the invasion of Afghanistan, and the war against Iraq.

Under President Bush II, the undertaking of a hegemonic project in the Middle East has proved to be very costly, measured in rising American casualties in Iraq and Afghanistan, a rise in anti-American terrorism worldwide, the overstretching of U.S. military forces, and the increasing spending on defense and homeland security that are responsible for the ballooning budget and account deficits: clear signs of an "imperial overstretch." The occupation of Iraq and the staunch support for the policies of Israeli Prime Minister Ariel Sharon have ignited anti-American sentiments in the Arab world, in many Moslem countries, and even among the majority of the European public. These policies have wrecked the traditional strategic alliances with France, Germany, and other governments in Europe, creating a transatlantic rift that will be difficult to repair.

My goal in this book is not to engage in the drawing up of entertaining alternative "What If?" historical scenarios. Either Bush I or Clinton could have decided to adjust U.S. policy in the Middle East to respond to the changing geo-strategic and geo-economic realities of the post–Cold War era. They did not. It is impossible to press the rewind button on history.

What I am proposing is not to change the past, but to try to affect the future. A debate in Washington and around the country about U.S. foreign policy in the Middle East should begin today. The growing costs of the war in Iraq and of advancing neoconservative imperial designs in the Middle East should encourage members of the foreign policy establishment and the general public to start a debate that should have taken place after the Berlin Wall fell. This debate should not focus exclusively on the direction of American policy in the Middle East, that is, whether we are exhibiting a "pro-Israeli" or a "pro-Arab" bias, or on the methods with which this policy is being pursued, such as unilateralism vs. multilateralism. Instead, Americans should ask themselves more basic questions: Why are we involved in the Middle East? Why are we trying to maintain hegemony in that region? Does this costly intervention help secure core U.S. national interests? Or does our continuing political-military presence in the region run contrary to Washington's geo-strategic and geo-economic interests?

While the White House, Congress, and the members of the policy community in Washington seem to be mostly interested with the "how," that is, with finding out the most cost-effective ways to advance traditional American Middle East policy, my main concern is with the "why," that is, why should we continue to preserve the tenets of Cold War-era policy if, as I suggest, it has not proven to be cost-effective in terms of current U.S. interests but, in fact, is very damaging to the security and welfare of the American people. The attacks on the American homeland on September 11, 2001, by Middle Eastern terrorists opposed to U.S. policies in the region, the ensuing war on terrorism, and the invasion of Afghanistan and Iraq have demonstrated the rising costs involved in preserving American policy in the region resting on attempts to impose hegemony. It is not too late for the United States to reassess its policies in the Middle East.

Why is there such resistance to such a reassessment? Indeed, why are those responsible for making American foreign policy unable even to see the need for such rethinking?

AMERICA'S COLD WAR—ERA MIDDLE EAST PARADIGM

Current American policy toward the Middle East results from entrenched assumptions of long standing. During the Cold War there evolved what I call a

Middle East Paradigm (MEP) that guided U.S. administrations beginning in the late 1940s. Central to this MEP was the belief that competition with the Soviet Union made American involvement in the Middle East a costly but necessary way to protect American interests as the leader of the Western alliance.

The historical core and theoretical foundations of American policy in the region during the Cold War revolved around three factors that provided a separate and legitimate rationale for U.S. involvement in the region. But they also operated together as part of a policy dynamic that helped produce and depended on political, institutional, and bureaucratic interests. The three factors include:

- *Geo-strategy:* As part of a strategy to contain the Soviet Union and its allies in the region, the United States replaced Great Britain and France—military and economically weakened in the aftermath of World War II—in the role of protecting the interests of the Western alliance in the Middle East. The Soviet Union was an aggressive global power with a huge economic and military force and a crusading ideological disposition that was perceived to be as threatening to America and the West in the Cold War as Nazi Germany and Imperial Japan had been in World War II. Hence the willingness on the part of the United States to pay the high costs of the containment strategy in the Middle East and worldwide.

- *Geo-economics:* Since the end of World War II, the United States assumed the responsibility of protecting the free access of the Western economies, including those of North America, Western Europe, and Northeast Asia (Japan and South Korea) to the energy resources in the Persian Gulf through a costly partnership with Iran, Iraq, Saudi Arabia, and other oil-producing states in the region. The American readiness to provide its allies with a free ride in the form of protecting their energy resources can be explained in the context of the Cold War strategy.

- *Idealism:* Since Israel was established in the aftermath of the European Holocaust in 1948, the United States has underscored its historic and moral commitment to ensure the survival of a democratic Jewish commonwealth in the Middle East by helping Israel to maintain its margin of security as it coped with hostile Arab neighbors. While this commitment reflected a certain element of idealism in U.S. foreign policy, as opposed to basic geo-strategic and geo-economic interests, and responded as well to domestic political pressure, it eventually became an integral part of the U.S. Cold War–era policy in the Middle East, that is, of its MEP. One important outcome of that policy has been a need for the United States to juggle its commitments to Israel and to the pro-American Arab oil-producing states, while simultaneously trying to resolve the Arab-Israeli conflict.

These are the foundations of the Middle East Paradigm. The term "paradigm" has been borrowed from the work of renowned historian of science Thomas S. Kuhn, who coined it in *The Structure of Scientific Revolutions* to describe a set of received beliefs that a scientific community needs in order to practice its trade. A paradigm rests on "universally recognized scientific achievements that for a time provide model problems and solutions to a community of practitioners," Kuhn wrote.[1] Applying the term "paradigm" in their work, political scientists and journalists have been using it to represent a set of received beliefs and assumptions that for a time provide model problems and solutions to a community of policymakers and analysts and that are based on the previous achievements of the members of such a community. Here the policy paradigm I am referring to is the set of received beliefs and assumptions that have guided those making and analyzing U.S. policy in the Middle East for most of the second part of the twentieth century.

My main contention in this book is that the changing realities in the world and in the Middle East—the collapse of the Soviet Union, the changes in Euro-American relationship, and the transformation of the Arab-Israeli conflict into a local dispute—have made the MEP obsolete. The costs of maintaining the MEP are proving to be even higher than they were during the Cold War. The original rationale behind the MEP was to advance U.S. interests. It no longer does. Instead, American national interests are actually being damaged by our continuing involvement in the Middle East while most of the benefits are extracted by global as well as regional players and domestic interest groups that thrive on American intervention in that area of the world.

THE MEP AND THE STRUGGLE OVER THE EUROASIAN WORLD-ISLAND

The MEP should be placed in the context of the historical narrative of American involvement in the important geo-strategic and geo-economic area of the Middle East and its peripheries in the Eastern Mediterranean and Central and South Asia. These areas, given their oil resources and location, have been the focus of the struggle between the major global powers during most of the twentieth century. British geo-political strategist Sir Halford J. Mackinder predicted at the start of the twentieth century that the era would be dominated by conflicts over the "world-island" of Europe and Asia between Western commercial and maritime powers and land-based governments that dominated the Heartland. The geo-strategic Greater Middle East rimlands and their energy resources would become pivotal in these global conflicts that would determine the fate of Western civilization. As Mackinder put it, "Who Rules East Europe commands the Heartland. Who rules the Heartland commands the World-Island. Who rules the World-Island commands the world."[2] Both World War I and II as well as the Cold War could be seen as recurring attempts by two maritime powers, Britain and the United States, or the Anglo-American Island Powers and their allied military blocs to prevent the emergence of a Euroasian combination (German-Ottoman; German-Japanese; Soviet-Chinese) as a rival that would determine and control what is the world's political, economic, and strategic heartland. That these great rivalries had acquired ideological dimensions, as clashes between liberal and authoritarian regimes, should not divert our attention from the centrality of the geo-strategic and geo-economic components in the three great global wars of the last century. In that context, both the great land powers and the great maritime power competed over the control of the geo-strategic edges of Euroasia—the Middle East and its peripheries. At the same time, the increasing dependency of the economies and militaries of all industrialized nations on oil forced all of them to focus on Middle Eastern energy resources as a core geo-economic objective.

The high costs of U.S. military intervention and peacemaking in the Middle East were justified as part of the larger global strategic and ideological struggles in which the Western powers were involved during most of the twentieth century, during which the Middle East and by extension the conflict between Arabs and Jews in the region gradually turned into a central battleground for the rivalry between the major global powers struggling for influence and control. The United States played the leading role in the protection of Western interests both worldwide and in the Middle East beginning in the late 1940s, when the Truman Doctrine and the support for Greece and Turkey in the Eastern Mediterranean marked the start of the Cold War. The United States continued in this principal role until the end of the rivalry between the superpowers, following the defeat of the Soviets in Afghanistan at the hands of Islamic guerrillas supported by American administrations committed in the Carter and Reagan Doctrines to protecting the Persian Gulf. Hence, the Cold War started and ended in the peripheries of the Middle East. Western victory was achieved through American leadership and containment of the Soviet-led bloc.

Western and American involvement in the Middle East intertwined with the conflict between Jewish and Arab nationalism in that part of the world. The conflict between the West and its two main rivals, communism and fascism, is recalled as the central ideological drama of the historical epoch that began with the Guns of August in 1914 and ended with the collapse of the Soviet Union in

1991. One of the most captivating political sub-plots of the age, which historian Eric Hobsbawm described as the "Short Twentieth Century" (1914–1991),[3] was the encounter between Zionism and Pan-Arabism that gave birth to the Arab-Israeli Conflict and the role that the West played in it. Both the Jewish and Arab national movements, Zionism and Pan-Arabism, each attempting to provide a modern secular identity to an ancient religious community, the Jews and the Arab-Moslems, succeeded in mobilizing diplomatic and military support for political independence by riding on the political waves and economic forces of the era and by allying themselves with its major global powers. It was the competition between two great superpowers over the Middle East, with its critical geographical significance and oil resources, that endowed the Arab-Israeli conflict with geo-strategic and geo-economic importance, turning it into one of the central diplomatic-military episodes of the Cold War. At the same time, idealistic and religious factors, including the traumatic impact of the Holocaust, Christian attachment to the Holy Land, coupled with the role that pro-Israeli Jewish communities played in the political and intellectual life of the West, helped to mobilize international public opinion and transform the war between Jews and Arabs in the second part of the last century into one of the world's greatest international media spectacles.

Washington, driven by these and other international and domestic pressures, and against the backdrop of Soviet-American competition, rising international oil prices, and concerns over possible annihilation of the Jewish state, was forced during the Cold War to expand its commitments in the Middle East as part of a strategy aimed, as noted, at containing Soviet expansionism in the Middle East, securing access to its oil resources; and, third, ensuring the survival of Israel. It was not surprising, therefore, that maintaining the U.S. leadership role in the Middle East became a core U.S. national interest and was reflected in U.S. willingness to risk a nuclear war with the Soviet Union, to endure a costly oil embargo during the 1973 Middle East War, and to expand, since that war, enormous diplomatic resources to resolve the Arab-Israeli conflict and achieve stability in that region. Those policies were energized by the sense that if the United States failed to "do something" and try to resolve this or that Middle East crisis, it would be creating the conditions for Soviet advancement in the region, courting an Arab oil embargo, or making it more likely that Israel would be threatened in a war with the Arabs. It is the scenario of the 1973 Middle East War and the images it produced— the threat of a nuclear confrontation between the United States and the Soviet Union, the high economic price resulting from an Arab oil embargo, Israeli-Jews fighting for their lives—that has left an enduring impact on the thinking of American presidents, lawmakers, and journalists. Hence, the knee-jerk reaction that "we have to do something, or else" exhibited by U.S. policy and opinion makers when something dramatic has taken place in the Middle East, such as violence in the West Bank, demonstrations in Saudi Arabia, or an assassination of an Arab leader. Their reactions and policies have been and still are conditioned by the MEP.

OBSOLETE FOREIGN POLICY PARADIGMS AND OLD GENERALS

Challenging the American public and policymakers to break out of the mold of obsolete and costly thinking and take a fresh look at taken-for-granted premises of U.S. foreign policy, in general, and in the Middle East, in particular, can sometimes be an impossible mission. To paraphrase and apply what General Douglas MacArthur once said about old generals, aging foreign policy paradigms do not simply fade away.

It takes time for great powers and their elites and publics to re-adjust their foreign policy paradigms to changes in the geo-strategic and geo-economic balance of power. It is usually the outcomes of international crises and wars that make it clear that a great power lost the game, and that another great power is emerging. And even then, there could be a long lag before we recognize the construction of a new foreign policy and the ensuing conventional wisdom about "who is up, and who is down" in the international system. Reading old copies of the *New York Times* or other major newspapers from the late 1940s and early 1950s one could get the impression that Britain and France were still great world powers at that time, despite the fact that World War II had decimated those two empires militarily and economically. It was only following the 1956 Suez debacle, the French withdrawal from Southeast Asia and North Africa, and the loss of the last British imperial outposts in the Persian Gulf, that Britain and France were starting to be perceived as nothing more than mid-sized European powers, occupying a space far below the American and Soviet top dogs in the global ranking order. At the same time, the United States and the Soviet Union, through the process of building their economic and military power and through their competition in the Middle East and elsewhere, were identified as the "superpowers," with Britain and France relegated to the role of allies of the American superpower. The foreign policy paradigm of multipolarity was replaced with one based on the notion of bipolarity.

Sheer inertia that is so much a part of human nature may explain why we sometimes continue to obsess with that with which we are familiar and accept the status quo. Political, bureaucratic, commercial, and media players have vested interests in ensuring that certain international issue-areas remain on the top of the policy agenda. These international issue-areas continue to receive presidential attention, budget spending, and press coverage, even if most Americans cease to be affected directly by them. After all, it was quite difficult for the members of the inside-the-beltway crowd in Washington, ranging from the Foreign Service and the military to think tankers and journalists, to get used to the idea that the Cold War was over. They have yet to recover from their post–Cold War depression, having been forced to live in a dull world without Checkpoint Charlie, arms control summits, Soviet studies, and other Cold World thrills, not to mention those huge budgets that went to pay for big and small wars, intelligence games, and aid packages to this or that "friendly" dictator. All of which explains perhaps why these former Cold War warriors seem to be afflicted by what could be described as the Enemy-Deprivation Syndrome, as they search for new "threats" to analyze, cover, and contain, whether it's China, Saddam Hussein, or Islamic terrorism. The media and opinion makers transmit the foreign policy paradigm to the general public, who in turn absorb it as conventional wisdom. Not surprisingly, many Americans probably assume now that the United States has always been involved in the Middle East in protecting "Oil and Israel" and in trying to make peace between Arabs and Jews. They would probably be surprised to learn that there has never been a formal military alliance between Israel and the United States and that Americans do not receive most of their energy imports from the Middle East.

We sometimes assume that foreign policymaking is a process in that leaders try to make decisions in a rational way, based on cost-effective calculations. It is also often assumed that political scientists, policy analysts, and journalists help leaders make decisions by providing them with all the necessary information and "right" ideas that develop eventually into coherent foreign policy paradigms. But there is a crucial difference between the evolution of a foreign policy paradigm and that of scientific paradigms that Kuhn proposed. A shift in professional commitments to shared assumptions, or to a scientific paradigm takes place when an anomaly "subverts the existing tradition of scientific practice" leading to what Kuhn described as a "scientific revolution," that is, "the tradition-shattering complements to the tradition-bound activity of normal science." Kuhn noted that new scientific paradigms require the reconstruction of prior assumptions and the re-evaluation of prior fact. That can be a difficult and time-consuming process that is strongly resisted by the established scientific community.[4]

Changes in scientific paradigms take place in response to observations of a certain reality that is not influenced directly by the work of the scientist. The scientist does not make objects gravitate to earth. He or she can observe them doing this while recognizing that the process of observing the phenomenon will not change the physical reality. But when it comes to politics and other areas of human action, including foreign policy, the experts who generate the paradigms that become the basis for the formulation and implementation of policy are not only involved in a process of observing reality. In fact, by disseminating information and constructing ideas that are then transformed into policies, these experts help shape political reality. Unlike the physical scientists, they can make objects fall. It is their paradigms that help create the stage for international crises and encourage nations to go to war.

Discussions of U.S. foreign policy decisions tend to create the impression that such decisions were rational responses to events beyond the control of the policymaker and that he or she was simply reacting to a natural phenomenon. The terrorist attacks on the Pentagon and the World Trade Center supposedly came out of the clear blue sky and U.S. policymakers were forced to come up with a policy, with military and diplomatic responses. But those who were being asked to draw the outlines of such a policy and implement it were the same policy analysts and policymakers who had shaped the long-standing U.S. approach in the Middle East and shared this policy paradigm, the MEP. It was this paradigm that led to the creation of the Islamic Mujaheddin in Afghanistan, to the U.S. military presence in Saudi Arabia, to the American support for Israel. It was those earlier U.S. policies in the Middle East and South Asia that helped set the stage for the events of 9/11. To put it differently, the events of 9/11 were in part a result of specific policies and the paradigms that produced them, much as the Soviet Union's invasion of Afghanistan led to its own unraveling and the release of centrifugal forces that continue to threaten the Russian Federation.

Only when the costs of maintaining a certain foreign policy prove to be higher than its benefits in terms of national interests and as measured in lives and money—and when that reality becomes obvious to both the elites and the public—are policymakers forced to bid reluctant farewells to the outdated and expensive diplomatic and national security paradigms that they took for granted.

It is difficult to imagine that those who had promoted these policies and existing paradigms would have been ready to admit after 9/11 that they observed an anomaly that subverted the existing tradition of the American MEP and were ready now to welcome a revolution in American foreign policy. In fact, as the post-9/11 events demonstrated, when it comes to foreign policy, the tendency among practitioners is to invest even more resources in sustaining the existing paradigm. That process helps create the conditions for new international crises and wars, which require policy analysts and policymakers to continue to circle the wagons around the vulnerable paradigm. The promotion of an even higher level of U.S. intervention in the Middle East after 9/11 is just another example of policy analysts and makers trying to protect the MEP.

So it is not surprising that if and when an individual dares to challenge the MEP, to suggest that it should be reassessed and propose a new MEP based on the notion of American disengagement from the Middle East, he or she is treated at best as a political Cassandra, or at worst as a political extremist, as an "isolationist," the term that members of Washington's foreign policy establishment usually use to bash those who disagree with them. Disengagement from the Middle East, you say? But what about "the oil?" Or "Israel?" Or "terrorism?" The United States is supposed to "do something" about that. At least, that is what the old MEP conditioned Americans to expect.

THE HIGH COSTS OF THE MEP

American policies in the Middle East involved the employment of huge military and financial resources and included the formation at various times of military alliances with Iraq, Iran, Turkey, and Pakistan; covert operations in most of the countries in the region, including the support for bloody military coups; direct military intervention in Lebanon; East-West confrontations, including one of the most dangerous ones during the Cold War in 1973; and very large economic and military assistance programs. Almost all of these policies promoted geo-economic and geo-strategic U.S. interests, and, with the exception of the support for Israel, had very little to do with the advancement of idealistic U.S. goals of spreading democracy and human rights. In fact, most of the regimes that the United States befriended in the Middle East, including at one time Saddam Hussein's Iraq, were some of the worst violators of American values of political freedom, liberalism, secularism, women's rights, and a free press.

Richard Perle and David Frum, in a brief Introduction to the Middle East 101 that they provide in their book, *An End to Evil*, depict the United States as having played a benign and enlightened, if not altruistic role in the region since 1945.[5] But there was nothing benign or enlightened, for example, about the U.S. move in 1953 to depose Prime Minister Mohammad Mossadegh and install Mohammad Reza Shah Pahlavi to the Peacock Throne in Iran or about the U.S. alliance with the authoritarian and corrupt Arab regimes in the Persian Gulf and Egypt and the massive military and economic assistance to the Jewish state. After all, this extensive U.S. intervention in the Middle East ignited the Arab oil embargo in 1973, led to a dangerous nuclear standoff with the Soviets during the Yom Kippur War, helped create the conditions for the 1979 revolution in Iran, and served as a backdrop to a list of Middle Eastern wars and anti-American terrorism.

Indeed, the costs of intervention in the Middle East for any outside global power are very high. It is a region where the boundaries between local, national, regional, and international issues are blurred, where most governments do not enjoy political legitimacy, and where a variety of identities—tribal, ethnic, religious, and national—compete for the allegiance of the people. An intervention by an outsider to advance its interests through an alliance with regional and local players usually results in efforts by other unsatisfied regional and local players to form counter-alliances and secure the support of other outside powers. Hence I use the model of a kaleidoscope to describe politics in the Middle East, reflecting the never-ending shifting alliances and realignments that a global power like the United States has to deal with when it gets involved in the region. I detail some of the costs that such involvement produced for the United States throughout the Cold War, as it tried to manage its relationship with client states like Israel, Egypt, and Saudi Arabia—as well as the relations between those clients—as part of a strategy to contain the Soviet Union and its clients in the region.

The costs of American engagement in the Middle East were acceptable during the Cold War as a way to protect core U.S. national interests. That this engagement took place in the context of the bipolar system and as part of a containment strategy meant that while the risks were very high in terms of the potential threat of nuclear war, in reality the costs were manageable, since the two superpowers were constrained by each other in their ability to expand their presence in the region and were able to restrain their respective client states and ensure that the costs did not become unbearable. The United States, like the Soviet Union, adopted an opportunistic policy aimed at preventing the rival superpower from controlling the Middle East. It certainly did not attempt to establish hegemony or create an imperial system in the region.If policymakers ever considered such ambitious and expansionist designs, they were aware that the systemic checks set by the reality of the Cold War would not have permitted them to promote an imperial strategy.

BUSH THE FIRST AND CLINTON: THE RISE TO AMERICAN HEGEMONY IN THE MIDDLE EAST

That with the end of the Cold War and the collapse of the Soviet Union the United States failed to take steps to reassess its military and diplomatic presence in the region meant that the old MEP remained alive and well. U.S. administrations attempted to contain regional powers like Iraq and Iran, and tried to resolve the Israel/Palestine conflict; but without a counter-balancing challenge from a competing global power, the decision by Washington to continue its high-profile engagement in the Middle East meant that the United States emerged as the only dominant outside player in the region. Hence, protecting the MEP under President Bush I and President Clinton left the United States no choice but to bear the costs of maintaining hegemony in the region. And until 9/11, those costs, including those involved in carrying out the Gulf War, seemed to be relatively manageable. But the terrorist attacks on the American homeland and the occupation of Afghanistan and Iraq demonstrated that Pax Americana in the Middle East would not remain cost-free; the costs would actually become higher than they were during the Cold War. There are no free empires!

Some observers have argued that American policy in the Middle East has been seized by domestic lobbies as a way of explaining why it does not reflect U.S. national interests. I describe some of the domestic political constraints that operate on U.S.-Middle East policy, including pressures from those in Washington who lobby in support of Israel and Saudi Arabia, and challenge some of the main arguments promoted by these lobbies, such as the notion that the United States is dependent on Middle Eastern oil resources or that Israel's long-term survival depends on American support. At the same time, I emphasize that the endurance of the MEP has to do with more than just the power of the "Israel lobby" on Capitol Hill or the machinations of Saudi Arabia and its business allies in Washington. The members of the two main wings of the American foreign policy establishment—the liberal internationalists who influence the thinking of Democratic presidents, and the conservative realists who still remain influential among members of the moderate Republican elite—have been committed to maintaining the MEP as a basis for U.S. policy in the Middle East. Without the willingness of those forces to support American involvement in the region, neither Israel's friends in the American Jewish community and the Christian Evangelical movement nor the heads of American oil companies would have succeeded in forcing the United States into its costly intervention in that part of the world.

Indeed, when Saddam Hussein invaded Kuwait in 1990, America's foreign policy establishment was provided with an opportunity to keep alive the Cold War era's MEP and reassert the American position in the region. U.S. policies in the Middle East from the Gulf War until 9/11 were characterized by a growing diplomatic engagement and drive toward U.S. military hegemony in the Middle East. This process helped perpetuate the status quo and secure in power unpopular authoritarian regimes. The United States played a leading role in trying to resolve the Israel/Palestine conflict while discouraging in the process the creation of legitimate sources of power and the formation of regional balance of power systems, and denying the Europeans any significant strategic role in the Middle East.

These American policies that reflected the commitment to the MEP were promoted in different ways but with similar outcomes by the foreign policy architects of the administrations of Bush I and of Clinton.[6] These two presidents were able to protect the U.S.-dominant position in the Middle East through a traditional policy mix of realpolitik (in the case of Bush I) and old-fashioned internationalism (during the Clinton presidency) that resulted in what could be described as the deluxe Pax Americana project in the region. Working through the United Nations (UN) and the North Atlantic Treaty Organization (NATO) and by counting on the backing of the pro-American Arab regimes in Egypt and the Persian Gulf, both Bush I and Clinton succeeded in placing Washington in the Middle East's driver's seat without paying the kind of very high military and economic costs that would have made such policies seem unbearable to the American public. Hence, American hegemony in the Middle East could have been preserved without harming Bush I's efforts to end the Cold War and bring the moribund Soviet Union into the Western fold and while permitting Clinton to promote the globalization agenda and a Pacific-oriented commercial diplomacy.

Bush's removal of Saddam Hussein from Kuwait and President Clinton's dual containment of Iraq and Iran allowed the United States to prevent two major military powers in the region from challenging the American position and threatening Saudi Arabia and other oil-rich Arab states. But it also made it impossible for regional players to establish new balances of power to deal with their own security in a way that would not have required American leadership. The U.S. drive toward the dominant position in the Middle East was achieved without forcing the United States to invade the capitals of countries in the region and to retain large numbers of American troops. That explains why both Bush I and Clinton rejected the advice to help Kurdish and Shiite rebels topple the regime in Baghdad, a move that would have brought about the disintegration of Iraq and spread instability to other countries in the region. Instead, the United States maintained a low-profile, over-the-horizon military presence in the Persian Gulf, imposing military and economic sanctions against Iraq and Iran, using limited military force to punish Iraq for alleged transgressions, and upholding two "no-fly zones" for Shiite Muslims in the south and Kurds in the north, with the latter turning into a quasi-autonomous Kurdish area. Those policies seemed sufficient to deter Iraq and Iran; and while the Europeans were critical occasionally of these policies, they could not muster the will or power to oppose them and come up with a coherent alternative agenda.[7]

The launching of the Madrid Peace Conference by George H. W. Bush and the indirect support Clinton was giving to Israeli-Palestinian moves toward reconciliation, known as the Oslo Peace Process, created the sense that America was "doing something" to resolve Arab-Israeli differences. These policies as well as the diplomatic "fire brigades" Clinton dispatched to the Middle East to deal with the occasional outbreak of Israeli-Palestinian violence helped relieve the concerns of the pro-American Arab regimes and made it difficult for Europe to exploit U.S. support for Israel as a way of winning diplomatic brownie points with the Arabs.[8] In that sense, the Bush and Clinton administrations were able to juggle the sometimes conflicting commitments to Israel and the Arab allies in what looked to be a successful diplomatic balancing act. Similarly, neither Bush I nor Clinton was forced to pay the major domestic political costs involved in trying to pressure the Jewish state to make painful concessions as part of a peace agreement and in a way that would antagonize Israel's supporters on Capitol Hill and elsewhere and harm their respective political standings in the electorate.

While Presidents Bush I and Clinton were doing their best to preserve the status quo on the two fronts of the Middle East, the Persian Gulf and Israel/Palestine, with limited costs, they seemed to be expanding U.S. hegemony over former Soviet Moslem republics in Central Asia and their rich energy resources. A weak post–Cold War Russia and a contained Iran—each of which have clear strategic and economic interests in the region—were not in a position to challenge the growing U.S. involvement in Central Asia.[9] On the other hand, the notion that Washington was unwilling to risk too many American military and economic resources became quite obvious as Washington projected a detached and low-key approach to the continuing political instability in Pakistan and the disintegration in Afghanistan, both of which did not seem to directly affect American interests.[10]

To put it differently and in a post-9/11 perspective, U.S. policymakers were doing what seems to come naturally to them, ensuring that the MEP would remain in place as a guide for American policy in the Middle East. The MEP continued to fly on automatic pilot. But it also dragged with it a lot of baggage, by helping to create the conditions that helped strengthen Osama Bin Ladin and his terrorist network—continuing the alliance with the Mujaheddin guerrillas in Afghanistan, tolerating Pakistani and Saudi support for the Taliban, maintaining a military presence in Saudi Arabia and the Persian

Gulf, imposing sanctions on Iraq, and helping Israel preserve the status quo in Palestine.

Here are some examples of what American policymakers could have done if they had made a decision to dispense with the Cold War–era Middle East paradigm. They could have declared victory in the Cold War and started reducing American military and diplomatic commitments in the region. That would have created incentives for regional and local players to reform their bankrupted political and economic systems and deal with legitimate security problems. A low-key U.S. position in the Middle East would have also encouraged the Europeans to pay the costs of protecting their own interests in the region. If Washington lacked the will and the power to bring an end of Palestinian-Israeli violence, it could have encouraged the Europeans to contribute more time and resources to mediate a peace agreement in Israel/Palestine.

9/11 AND THE SECOND INTIFADA: EXPOSING THE REAL COSTS OF HEGEMONY

But American policymakers were not ready to do that, and with the costs of those policies still being perceived as relatively low by most Americans, there was no public pressure on Washington to disengage from the Middle East. So on 9/11 the automatic pilot carrying the MEP on the road toward costs-free hegemony lost control. It suddenly became obvious that the attempt to maintain the Pax Americana project in the Middle East with relatively minimal costs was not going to work in the long run. The Middle Eastern chickens were bound to come home to roost—sooner or later. Some critics describe the devastating outcomes of U.S. conduct in the Middle East as "blowback," as the unintended consequences of American policies.[11] Another way of describing what happened is to suggest that the best and the brightest, who were managing American policy in the Middle East, assumed that the costs of maintaining the MEP in order to advance their policies would not require using new and very expensive policy methods or the investment of enormous military and diplomatic resources that are more in accordance with the needs of full-blown empire.

But it was not only 9/11 that made it clear to the public that Pax Americana in the Middle East entailed major costs. The collapse of the Camp David Israeli-Palestinian peace summit and the start of the new Intifada in 2000 demonstrated that the U.S. diplomatic juggling act between the Israelis and the Arabs over the future of Israel/Palestine necessitated a huge investment in terms of presidential time, diplomatic resources, and domestic politics. From what looked like a win-win game during most of the 1990s, that of trying to go through the Palestinian-Israeli diplomatic motions and making everyone happy, the White House suddenly found itself in the middle of a lose-lose game. If it could not "deliver" Israel, it would antagonize the Palestinians and the Arabs, and if it did pressure Israel, it could damage its support on Capitol Hill as well as support from critical constituencies in the coming presidential and congressional elections. And by failing to do either, after creating expectations that it was about to finally bring an end to the conflict between Jews and Arabs in the Holy Land, the Clinton administration admitted that it could not perform its role in peacemaking duties as regional hegemon. The ensuing violent Palestinian Intifada, which broadcast live 24/7 on Arab-language cable news stations, was directed against both Israel and the United States. It intertwined with the general upsurge of anti-Americanism in the Middle East. From that perspective, the failure in Camp David can be seen as a prologue to 9/11, another clear indication that American hegemony in the Middle East could not remain cost-free as it did during most of the 1990s.

BUSH II AND THE NEOCONSERVATIVES

A paradigm that was perhaps required for U.S. policymakers as a way of preserving the strength of American interests during the Cold War is now drawing the United States into one of the most costly and bloody quagmires since the Vietnam War. Much of the media reporting and scholarly analysis of the war in Iraq has been focused on the role that neoconservative intellectuals and policymakers, or "necons," have played in formulating and implementing U.S. policies in the Middle East. This is not the place for another anti-neocon tract that bashes a secret "cabal" of Leon (Trotsky) fans and Leo (Strauss) groupies for "hijacking" post-9/11 U.S. foreign policy. The neocons are simply the logical extreme of America's Middle East paradigm that evolved during the Cold War. The neocons are central to this analysis because of the crucial role they have played in reviving and re-energizing the MEP following the shocks it experienced during the Second Intifada and 9/11, which demonstrated the growing costs of maintaining U.S. hegemony in the Middle East. Indeed, applying Kuhn's line of thinking, it can be argued that the Second Intifada and 9/11 were the kind of earthquakes that should have forced the members of the community of foreign policymakers and analysts to recognize that the old paradigm provides them with neither sufficient explanations to the problems America faces in the Middle East nor with the necessary solutions to them. The neocons were there in the White House and the Pentagon, in think tanks and editorial boards, to provide Washington with a strategy to protect the exposed paradigm and to sustain U.S. involvement in the Middle East with the full force of American military and diplomatic power—and as part of an American imperial project that disregarded the concerns of regional players and the interests of European allies. In a way, the neocons were basically arguing that the cost-free policy methods advanced by Bush I and Clinton were not viable anymore if one wanted to protect the MEP and ensure U.S. dominant position in the Middle East.

The neoconservative policymakers who have guided U.S. Middle East policies since 9/11 under the administration of George W. Bush proposed and utilized policy methods to protect the MEP that were different than those applied by Bush I and Clinton and their policy advisors. Instead of an off-shore balancing strategy in which the United States maintained its hegemony through mostly indirect military engagement in the Middle East, the neocons promoted a strategy based on direct and unilateral American presence in the region, with the occupation of Afghanistan and Iraq being the first steps to the promotion of American imperial policy, including the possible military moves against Syria and Iran. By extension, the control of the oil resources in the Persian Gulf would not depend anymore on the goodwill of governments in the region, but would be determined exclusively by American military power. The neocons also replaced the policy based on the need to juggle American commitments to Israel and to its Arab partners with one based on total support for the Israeli position, with America continuing to work to resolve the Israel/Palestine conflict—but under the terms set by a nationalist Israeli agenda. The result has been the political and ideological marriage between the American Empire and Greater Israel. Finally, neoconservatives based their strategy of unilateral American military presence in the Middle East on the assumption that the European allies should not play any role in determining the future of the Middle East. In fact, Europe was seen as a global rival that should be expelled from the region. As the neoconservative narrative described it, an American-Israeli alliance in the Middle East would now be able to stand up to the global threat posed by a Euro-Arab axis in the region.[12]

The main challenge to the neocons comes from the liberal internationalist and conservative realist foreign policy practitioners and analysts who are bound to have a major impact on future U.S. policies, if and when, as I predict, the neoconservative methods to preserve the MEP prove to be a disaster. The challenge to the neoconservatives from rival wings of the American foreign policy establishment is not based on a rejection of the MEP, however, but on the suggestion that a more cost-effective set of methods be deployed so as to reconstruct another deluxe Pax Americana in the Middle East. By working through multilateral institutions like the UN and NATO that will share the economic and military burden of occupying Iraq and Afghanistan, the United States will still be able to maintain its hegemony in the region. American interests in the region will continue to be secured by co-opting the Saudis and other Arab regimes dependent on American assistance, and by re-projecting a balanced policy in dealing with the Israel/Palestine conflict. America will remain committed to Israel, but will also be able to force it to make the kind of concessions that the Saudis and other Arab governments and the Europeans demand. Hence the debate between the neoconservatives and their more international- ist and realist rivals seems to be over the means to achieve the primacy of the U.S. position in the region, between the advocates of a full-blown empire and the proponents of an "Empire Lite."

THE IMPORTANCE OF BEING CONSTRUCTIVELY DISENGAGED

There is another way of looking at the future of U.S. policy. Changes in the global balance of power and the constellation of forces are bound to lead to U.S. disengagement from the region, and the main question that remains is not whether such a disengagement will happen, but under what conditions it will take place. For a variety of historical, political, and institutional reasons, in- cluding the force of inertia, it has become very difficult for U.S. policy- and opinion makers to dispense with the old MEP until the costs of maintaining it in terms of lives and dollars become so obvious to the American public that it will then force the administration and Congress to start a process of disen- gagement from the Middle East. The sooner that process takes place, the less painful the process of disengagement from the region will be.

There is a difference between what I call "constructive disengagement," a scenario in which the Americans take steps to end their hegemonic project in the Middle East and start shifting the economic and military burden of secur- ing order and stability in the region to the Europeans, and the route of "de- structive disengagement," in which regional and global pressures, taking the form of new Middle Eastern crises and wars, force the United States to cut and run from the Middle East.

An example of "constructive disengagement" is the mostly orderly and peaceful way in which Britain took steps to shrink its military commitments in Central and South America as part of a cooperative strategy, with the United States assuming the responsibility of a "balancer of last resort" in those regions in the years following the enunciation of the Monroe Doctrine, and especially after the American Civil War and, even later, after President Theodore Roosevelt's "Corollary" to the Monroe Doctrine. The end result was that the Americans and the British moved toward adopting a common approach toward their interests not only in Central and South America, but in the entire Western Hemisphere.[13] At the same time, the process by which Britain reduced its military and diplomatic commitments in the Middle East during the twentieth century and especially since the end of World War II demonstrates the high costs involved in "destructive disengagement." British sacrifices during World War II to maintain its position in the Eastern Mediterranean and the Persian Gulf accentuated the dilemmas involved in sustaining its empire in the region, especially as the Americans applied their economic and military pressures on London to give up its overseas colonies and outposts. The humiliating 1956 Suez Crisis served as the diplomatic-military straw that broke the British camel's Middle Eastern back and created the conditions for the United States to assume the full responsibility and costs of leading and protecting the interests of the Western alliance in the region and in opposition to the expansionist Soviet moves there. Britain eventually accepted the primacy of the United States in protecting Western interests in the Middle East, but only after paying a high price in British lives, money, and prestige.

NEEDED: A NEW MEP

Great powers play the central role in shaping international relations and regional politics. Hence, a study of the interaction between the Middle East and the international system is one that analyzes the relationship between great powers and local and regional players. Indeed, America's MEP and its intervention in the region can be understood only in the context of the American-Soviet rivalry of the Cold War and the way local and regional players benefited or were set back by this competition. This realpolitik-type narrative is predicated on the premise that the American drive for hegemony in the Middle East inevitably produces challenges by the countervailing force of other global powers cooperating with regional and local players. I expect that unless American policies change sometime soon, a Euro-American rivalry in the Middle East in this century could acquire some of the elements of the Soviet-American confrontation in the region in the last century. Even under a best-case scenario, such a rivalry could not be avoided, but perhaps managed more effectively and postponed for a while. From that perspective, the Euro-American rift was not a sub-plot in the story of U.S. policy in the Middle East between the Gulf War and the war against Iraq; rather it is the main plot and the main driving force behind the American strategy—and it could determine the future interaction between the Middle East and the international system.

As I argue in the book, the rift between the United States and the Europeans during the war against Iraq in 2003 is in a way a mirror image of the tensions between them during the war against Egypt in 1956. It is possible that administrations in Washington will take steps to repair those rifts and achieve a détente of sorts with the Europeans in the coming years. A foreign policy drawn up by an internationalist or a realist U.S. administration based on some level of cooperation with the Europeans in dealing with the Middle East would be most welcome. The application of such policy methods will be less harmful to U.S. interests than continuing to pursue the neoconservative approach, which will only make the Euro-American rift unbridgeable and possibly lead to growing challenges to the U.S. position in the Middle East with rising costs in lives and money to the American people. In short, the needed foreign policy would be a cost-cutting one, which would still be based on the assumption that the United States can maintain its primacy in the region by applying the methods utilized by Bush I and Clinton. At the end of the day, it will still be a policy based on U.S. hegemony that will face regional and global challenges. The Europeans will continue to enjoy the benefits provided by American involvement in the Middle East, including free access to the region's oil resources. But at the same time, they will be competing with the United States for influence in the Middle East and exploiting its problems there.

To put it in economic terms, most of the members of the American foreign policy establishment assume a monopoly of American diplomatic and military power in the Middle East and worldwide; the internationalists and the realists are willing to offer the Europeans a share in the market, but under the condition that the United States continue to own most of the stock in the Middle East and elsewhere. They all want the United States to remain in the driver's seat; the realists and the internationalists will permit the Europeans to change the oil, replace the tires, and perhaps even pick up the kids from school. What I am proposing here is the creation of a global oligopoly, in that the United States divides the market with the Europeans. It allows them to take turns in driving the car; more important, the Europeans can have a say in determining where the car is heading. In this multipolar system, the United States will be ready to turn over the Middle East "market share" to European control. Such a process could be gradual and "constructive" and in the first stage could take the form of an interim Euro-American condominium in the region.

But I think that it is more conceivable that tensions over the Middle East will intensify in the coming years and will take the form of political-military and economic competition. A more unified and assertive EU will take advantage of the setbacks that the United States will have to contend with in trying to maintain its primacy in the Middle East through its military presence in the Persian Gulf and continuing efforts to manage the Israel/Palestine conflict. Indeed, as realist foreign policy political scientist John Mearsheimer points out, in an international system characterized by anarchy, great powers "are always searching for opportunities to gain power over their rivals, with hegemony as their final goal."[14] As the international system lacks legitimate and effective mechanisms to recognize and validate changes in the balance of power, crises and wars end up determining the outcome of those changes. This could certainly happen in the case of a Euro-American rivalry in the Middle East.

Critics would probably challenge my line of reasoning by arguing that the attacks on New York and Washington by a Middle Eastern terrorist organization and the ensuing war on terrorism demonstrate that the United States has no choice but, and in fact, now has an obligation, to increase both its military and diplomatic commitments in the Middle East, including trying to resolve the Arab-Israeli conflict, especially since—their argument would go—the EU doesn't have the political will or the military capability to deal with the twin threats of terrorism and weapons of mass destruction (WMD) emanating from the Middle East.

I will turn this criticism on its head: The refusal by American decision makers, Republicans and Democrats, to reassess U.S. involvement in the Middle East in the aftermath of the Cold War and to adopt instead a policy aimed at maintaining American hegemony in the region by pressing for specific policies in the Persian Gulf and Israel/Palestine helped produce the kind of anti-American sentiments in the Arab world that brought about 9/11 and the rise of terrorism against the United States. This U.S. policy also prevented the Europeans from increasing their influence in the Middle East and the regional players from developing new balance-of-power systems. Hence there is a direct line that connects the Gulf War in 1991 to the war against Iraq in 2003 and it takes the form of America's MEP, which I challenge in this book. It is not too late, I believe, to reassess this paradigm and to adopt an alternative approach, to choose a new MEP.

2

TILTING THE MIDDLE EAST KALEIDOSCOPE

THE RISING COSTS OF AMERICAN INTERVENTION FROM THE COLD WAR TO THE IRAQ WAR

After a storm, be it political or meteorological, passes over the Middle East, the region returns to its eternal stillness, as though nothing has happened. The people come out of hiding, remove the sand from their faces, shake the dust from their clothes, and return to the desert's routine: the daily struggle over water wells and grazing spaces. The desert's tribes go back to the ritual of signing and breaking alliances, and their leaders meet at night before the fire to contemplate the next raid against their hostile neighbors.

It is in front of the burning fire that the American guest is treated to another ritual of Middle Eastern hospitality. The tribe's elders listen to his advice and nod with polite approval as the foreigner, the child of some faraway green-pastured land, suggests that the time has come to replace primal desert hatred with eternal peace. As the American guest outlines his vision of a new Middle Eastern order, the product of the Western mind, with its contemporary images of board room directors raising glasses of scotch after the signing of successful business deals, the Arab elders, adhering to Moslem religious rules by sipping their orange juice, recall the other foreigners who have passed through the region: the Greeks, the Romans, the Crusaders, the British, the French, and now the Americans. Those foreigners and others all hoped to recreate the Middle East in their own image, only to retreat from the region humiliated and exhausted, abandoning their regional allies and leaving nothing more than their imprint on some precious archaeological item.

THE SAME OLD–SAME OLD MIDDLE EAST . . .

As the dust settles in the Middle East following the transition of power in Iraq from the United States to an Iraqi leadership, Washington is finding to its chagrin that, notwithstanding all the great expectations, no New Iraq has been born and that the post-Saddam Middle East looks quite familiar. Despite the continuing dominance of strong governments in that part of the world, the lives of most men and women continue to be, as Thomas Hobbes put it, "solitary, poor, nasty, brutish and short." Most of the changes that have taken place in the Middle East are not the reflection of the grand designs drawn in the White House and neoconservative think tanks and editorial boards: The hoped-for creation of a politically democratic and stable Iraq that would serve as a shining model for the entire Middle East and its peripheries has failed to materialize.

But it is not the first time that a storm passed over the Middle East to leave behind misery, destruction, and broken dreams. Following the end of the Gulf War in 1991 and the Madrid Peace Conference there were high expectations in Washington that a new American-led order would be established in the Middle East. The Madrid Peace Conference and the ensuing Oslo peace process were supposed to lay the foundations for a New Middle East, one in which Israelis and Palestinians would make peace and the region would be integrated into the expanding and prosperous global economy, with young and hip Israelis and Palestinians making money, surfing the Internet, watching MTV, and doing a lot of "cool stuff" in a new high-tech start-up in Israel's Silicon Wadi (valley). That was certainly the New Middle East vision promoted by Shimon Peres[1] and echoed by the leading fan of globalization and Oslo in America, *New York Times* columnist Tom Friedman.[2]

Ten years later and it is the same old, same old Middle East. The conservative—or are they "moderate conservatives"?—Ayatollahs are still in power in Teheran and all the indications are that they, and not the "moderates," are strengthening their grip over power, notwithstanding the dreams shared by American neoconservatives about enacting another regime change that would unleash a democratic revolution in that country.[3] The Hashemites are still in control in Jordan, with its Palestinian majority, and their traditional rivals, the

Saudis, remain firmly in control of that oil-rich country. As the Saudis confront deadly terrorist attacks from antiregime terrorist groups, they "round up the usual dissidents"[4] and continue to confound all those forecasters with their doomsday scenarios about the royal family's imminent collapse.[5] The military is still in charge in Egypt and authoritarian regimes, both "soft" and "hard," are in power all over the Arab world, as "the Arab League's twenty-two states remain the most uniformly oligarchic slice of the world," where not a single Arab leader has ever been peacefully ousted at a ballot box.[6] And there is even more violence in the Holy Land.

If anything, things seem to be getting worse in Mesopotamia, in Israel/Palestine, and in the Greater (or Broader) Middle East in the aftermath of the ouster of Saddam Hussein. In Iraq, as in Israel/Palestine, the blood is still flowing and the politics seem more treacherous, leading one of the advocates of the ouster of Saddam Hussein to conclude that "the American project to replace [Saddam Hussein] with the Middle East's first democracy is in new peril, and the road ahead may yet be more hazardous than the distance already traveled."[7] The road to Jerusalem should have led through Baghdad, according to those who had predicted that the ouster of Saddam Hussein and the establishment of a democratic Iraq would produce spill-over effects in the entire Middle East, including in Palestine, where, according to their fantasies, a democratically elected leadership would conclude a peace agreement with Israel, and the two-state solution, with a secure Israel and an independent Palestine living side by side, would become a reality.

Instead, it seems that Baghdad is looking more and more like Jerusalem, where suicide bombing does not come as a shock; the "Sunni Triangle" now resembles the Gaza Strip, as government and American soldiers battle Arab insurgents and rock-throwing kids; and the anti-American Shiite violence in southern Iraq recalls the anti-Israeli attacks in southern Lebanon during the Israeli occupation there.[8] And while the alliance between the American Empire and Greater Israel, formalized during the Bush-Sharon meeting in April 2004 in Washington, is ensuring that the idea of the two-state solution becomes a distant dream in Israel/Palestine, there is a growing expectation that a three-state solution (Arab-Sunni; Arab-Shiite; Kurdish) could become a realistic option in Iraq.[9]

Recall the rosy scenarios promoted by the White House, the neoconservative ideologues and their cheerleaders in the American media:[10] The ouster of Saddam was supposed to usher in a new era of political freedom in Iraq, one in which the country and its people would be united behind a pro-American and democratically elected government. Iraq would be pluralistic, secular, committed to women's rights, and would help spread political and economic freedom all over the Middle East.[11] Instead, as the images from Iraq suggest, the repressive military dictatorship of the Baath party has given way to political chaos. Real power in the country is not controlled by Ahmed Chalabi and other American puppets and certainly not by a group of Jeffersonian Democrats,[12] but is in the hands of the religious figures, tribal chieftains, and their militias, which dominate the three main ethnic and religious groups that constitute the imaginary "Iraqi nation."[13] There are the violent gangs, linked to former Baathists and radical Islamists, that rule the neighborhoods and streets of the "Sunni Triangle," and to whom the American invasion is seen as part of a strategy to destroy the power of the Sunnis and deprive them of the political and economic privileges they enjoyed under Saddam Hussein.[14] The religious Shiite figures range from the "moderates" (who just hate Americans) led by Grand Ayatollah Ali Sistani,[15] to the "radicals" (who want to kill Americans), headed by Muqtada al-Sadr's Shiite militias.[16] But they are all content to see the Americans fight the Sunnis and weaken their power. The Shiite leaders, representing 60 percent or so of Iraqis, who were repressed especially brutally by Saddam Hussein, hope to establish an anti-Western clerical regime in Baghdad with possible links to their coreligionists in Iran. And the Kurds enjoy their current U.S.-protected autonomy and look forward to cleansing their areas of Arabs and Turkomans, as they continue to cling to their dream of establishing a Greater Kurdistan.[17] Indeed, reflecting the ethnic and religious tensions in Iraq, a fragile coalition of Shiite political parties committed to an Islamic fundamentalist agenda and with ties to Iran and a nationalistic Kurdish bloc, facing strong opposition from the Sunnis, came to power in Baghdad in April 2005.

That is the current reality in post-Saddam Iraq. Is that another example of "unintended consequences?" It certainly does not match with the Wilsonian fantasies concocted by the neocons. If anything, it resembles Yugoslavia after the death of Marshall Tito, with the added concern that the election of an Islamist government in Baghdad and the disintegration of Iraq will play into the hands of anti-American terrorists and force regional players like Turkey, Iran, and Saudi Arabia to get involved in a potential bloody civil war. The rise of a clerical Shiite regime in Baghdad and the secession of the Kurds from Iraq, which are two realistic scenarios being considered now, are the kind of changes that are bound to spill over into other countries in the region. They could reawaken demands for Kurdish independence in Turkey, Iran, and Syria and force Ankara to intervene in Iraq to protect the Turkoman minority in the north and deny the Kurds control over the oil resources of Kirkuk. In fact, there are already signs that the Kurdish show-of-force in Iraq is spilling over into Syria, where grievances simmering within the Kurdish minority (of two million) for several decades is finally boiling over in the aftermath of the war in Iraq.[18] The rise of a Shiite state in Iraq would play into the hands of their coreligionists in Iran and Saudi Arabia, while the collapse of the ruling Sunni minority in Baghdad would send shockwaves across the entire Arab world, with its mostly Sunni population. The result of all these and related developments will not be the rise of the first liberal democracy in the Arab world but probably the creation of a mini-Afghanistan (or mini-Afghanistans) in Iraq and perhaps in other countries in the region, in which ethnic, tribal, and religious groups would fight one another, with support from regional and global players. At the end, the best-case scenario would make Iraq look like Yugoslavia today, a collection of three or more protectorates: an Arab-Sunni state at the center, in which the Arab League and the EU maintain security; an Arab-Shiite state in the south under UN supervision and with links to Iran; and a Kurdish protectorate, where the United States and Turkey retain spheres of influence. And that is the best-case scenario.

Sound depressing? But this is the Middle East that has proven to be and will prove to be once again a graveyard of great expectations for outside powers as well as regional players. Since the fall of the Ottoman Empire outside powers have all been trying again and again to make and remake the Middle East. And at the end, in the words of the Rolling Stones, "They can't get no satisfaction!" Recall the many grand schemes to remake the Middle East: whether it was Shimon Peres's mirage of a New Middle East that was buried during the violence of the Second Intifada, or Ariel Sharon's fantasy of a New Order in the region after the Lebanon War, which only embroiled Israel in a long and bloody quagmire in southern Lebanon and a humiliating withdrawal and the rise of Shiite terrorism directed against Israel and the United States. Or consider Nasserism, the nationalist ideology pursued by the late Egyptian President Gamal Abdel Nasser, who promised to unite the Arab world under Egypt; that only led to a succession of military dictatorships, bankrupted economies, and inter-Arab and intra-Arab fighting. Or the ambition of Khomeinism promoted by the late Ayatollah, who wanted to spread Iran's version of Islam in the entire Middle East; his policies only isolated Iran in the Middle East and ignited a war with Iraq. Recall how the Six Day War in 1967 was supposed to bring a new era of peace between Israel and her Arab neighbors; it led directly to the 1973 War and to two Palestinian uprisings. Or the way the Egyptian-Israeli peace accords were expected to change everything in the Middle East and establish the foundations for a pro-American Arab-Israeli coalition; they resulted in a "cold peace" between the two countries. And indeed, there was that euphoric mood in Washington following the first Gulf War and the Madrid Peace Conference; those supposedly earth-shaking events were followed by another war against Iraq and a bloody war in the Holy Land. So much for the rise of great expectations in the Middle East and the regional and global powers that produce them.

BEWARE OF NEW "BLOWBACKS"

That the U.S. Wilsonian mission in Mesopotamia has resulted in an Iraq on the verge of a bloody civil war between Arab-Sunnis, Arab-Shiites, and Kurds that could threaten the stability of the entire Middle East should not have come as a surprise to any observer of the Middle East. In fact, it follows the same familiar pattern that led to the Gulf War and eventually to 9/11. The U.S. assistance to Iraq during the Iraq-Iran war was part of a strategy to contain Teheran and defend U.S. interests in the Persian Gulf. It ended up helping to bolster the power of Saddam Hussein and strengthened his resolve in confronting and eventually invading Kuwait. That in turn led to the American decision to force Iraq out of the oil-producing kingdom. At the same time, the U.S. financial and military backing for the Mujaheddin guerrillas in Afghanistan, as part of a strategy to undermine the Soviet occupation and protect the regional gas station also-known-as Saudi Arabia, and the American military presence in Saudi Arabia in the post-Gulf War interlude helped produce Osama Bin Ladin's Al Qaeda and brought us the infamous "blowback" in the form of 9/11. And that led directly to the war on terrorism, the invasion of Afghanistan, and the occupation of Iraq.

And now the ousting of Saddam Hussein and the American invasion of Iraq are helping to boost the religious and political power of the Shiite majority of Iraq to energize the drive toward self-determination of the Kurds in that country and to radicalize the secular Sunni minority.[19] So Americans should perhaps get ready for the possible next set of four intertwining "blowbacks," which include:

- An alliance between a Shiite-controlled government in Baghdad and the "conservative" and "moderate" Ayatollahs in Teheran. Such an alliance could serve as a destabilizing force in the Middle East by providing support to Shiite secessionist movements in the Arab oil-producing states in the Persian Gulf as well to the anti-Israeli Hizbollah group in Lebanon, forming the foundations for the new anti-American terrorist nexus with potential access to WMD. Iran, with its Shiite majority and regional ambitions, has already been playing a major role in supporting Shiite groups in Iraq.[20] And the expanding political and military power of the Shiites in Iraq, the Persian Gulf, and the Levant could help Iran establish its role as the regional hegemon in the Persian Gulf, with the remnants of Iraq and a weakened Saudi Arabia and the other Arab oil-producing states in the area being transformed into satellites of an oil-rich Iran that is equipped with nuclear weapons. Such developments could create the conditions for a major military (nuclear?) confrontation between two nation-states with vigorous religious features—Moslem-Shiite Iran and Jewish Israel.[21]

- An assertive Kurdish leadership in northern Iraq could attempt to advance a Greater Kurdistan agenda that would threaten the interests of Turkey, Iran, and Syria with their large Kurdish minorities.[22] The Kurds could try to get control of the oil resources in Kirkuk and discriminate against the Arab and Turkoman minorities in its territory. Washington would have to decide whether to back a Turkish move into northern Iraq, antagonizing the Kurds, and turning them into an anti-American force.[23] Indeed, recall how the Mujaheddin in Afghanistan have evolved from a pro-American movement to one that regards the United States as the enemy. Alternatively Washington could oppose the anti-Kurdish Turkish move that would probably be backed by Iran and Syria, and find itself pressed into a confrontation with a long-time ally. The assertiveness of the Kurds in northern Iraq is also creating another new source of regional tensions in the Middle East. Israeli military cooperation with the Kurds there as part of a strategy to use them against Syria and Iran has ignited anger in Ankara and is threatening to weaken and even destroy the military partnership between the Turks and the Israelis and threaten the balance of power in the region.[24]

- The continuing radicalization of the Sunni minority in Iraq could only produce even more anti-American sentiments among members of the Sunni majority in the Arab world and make it difficult for the regimes in Egypt, Jordan, and Morocco to maintain their pro-American stand.[25] The "Sunni Triangle" in Iraq could become a magnet to radical Sunni religious groups that will try to spread their message and power to Jordan, Syria, and Saudi Arabia. An Arab Sunni state consisting of parts of Iraq, Jordan, and Syria could become the political and military base for Osama bin Ladin and associates, and other radical Arab-Sunni groups, from which they would threaten Saudi Arabia, Israel, and the United States.

- Then there is another possible scenario that should worry U.S. policymakers: The continuing American occupation of Iraq could encourage unity among the Sunnis, Shiites, and the Kurds and help form a new sense of Iraqi nationalism—one that would direct its power against the United States. There are signs that such a process might be taking place in Iraq as a result of the American policies, which would be the ultimate irony: America "liberates" the Iraqis to see them turning against it, giving birth to anti-American Iraqi nationalism.[26]

Finally, while the above "blowback" scenarios could happen in the more distant future, U.S. policymakers have to consider a more immediate and clear outcome of the war in Iraq and its impact on the Greater Middle East. Military and intelligence analysts seem to agree that the war in Iraq diverted resources from the struggle against Osama bin Ladin and his Al Qaeda organization.[27] Former CIA official Michael Scheuer argued that the invasion of Iraq helped bin Ladin rally support among Moslems by "convincing them that Islam is under attack from the United States and that it is their responsibility to defend their faith."[28]

American experience in the post–Saddam Hussein Middle East is an outgrowth of its hegemonic strategy in the region in the aftermath of the Cold War and it recalls U.S. performance in the Middle East during most of the rivalry with the Soviet Union. The costs now seem to be higher than during the Cold War. But the United States is forced once again to adopt the same modus operandi, of dealing with a reality in which, despite its top-dog position, it is not even able to wag its own tail. And it is not always sure who is actually wagging it. A local partner? A regional adversary? An outside spoiler? Indeed, the inconsistent choices that American policymakers made in dealing with the insurgents in the Sunni city of Fallujah—refraining from attacking the insurgents in the city and turning over control to a local militia that included former Baath officers in May 2004 and then launching a crushing invasion of the city in November 2004—could serve as a metaphor for U.S. policy in the Middle East. A global power with a mighty military force finds itself entangled in the regional and local politics of a country. It is unable to translate its military power into a clear political victory and it hopes instead to achieve the least-worst scenario. The choice it ends up facing is between permitting anti-American forces to patrol the streets of Fallujah[29] and destroying the city with American firepower.[30] To quote the wise words of that famous Middle East analyst, Yogi Bera, "It's déjà vu all over again."

THE MIDDLE EAST AS A KALEIDOSCOPE

The United States is discovering after the war in Iraq what many outside global players as well as local and regional players have learned the hard way: It is impossible for any actor to impose its particular agendas on the Middle East. In the Middle East, everything is related to everything else; the boundaries between local, national, regional, and international issues are blurred. A player with great expectations arrives on the Middle East scene, trying to make peace between rivals, spread democracy in this country or socialism in another one, or attempting to use nationalist and religious banners to create a sense of unity. But such efforts are bound to result in counter-efforts by unsatisfied players to form opposing regional alliances and to secure the support of other local players and global powers. What you intended does not always happen in a region where "unintended consequences" are the name of the game—not an exception to the rule. As Middle East historian L. Carl Brown proposed, "just as with the tilt of the kaleidoscope the many tiny pieces of colored glass all move to form a new configuration, so any diplomatic initiative in the Middle East sets a realignment of the players."[31]

The Middle East and its peripheries, or the Greater Middle East, which stretches from the Balkans to the borders of China, is described by political scientists as the most "penetrated" area of the world—in which numerous tribal, religious, ethnic, national, regional, and extra regional political players combine and divide in shifting pattern of alliances. Applying Brown's kaleidoscope model to the Middle East, one can see why diplomacy in the region is characterized by a mishmash of local, regional, and global issues, never-ending conflicts, and unsolved problems. Chaos and instability have, indeed, been the rule and not the exception since the fall of the Ottoman Empire. Outsiders who want to play the Middle East game should expect to become part of the chaotic system—not vehicles to stabilize it. The kaleidoscope has been turned after America invaded Iraq and a new configuration has emerged. But as always, the configuration includes similar players—local (Shiites, Sunnis, Kurds, Turkomans, tribal groupings) and regional (Turkey, Iran, Syria, Jordan, Israel)—and comparable problems (religious and ethnic strife, national identity, outside interference) that will drive the region into yet another time of chaos out of which will emerge a new, equally temporary and unstable, configuration.

The role foreign powers play in the Middle East remains critically important for the outsiders as well as for the locals. The politics of a thoroughly penetrated system such as the Middle East is not adequately explained, even at the local level, "without reference to the influence of the intrusive outside system."[32] Yet, as American and Soviet experience in the region suggests, and as the current American involvement there has dramatized, the outside actor can rarely control the politics of such a system and frequently becomes involved in issues that have nothing to do with its original interests in the region. A major power's ability to impose policies on local players or exclude other major powers is limited. Even a superpower can sometimes fall hostage to the machinations and ridicule of local powers.

The Middle Eastern elites use outside powers, including the United States, to advance their domestic and regional interests. Those elites lack either stable and legitimate political systems, or economic structures capable of sustaining their bottomless budgets, or both. It is external, especially American, support that allows the political elites to win domestic support for their policies. Washington's sponsorship of the negotiations that culminated in the Egyptian-Israeli peace accords enabled Cairo and Jerusalem to mobilize domestic and regional support for the accord. Their political elites could justify political and territorial concessions that would not have otherwise been acceptable to either their domestic rivals or supporters, by citing American diplomatic commitments and lucrative economic and military aid packages. While Washington may have enhanced its international prestige as a result of the Egyptian-Israeli peace agreement, that accord did not compensate the United States for the "loss" of Iran by creating a pro-American Arab-Israeli axis. The peace agreement may have actually contributed to instability by freeing Israel's military forces to invade Lebanon in 1982 and creating more hostility among the Palestinians and other Arabs who were angered by America's inability to "deliver" Israeli concessions. Moreover, the peace agreement resulted in increased American financial and military commitments, especially the new obligation to supply Egypt with a level of aid similar to that given to Israel.

Or take the events that followed the Israeli invasion of Lebanon in 1982 and the Israeli–Palestinian wars there. The United States deployed its forces there in order to help end the war, in a move that was supposed to strengthen the American position in the region. Instead, it brought about the bombing of the Marine barracks in Beirut and ignited a major confrontation with Lebanon's previously quiescent Shiite community, bringing Syria and Iran into the picture and leading to other anti-American terrorist acts, such as the 1985 hijacking of TWA Flight 847. The spiral of violence prompted the Reagan administration's misguided arms-for-hostages scheme, which contributed to the policy calculations that led to American intervention on the side of Iraq in its war with Iran in 1988. That move in turn set in motion a chain of events that eventually produced Gulf War.

Supporting a local elite makes an outside power such as the United States a symbol of evil in the eyes of opposition forces. It creates political and economic expectations that cannot be fulfilled, thereby causing the outside power to be derided by those who originally sought its aid. American support for Israel has been one of the factors that have created so much hostility toward the United States in the Arab and Moslem worlds. U.S. backing of the dictatorial regime of the Shah of Iran, whom Washington helped to restore to power in 1953, turned Washington into an object of hatred in the eyes of most Iranians and helped accelerate developments that led to the 1979 Iranian revolution. The United States has still not recovered from that experience, as seen by the unsuccessful efforts to mend its relationship with Iran.[33] Similarly, the alliance between Washington and the Christian Maronite minority in Lebanon after the

1982 Israel invasion of that country, and its embroilment in the Maronite–Shiite civil war, resulted in the bloody Shiite campaign to evict the United States from Beirut.

American relationships with the Shiites and Kurds in Iraq between the Gulf War and the war against Iraq in 2003 also demonstrated the dangers that Middle East clients pose to their patrons. During the Gulf War, President Bush I encouraged the Kurds and the Shiites to take up arms against Saddam Hussein and topple the regime in Baghdad. But taking into consideration American interests in the Persian Gulf in backing Saudi Arabia and in containing Iran's Ayatollahs and its alliance with Turkey, Washington could not permit the disintegration of Iraq and the possibility that chaos there would spill over into other parts of the region. The Americans therefore ended up providing only limited support for the two groups, abandoned them when they seemed to be moving to win their objectives of seceding from the central control of Baghdad, and permitted Saddam Hussein's troops to suppress their respective rebellions. The outcome produced anti-Americanism among the Shiites and led to new American military commitments to protect the Kurds and the Shiites through the "no-fly zones" and new military and economic commitments and created the conditions for Kurdish political autonomy in the North. The Americans paid high costs—including in moral terms—by promoting these policies, by tilting the Middle East kaleidoscope. But the new configuration that emerged and the way the little pieces interacted seemed to fit what George H. W. Bush and his advisors considered to be the best way to promote U.S. interests in the Middle East in the aftermath of the Cold War, that is, by securing a Pax Americana there. America's Middle East Paradigm (MEP) survived, but long-term U.S. interests were damaged.

THE COLD WAR: A WIN IS NOT A WIN

A clear distinction should be made between the nature of the costs that the United States paid during the Cold War as it tilted the kaleidoscope and those it has been forced to bear following the disappearance of the Soviet Union as a threat to American interests in the region. Tilting the Middle Eastern kaleidoscope during the Cold War as part of strategy to serve U.S. interests as determined by the MEP was costly—but justifiable.

It is the kaleidoscope model that explains why both the United States and the Soviet Union were unable for most of the Cold War to establish a dominant position in the Middle East and eject the other from the region; and why they were not even able to create recognized spheres of influence like those that existed in Europe and Asia. The two superpowers discovered that in order to be a successful player in the Middle East, an outside power had to avoid moving beyond the point at which easy victories cease, to resist the temptations to try to eject great power rivals, and to settle instead for an implicit balance of power.[34] Some examples of overreach by the United States in the Middle East during the Cold War include:

- The efforts by Secretary of State John Foster Dulles to foster the pro-Western Baghdad Treaty, which excluded Cairo, resulted in the Egyptian-Czech arms agreement and the beginning of a major Soviet presence in the area.
- The Eisenhower Doctrine sought to build a bulwark of alliances against Egypt's increasing influence but failed to impose its agenda on the Middle East since it did not accord with clearly expressed regional interests, especially with those of the rising forces of Pan Arabism represented by Egypt's President Nasser. It assumed that ad hoc alliances with the more conservative elements in the Arab world, while trying to mediate the conflict between Israel and the Arabs, would provide Washington with enough leverage to impose its agenda on the region. The Soviets were able to successfully exploit the contradictions in American policy by backing Nasser and his Arab nationalist crusade.
- President John F. Kennedy adopted a more creative approach as he tried to juggle the three components of U.S. policy in the Middle East—its commitments to Israel, its relationship with Saudi Arabia and the conservative Arab regimes, and its efforts to establish ties with Nasser and the Arab nationalist agenda in Algeria and elsewhere. That proved to be another exercise in futility, since JFK ended up antagonizing Nasser by backing his opponents during the civil war in Yemen. He failed to prevent Israel from promoting its interests by taking steps to acquire nuclear military capability. Again, the Soviets took advantage of these setbacks by strengthening their military and diplomatic ties with Egypt, Syria, and Iraq.
- The American policies that facilitated the Egyptian-Israeli peace treaty during the Carter Administration repeated some of the same errors. These policies attempted to exclude the Soviet Union from the peace process and the Palestinians from the peace agreement. By neutralizing the military threat to Israel, the accord encouraged Israel to attack Lebanon in 1982. That resulted in the Israeli-Palestinian war in Lebanon and the success with which a Soviet client, Syria, sabotaged other American peace efforts after that war.

In these and other instances, the Americans did achieve some short-term gains—Presidents Eisenhower and Kennedy were able to contain Nasserist threats to the more conservative forces in Lebanon and Yemen, respectively.

President Carter achieved a major diplomatic coup in mediating a historic peace agreement between Israel and Egypt. But each gain produced counter-moves by local, regional, and global players that posed new threats to American interests.

The Soviet experience in the Middle East was not very different from that of the Americans. The Soviets may have realized immediate gains from their 1955 arms agreement with Egypt because it reflected Egyptian and regional interests. But they did not succeed in using Egypt as the vanguard of a more assertive policy in later years because their interests did not jibe with those of Egypt's leaders. The result was Egyptian President Anwar Sadat's expulsion of the Soviet leaders and his opening to the United States after the 1973 war. In a way, the Soviets' dilemmas were mirror images of the American problems. Their success in making inroads into the Arab world since 1956, and particularly since the 1967 Six Day War, depended on their adoption of a hostile approach toward Israel, including breaking diplomatic relations with the Jewish state in 1967; that made it impossible for them to serve as mediators between the Arabs and the Israelis. Similarly, their failure to win the support of the more conservative states in the Arab world, led by Saudi Arabia, explains to a large extent why they could not exploit the limited military success of their ally, Egypt, during the 1973 war. The Egyptian alliance with the Saudis during that war provided them with a new opportunity to establish ties to the Americans and to use their services to reach an agreement with the Israelis. Overall, both the Americans and the Soviets discovered that their global interests in the Middle East were constrained by the way local and regional players perceived their interests, which did not always accord with those of their respective patrons.

Hence, like the Soviets, U.S. policymakers recognized the constraints operating on their power in the Middle East during the Cold War. Efforts to manipulate local and regional players to promote American interests vis-à-vis the Soviets could not succeed unless they accorded with the interests of those Middle Eastern actors. Indeed, actors like Egypt were able to play one superpower against the other, while Israel and Saudi Arabia succeeded by utilizing their own sources of power—a strong domestic lobby in the case of the Jewish state, and the control of oil resources in the case of the Saudis—to set obstacles in the way of U.S. policy moves. The result was that American efforts to exclude Moscow and its clients tended to backfire. Better results ensued when Washington adopted a less grandiose approach that took the interests of the Soviets and other regional actors into consideration. The breakdown in American-Soviet diplomatic cooperation in resolving the Arab-Israeli conflict in the late 1960's encouraged Moscow to support Egypt's attempts to challenge the status quo as demonstrated first in the War of Attrition and later the 1973 Yom Kippur War. After that war Washington involved the Soviets in the diplomatic process leading to a series of Egyptian-Israeli agreements. But the ensuing pressure from Egypt's President Anwar Sadat encouraged Washington to marginalize the role of Moscow in the Egyptian-Israeli negotiations and provided the Soviets with an opportunity to increase their influence over Syria and the Palestinian Liberation Organization (PLO) and to promote anti-Americanism in the Arab world. Sadat proved to be the ultimate Middle Eastern master of exploiting the Soviet-American competition to his advantage, first, by using Soviet military and diplomatic support to launch the 1973 war against America's client, Israel, and then by drawing the United States, after that war, onto Egypt's side as the main supplier of economic and military assistance. The leading U.S. position in managing the Egyptian-Israeli détente after 1973 was perceived as a major diplomatic victory for Washington. But it also involved costly military and financial commitments on the part of the United States, including huge economic assistance packages to the former Middle Eastern enemies.

In a way, the bipolar balance of power in the Middle East was not entirely a zero-sum game. The presence of two competing superpowers in the Middle East during the Cold War increased pressure on them to expand their military and economic resources, got entangled in costly local and regional conflicts, and almost forced them into nuclear military confrontation during the 1973 war. But at the same time, each superpower could set constraints on their respective clients during times of crisis and diplomacy and press them to accept diplomatic and military moves that accorded with the common interests of Washington and Moscow. Hence the United States and the Soviet Union were on the verge of a nuclear military confrontation during the 1973 Middle East war. But they were still able to pressure Israel and Egypt to end their military hostilities and start negotiations.

WHY BALANCING AMERICAN POWER BENEFITS AMERICA

American high-school students are taught in their civics classes about the way the system of checks and balances strengthens the U.S. political and judicial systems by restraining the power of individuals and groups and helping to resolve domestic conflicts and achieve compromises between contending sides. Since one of the basic assumptions is that the international system is "anarchic" and that it lacks a central authority or government that is based on a sense of a common good and agreed-upon rules of the game, the system that the Founding Fathers advanced as the basis of American government cannot be applied in the international arena where no central government is in charge. But not unlike political players in the domestic political system, in the international arena the power of states is checked. The checks and balances in international relations are not achieved through a formal constitutional structure but in the form of a balance-of-power system.

In the international system, even the ability of a great power like the United States to achieve its interests is counter-balanced by the political-military and economic weight of other states. Hence, the structure of the international system—whether it was the bipolar system of the Cold War or the multipolar system of the nineteenth century—set some checks on the power of all of its members, including the major players. The bipolarity of the Cold War set limits on the ability of the United States and the Soviet Union to impose their respective agendas on the Middle East. At the same time, the collapse of the Soviet Union put the United States in a position in which it could preserve and expand its position in the Middle East without a direct challenge from a peer competitor. But the maintenance of U.S. hegemony in the Middle East has involved more than just protecting a stable status quo. The reality of many local and regional players competing for power in the Middle East forces Washington to use its military and diplomatic power to deal with active regional challenges to its supremacy. This American role can prove to be a very costly business. The good news from the American perspective is that unlike during the Cold War, those regional challengers cannot rely on the support of a rival global power like the Soviet Union. But that is also bad news for Washington, since without another global power to check its moves in the Middle East, the United States has transformed into a hegemon that is alone responsible for maintaining a stable balance of power in the region.

Indeed, the costs of U.S. intervention in the Middle East seem to rise when there is no outside global player that has enough power to challenge the American military position directly or in alliance with regional players. In a way, the costs of nuclear war with the Soviet Union were perceived as so high so that such threats served to set clear constraints on the use of American (and Soviet) power in the Middle East during the Cold War and forced each superpower to restrain their Israeli (and Egyptian) clients. This is the kind of peer competition that has been missing from the Middle East game board since the collapse of the Soviet Union. The reality of a unipolar international system has encouraged the United States, starting with the Gulf War in 1991, to maintain its supremacy in the Middle East and take actions to challenge the local and regional players.

The situation of unipolarity provided the United States with an opportunity to establish hegemony in the Middle East. But not every opportunity has to be taken. That there was not a consideration of reducing America's involvement in the region after the end of the Cold War was not surprising: Any effort to lower the U.S. profile in the region would have called into question the American commitment to its MEP and encouraged regional and local players to start forming their own balance-of-power system, independent of U.S. control. But hegemony also meant that without the checks imposed by a rival superpower, the costs for the United States have risen to the stratosphere. It is quite conceivable that 9/11, the Second Intifada, and the two wars against Iraq would not have happened if the Soviets had still been around.

Consider the following:

- Neither the Gulf War nor the war against Iraq would have taken place if the Soviet Union had still been playing the role of an assertive superpower that could both contain the United States and tame its client, Iraq. Nor would the Clinton administration's dual containment of Iraq and Iran have been a realistic option for U.S. policymakers in an international system in which the Soviet Union could offer political-military and economic patronage to both countries as a way of countering U.S. sanctions.

- Would an Israel allied with the United States and a Palestinian leadership under Soviet patronage have been able to deal more effectively with their differences in negotiations conducted under a Soviet-American collaborative setting in 2000? Under such conditions, each superpower would have been in a position to press its own client to make concessions. Instead, the United States was drawn into a summit in which the American president was forced into an impossible situation of acting as an "honest broker," a role that he could not play because of his country's close ties with Israel. In any case, both superpowers would have had to share responsibility for the failure of an American-Soviet peace summit on the Middle East, if the Palestinian-Israeli negotiations collapsed. Instead, anti-American sentiments increased in the Arab world as a consequence of the Camp David failure.

- Reflect on what did not take place in Afghanistan following the Soviet withdrawal from that country. According to former Texas Democratic Congressman Charlie Wilson, who was responsible for mobilizing Congress in support of the Pakistan-led anti-Soviet Mujaheddin in Afghanistan, the Russians, following their departure from that country, were interested in cooperating with the United States in stabilizing Afghanistan and preventing the strengthening of radical Islamic forces there. Russian officials told Wilson that the United States and Russia now had "a common interest in stabilizing Afghanistan and particularly in preventing radical Islamic elements from coming to power."[35] They argued that both the Americans and the Russians, who were now backing a puppet government in Kabul, should cooperate in containing the threat of militant Islam in Afghanistan and Central Asia. Wilson recalled that at that time he himself, despite his strong commitments to the guerrillas, was starting to worry over the possibility that the Moslem guerrillas, who were committing unspeakable atrocities and promoting anti-Western agendas, would come to power in Kabul and Wilson wondered whether American interests would not be better-off in the long run if the United States worked with the Russians to support the existing Afghani government. But against the backdrop of a collapsing Soviet Union that was not in a position to resist the United States anymore—and with Pakistan, Saudi Arabia and the pro-Mujaheddin lobbies on Capitol Hill pressing Washington to continue supporting the guerrillas—the opportunity for an American-Russian condominium in Kabul and the establishment of a neutral state in Afghanistan was lost. The road was open for a continuing civil war, and the eventual coming to power of a Saudi-Pakistani backed Taliban that provided the training ground for the masterminds of 9/11.

• Russian weakness has also made it possible for the Americans to expand their involvement in Central Asia, with the result that both the Bush I and the Clinton administrations were increasing U.S. commitments in a region that had never been seen as affecting core or even limited American interests.[36]

That the U.S. military campaign after 9/11 to oust the Taliban and invade Afghanistan was so successful had to do with the willingness on the part of Washington to cooperate with the Russians and other outside players, including India, and even Iran, in assisting the Northern Alliance coalition, and with Pakistan, in denying support for the Taliban and co-opting the leaders of the Pashtun majority in that country. An effective strategy of considering the interests of local and regional players and refraining from antagonizing competing outside powers permitted the Americans to tilt the kaleidoscope in a way that accorded with the short-term interests of the United States of ousting the Taliban and destroying Al Qaeda. Adopting such a realpolitik perspective that assumes the need to cooperate with other global and regional players helped secure the success of the American mission in Afghanistan. A coalition of tribal, ethnic, and religious groups in alliance with the United States and other outside powers toppled the Taliban and won the war in Afghanistan. Applying the realpolitik kaleidoscope model to Afghanistan also explains why America should not try to constrain outside players like Russia and Iran from maintaining their ties with regional and local players in that country. Trying to challenge the influence of other outside players would only result in a backlash, creating the potential for alliances between the Iranians and their Khazar Shiite allies or between the Russians and disgruntled Tajiks and other elements in the non-Pashtun ruling coalition.

OLD (IMPERIAL) MOVIES; NEW (IMPERIAL) MOVIE

While President George W. Bush and his aides focused on the alleged links between Saddam Hussein and Osama bin Ladin and the "grave threat" that Iraq's WMD were posing to the United States and the West as the concrete *casus belli* for invading Iraq, it was the political transformation of Iraq and the entire Middle East under the leadership of the United States that has emerged as the broader objective of the war on Iraq. There is a clear continuity between the strategic goals of Bush I and Clinton in the Middle East and throughout the world and that of Bush II: to build on the sense and the reality of American military supremacy and extend the "unipolar moment" that followed the collapse of the Soviet Union and its empire in 1991 by strengthening the foundations of American hegemony in the Middle East as part of an effort to ensure the survival of the MEP. But in contrast to the conditions in the 1990s, the post-9/11 policies were based on the assumption that a relatively cost-free Pax Americana in the Middle East was not viable anymore, and that direct military engagement was necessary if the foundations of the MEP were to be secured. The planes hitting the World Trade Center on 9/11 were the first and clearest indications that American hegemony in the Middle East entails major costs. According to the new strategy to protect the MEP, the United States had no choice, therefore, but to transform its hegemony-by-remote-control into a hands-on empire. That decision not only produced major costs for the United States but also set the stage for a direct challenge on behalf of the Europeans to American hegemony.

Hence the terror attacks of 9/11 seemed to provide Bush II and his neoconservative advisors with a rationale for such a policy and with an opportunity to win Congressional and public support for the invasion of Iraq as the first step toward the implementation of the assertive hegemonic project in the Middle East. Washington seemed to be following in the footsteps of former imperial powers that had tilted the kaleidoscope in a way that would fit with their global interests.

As noted earlier in the book, the main criticism of Bush II's policies by liberal internationalists and conservative realists has to do with the methods used to achieve the goal of U.S. primacy in the Middle East and not over the long-term hegemonic strategy; these critics proposed the need to maintain an international consensus and support for the Arab states by focusing on a resolution of the Palestine/Israel conflict and by utilizing multilateral institutions. Where they agreed with the neocons was on the United States' need to maintain a hegemonic project in the Middle East. That is what great powers tend to do when they face no constraints on their power. They try to expand their power until they suddenly face major obstacles in their way in the form of resistance by regional and global powers. But striving to achieve hegemony in the Middle East is not in U.S. interests and in the long run it will not be viable for the same reason the goal was not a realistic proposition during the Cold War. Other global powers working with unsatisfied local and regional players are bound to raise the costs for the United States in such a way that it will not be able to maintain its imperial Middle East scheme.

That the goal of achieving dominance in the Middle East is very costly and unsustainable in the long run is exactly the lesson that one draws from the British imperial undertaking in the Middle East in the early twentieth century, which should be placed on the top of the list of unfulfilled expectations of great powers in the Middle East.

Britain's own MEP, driven by strategic interests, the smell of oil, and religious sentiments, prompted the English-speaking people to invade the Middle East and try to establish a new and stable order at the start of the twentieth century. And now in the early twenty-first century we seem to be witnessing a similar hegemonic American undertaking in the region: The Anglo-Americans return to try to set up a new and stable order in the Middle East. One can say about the imperial designs of great powers in the Middle East what Oscar Wilde once said about second marriage: It is the triumph of hope over experience. In the old imperial movie, the British created Iraq. They put the Hashemites and the Saudis in power. They maintained influence in Egypt. They tried to end this or that cycle of violence between Arabs and Jews in the Holy Land. We know how that movie ended. To put it in economic terms, the costs of the British Empire in the Middle East were higher than the expected benefits. Resistance from regional players (including terrorism), challenges from global powers (including the U.S. ally), economic decline, and opposition at home led eventually to a long and painful withdrawal of Britain from the region, culminating in the 1956 Suez debacle. This time the name of the movie is the American Unilateral Moment in the Middle East. But we have a feeling that we have seen this movie before. The actors are different, but the script is familiar: The Americans are trying to recreate Iraq, navigate between the Saudis and the Hashemites, preserve influence in Egypt, and bring an end to another cycle of Arab-Jewish violence.[37]

But to invert Wilde, experience can sometimes triumph over hope. After all, not every love affair or one-night-stand leads to marriage, and not every intervention by a global power in this or that region of the world should lead to permanent military-political presence, nor should ties with this or that client create the basis for a long-term alliance. Moreover, the neoconservatives who were primarily driving this imperial project seemed to have added a Wilsonian soundtrack to the old realpolitik-oriented script and raised the costs of the American production by suggesting that the United States had the power and the will to create an Iraqi federation of Arab Sunni and Shiites and Kurds based on liberal principles and a process of trickle-down democracy, secularism, and pro-Americanism that would transform the entire Arab world and help bring peace between Israel and Palestine. Under the influence of neocons, President Bush embarked not only on an imperial undertaking to protect and advance perceived U.S. interests. He has launched what amount to an imperial crusade to reshape the Middle East and its peripheries.

"Sixty years of Western nations excusing and accommodating the lack of freedom in the Middle East did nothing to make us safe—because in the long run, stability cannot be purchased at the expense of liberty," Bush told the National Endowment for Democracy in November 2003.[38] Bush and his advisors introduced the Big Bang scenario for Iraq and the Middle East that the neoconservative intellectuals promoted: a new age of stability, democracy, and prosperity under American guidance. It's as though Queen Victoria and Woodrow Wilson got married and gave birth to a new breed of political creature, the Democratic Empire in the Middle East.

EMPIRE AND DEMOCRACY: THE VERY ODD COUPLE

But not unlike other dogmatic ideologues in history, the neoconservative intellectuals who argue that Iraq could be turned into a shining model of democracy for the Middle East are advancing their own wishful thinking and political agendas. The notion that Iraq and most of the Arab Middle East could be transformed in the near term into full-fledged democratic systems is nothing short of a fantasy. Much of the region is at the stage of political development that Italy and much of southern Europe were in the middle of the nineteenth century—something that bodes ill for both domestic and regional stability, and there is little that the United States can do about it. More important from the American perspective, implementing this ambitious strategy in its most basic form—establishing a one-person, one-vote system in Iraq—could bring to power the kind of anti-Western Shiite leaders who would ignite a religious and ethnic civil war in Iraq, undermining America's interests in the region. That kind of potential outcome demonstrates the tensions between the two concepts that drive the neoconservative project: democracy that permits free elections and imperialism that requires stability. A democratic empire is unlikely to be sustained in the long run. The power in control is left with two choices. If it wants to secure its imperial project, it has to give up on its democratic pretensions and engage in repression. If it aims at promoting democracy, it needs to abandon its imperial objectives and permit self-determination.

There is also a certain irony in the conservative Bush administration's engaging in nation building in the Middle East, of attempting to create a democratic empire in the Middle East, as opposed to a more limited realpolitik project of a traditional empire. If there was one thing that used to define American conservatives, it was their skepticism—if not hostility—toward the role of government in the management of human affairs. According to traditional conservative philosophy, the state and its political class have neither the moral right nor the administrative capability to direct people's lives, here at home or abroad. Yet American neoconservatives want government to manage distant and far-away lands. These conservatives seem to have become born-again government interventionists and social engineers when it comes to Iraq, Afghanistan, and millions of foreigners and other distant societies in the Middle East whose values are alien to most Americans.

Conservatives used to believe that government can play a limited role in the process of improving race relations in the United States. But the conservative administration of George W. Bush suggests that all you need is, yes, government—a few days and nights of aerial bombing, 140,000 U.S. troops, bureaucrats with good intentions, and economic aid from Washington—and, voilà! We have "nation building." And what's next? Religious freedom, individual rights, and democracy among members of a society that is just starting to enter the Age of Enlightenment. Give government a chance and thousands of years of deep-rooted hatred among tribal, ethnic, and religious communities in Iraq will come to a happy end. The same conservatives who have warned us in the past of the harmful, unintended consequences of government projects seem to ignore concerns that America's nation-building venture in Iraq could not simply fail but might also destabilize Iraq and the entire Middle East. Further, these conservatives apparently do not see that the U.S. occupation of Iraq could ignite more anti-American terrorism, not to mention the harmful impact it would have on the growth of U.S. government power and on the economy and civil rights in America. Indeed, there is a certain touch of the theater-of-the-absurd in watching spokesmen for a White House controlled by conservatives who had been proponents of "states' rights" in the South not many years ago, now proclaim the need to advance the legacy of Martin Luther King, Jr., in Iraq.

A conservative—as opposed to "neoconservative"—critique, one based on realpolitik perspectives of the Bush administration's Middle East agenda of a democratic empire, should be based on two arguments. First, that the project is not doable. As Australian conservative analyst Owen Harries pointed out, "democracy is not an export commodity" but is "much more a do-it-yourself project." Indeed, for several generations, Americans had been using their influence in the Caribbean and Central America in very small, neighboring countries, and even there they faced major obstacles in promoting democratic forms. So why will Americans, who are not particularly good at understanding other cultures and other societies, be able to achieve those ambitious goals in the Middle East?

The second argument advanced by Harris posits that "if you are the sole remaining superpower, you should be very careful and restrained in the use of your power." After all, the fate of dominant powers that are very active and assertive is that they are balanced sooner or later by coalitions of powers against them, and that this is likely to happen to a United States that insists on imposing its will on the world. A sense of "American exceptionalism" leads some Americans to believe that their country would be an exception to the notion that empires are bound to decline and fall. That process of decline and fall might have happened to Spain under Phillip II, it might have happened to France under Louis XIV and Napoleon, it might have happened to Wilhelm II and Hitler's Germany, it might have happened to the British and French empires, and it might have happened to the Soviet Union, but it would not happen to America, because we are, hey, so "cool" and different.[39]

THE COSTS OF EMPIRE

Indeed, some Anglo-Saxon historians like the British Niall Ferguson,[40] the Canadian Michael Ignatieff,[41] and the American Max Boot[42] have been promoting, if not celebrating, the rise of the American empire in the Middle East and the promotion of American values in the Moslem world.

In reality, this vision of imperial American power will not prove to be very compelling mainly because it will not be very successful. It is a vision of American power that is "recklessly utopian," as political scientist Corey Robin describes it. The neoconservative intellectuals have seized upon the terrorist strikes of 9/11 as an opportunity to advance their imperial fantasy as a way of striking at the libertarian or neoliberal agenda of the 1990s during which it was suggested that globalization and the accelerating process of free trade and free markets was undermining the efficacy of military power and traditional em-

pires. Neoliberalism advanced the notion that the Economic Man and the ideology of individual interest were winning over the Political Man and the commitment to a public or national interest, and that the end of communism and
the triumph of capitalism was accompanied by a "belief in the free market as a
harmonious international order of voluntary exchange requiring little more
from the state than the enforcement of laws and contracts."[43] Neoconservatives
challenged this neoliberal reverence for the Economic Man and the vision of
American-led globalization. They also attempted after 9/11 to replace it with a
fantasy of an American-controlled empire in which the Political Man and military might reign supreme.

But in a way, the notion of an American-controlled empire based on strong
military foundations was the intellectual mirror image of the idea of an American-led globalization. Indeed, not long ago, during the swinging '90s, we were
all celebrating the coming era of globalization. The "content providers" of the
decade wrote books and articles called "The Rise and Fall of the Nation-State"
and "The Borderless World." They predicted that the business cycle would die,
that the Dow would reach 12,000 (or was it 24,000?), that power would shift
from government to businesses, and that the merger between Time Warner
and AOL would change the world as we knew it. Rereading those forecasts
should provide us with some perspective about the scenarios being drawn
today, sometimes by the same pundits, who envisage the rise of a global American empire in which the United States, exploiting its unequaled military
power, will make the world safe for its interests and ideals. Click "American empire" on your Internet search engine and you'll be linked to hundreds of Web
sites, newspaper columns, magazine articles, and books that discuss and debate
Washington's new imperial role around the globe. An influential group of
American neoconservative intellectuals has been advancing the notion that
America should and will enjoy a long unipolar moment. Critics here and
abroad have been challenging this unilateralist American approach. The war
in Iraq is fodder for both sides.

But the talk about American empire in the first decade of the twenty-first
century is probably going to sound a lot like some of the hype about globalization in the last decade of the twentieth century that was produced by pundits
searching for catchy phrases and colorful metaphors to explain complex reality. Not that change is not real. The collapse of communism, worldwide economic liberalization, and the advancement of information technology have all
affected global politics and social systems. But the business cycle did not go
away. The bears returned to Wall Street. The AOL–Time Warner merger
flopped. And the nation-state is alive and well, its power even strengthened in

response to outside challenges, ranging from terrorism to SARS. Reality—and complexity—bites.[44]

Now, consider the notion that the duopoly of the Cold War, United States versus the Soviet Union, was replaced by a monopoly—the American empire. It is a fact that the United States is the strongest military power in the international system, in the same way that elements of globalization are a reality. But just as globalization has not smashed the nation-state, U.S. military supremacy need not transform America into an empire. Economic costs, public opposition, and potential challenges from other global players are getting in the way. Indeed, given the clash between the inward-looking democratic process and liberal traditions of the United States, on the one hand, and the high costs exacted in money and blood for lengthy interventions abroad, it can only be expected that the American empire will collapse before it could even be proclaimed.

Since the United States chose to act in Iraq without the authorization of the UN Security Council, without the support of NATO, and with only a handful of allies, it is now paying practically all the expenses of the Iraq occupation. "Even those who supported the unilateral intervention in Iraq seem by now to realize than it cannot be sustained," concluded former American Ambassador to Croatia Peter Galbraith. "The Bush Administration, having scorned the United Nations, is now desperate to have it back."[45] The Bush administration's expectations that the United States would not need many troops in Iraq and that the country's oil production would pay the costs of rebuilding Iraq proved to be illusionary. By May 2004, $150 billion had already been spent on Iraq (an amount equal to 25 percent of the nondefense discretionary Federal budget); one year of involvement in Iraq could cost about $100 billion. These costs demonstrate the constraints operating on the implementation of the American imperial project. In a context such as that of the kaleidoscopic Middle East, with its intertwining relationship between domestic, local, and global players, the costs that are imposed on an outside power that attempts to dominate the region tend always to be higher than expected.

That indeed was the experience of Britain during the twentieth century in the Middle East as it tried unsuccessfully to secure the foundations of its empire. Interestingly enough, there were just fewer than 150,000 British troops in Iraq in 1920 after the "liberation" of that country from Ottoman control, almost the same number of troops that the Americans had in Mesopotamia in 2004. Like the British in the early twentieth century, the Americans are facing in Iraq today ethnic and religious militias revolting against the foreign Anglo-Saxon occupiers. Contemporary Anglo-American imperialists such as Niall Ferguson recommend that the Americans strike back against the Iraqi insurgents with the kind of ruthlessness that the British applied in the last century. "In 1920, the British eventually ended the [Iraqi] rebellion through a combination of aerial bombardment and punitive village-burning expeditions," which were "not pretty," Ferguson recalls.[46] Moreover, like the British who had to confront an Arab "revolt" in the 1930s aimed against its Zionist project, the Americans are now finding themselves in a very similar situation: having to deal with a Palestinian uprising against Israel, with the costs incurred measured either by rising anti-Americanism among the Arabs if Washington supports the Jews in the Holy Land, or by domestic political opposition if the White House tries to appease the Arabs. Add to that the price the Americans are paying in protecting the power of the Hashemites and the Saudis and to prop up their protectorate in Egypt. It is not surprising that the situation sounds and looks like a rerun of a British imperial movie.

WHERE HAVE YOU GONE, SADDAM, THE ARAB "NATION BUILDER"?

Conventional wisdom among foreign policy wonks is that, all things considered, the Iraqi people are better off without Saddam Hussein. Even the harshest Bush-bashing pundit tends to qualify his or her criticism of the war in Iraq with the line, "there is no doubt that Saddam Hussein was an evil man and we should all be thankful that he and his cronies have been deposed, but . . ." In fact, you can already envision neoconservative columnists insisting a year or two from now that despite the fact that we weren't successful in establishing a democracy in Mesopotamia, we should appreciate the "legacy" that President George W. Bush has left behind. Our grand ambitions of making Iraq and the Arab world safe for political freedom weren't fulfilled. But at least we don't have another bloody dictator around anymore, right?

To respond to that question, one should press the rewind button of twentieth century history. There was a time in the West, 100 years ago, when liberal intellectuals in New York, London, and Paris were united in the certainty that the most antidemocratic and corrupt regime in Europe was Czarist Russia. The Czar and his cronies were regarded as leading reactionary figures opposed to reform, who repressed their people, launched anti-Jewish pogroms, and dominated a huge empire. It was not surprising then that when Czar Nikolai II abdicated in 1917, the event produced a sense of euphoria among liberals everywhere. They expected that now that the evil tyrant was gone, Russia would enter an age of political and economic progress. All things considered, the

Russian people were expected to be better off without Czar Nikolai II. Such reactions also followed the abdication of Kaiser Wilhelm II in the aftermath of Germany's defeat in World War I. That authoritarian and militarist figure was regarded by most Western observers as a warmonger responsible for the outbreak of the Great War. That he was now in exile and his rule was replaced by a republican system committed to democratic principles was seen at the time as another step in the worldwide march toward progress—together with the end of the Czarist rule in Russia as well as the collapse of the despised Austro-Hungarian and Ottoman Empires. The world was supposedly now better off without all these autocrats and despots.

We can vividly spot the weaknesses of these assumptions if we press the fast-forward button of history and are exposed to the revolting personalities of Hitler and Stalin and to the horrific images of Auschwitz and the Gulag, to the bloody scenes of the battlegrounds of World War II and the long history of the Cold War. And after following the terror of the civil war in Yugoslavia and the continuing mess in the Middle East, some may even feel nostalgic toward the Austro-Hungarian emperors and the Ottoman sultan.

This is not to dispute that Hussein was a monster like Stalin or Mao. He certainly was. The more relevant point to consider is whether whatever or whoever replaces him would be an improvement over the status quo ante. Might we—and more important, the Iraqi people—feel a sense of nostalgia toward Saddam Hussein years from now, forgetting that he was an odious dictator who brutalized his people, if the country degenerates into a bloody civil war à la Afghanistan, with warlords and terrorists? If parts of Iraq come under the rule of a theocratic Shiite regime, women and Christians wouldn't even enjoy the limited freedom they had under the secular Baath rule. Will the times and actions of Saddam be sanitized if Iran, equipped with nuclear weapons, becomes the hegemonic power in the entire Persian Gulf? What will happen if Turkey, Iran, and Saudi Arabia become embroiled in a regional war in which they would carve up Iraq? Finally, how will the past be reinterpreted if the United States is forced into a lengthy and costly occupation as part of a strategy to prevent these scenarios sketched above?

We should recall, however, that Czar Nikolai II was forced out of power by the Russian people and not by an outside power. And, notwithstanding President Woodrow Wilson's slogan of "making the world safe for democracy," World War I resulted from political and strategic considerations and was not aimed at "regime change" in Russia and Germany. The United States ousted Saddam Hussein, a man known for brutality against his own people and for his threats against his neighbors, in a war of choice. We have become responsible for whatever scenario might unfold in Iraq or its remnants, for better—or more likely—for worse.

It is true that the problems that threaten to tear Iraq apart, including Kurdish aspirations for political independence, Shiite dreams of dominance and their hopes to establishing a theocracy, and Sunni efforts to regain their lost power, are not of America's direct making. But it is the American ouster of Saddam Hussein and the invasion of Iraq that created the new configuration in Iraq that made all these developments possible. To put it differently, if Washington had refrained from tilting the kaleidoscope and permitted the old configuration to remain in place, the continuing status quo in Iraq would have kept the Pandora's Box of ethnic, religious, and tribal conflicts closed for quite a while. And while the death of Saddam Hussein and an ensuing civil war in Iraq might have created the conditions for the same kinds of problems Iraq is facing today, the United States would have not been blamed for such an outcome.

But the Bush administration has tilted the kaleidoscope by "liberating" Iraq, and the problems the United States is facing there and in the Middle East have less to do with the failure to plan for the occupation of Iraq and more with the systemic dilemmas that would have confronted even the most organized and efficient occupying force. Even if the U.S. occupiers had prevented the looting of the Iraqi National Museum and other public and government institutions, including hospitals and schools, and were able to deal effectively with other problems, like the lack of electricity and potable water, they would still be facing the same kinds of structural problems resulting from the collapse of a central power in a country divided along ethnic and religious lines.

U.S. failures in Iraq resulted from the faulty conceptual framework and unrealistic expectations that guided the administration of Bush II: that removing Saddam Hussein and decapitating his top leadership would create conditions for an orderly change of power and that the Iraqi people would not only greet the American "liberators" with flowers, but would be ready to unite behind a new leadership that would enjoy a sense of legitimacy and be able to impose law and order and begin the process of nation-building. All of these assumptions were based on the idea of an Iraq that existed only in the minds of the neoconservative ideologues, an Iraq, which like many of the political entities in the region are nothing more than superficial structures invented by outsiders, with borders that reflect the interests of European colonizers rather than authentic domestic concerns and dispositions.

In fact, the American occupation has interrupted a process led by Saddam Hussein and the Baath party of, yes!, nation building, in which tribal forces among the Sunni ruling minority allied with the Baath party and with the support of co-opted elements in the Shiite and Kurdish communities. This nation-building was aimed at centralizing political power in Baghdad and forming a new "Iraqi" identity that combines elements of Arab nationalism, Islam, and pre-Moslem Babylonian history and that meant the creation of a strong military and a centralized bureaucracy that served to protect Saddam Hussein and his cronies and to control patronage. This form of nation building required the suppression of minorities; the promotion of a culture of obedience through a controlled press and educational system; the appropriation of the country's main natural resource and sources of revenue, oil, by the central government; and the use of imagined and real foreign threats (the United States, Israel, Iran) as a way of mobilizing national support.[47]

The Iraqi model of nation-building has been pursued in most of the Arab world with some modifications that take into consideration local conditions, such as the lack of oil in Egypt and other countries in the region. It reflects the reality in which Iraq and most of these other countries are not real nation-states with a clear sense of national identity that can provide legitimacy to those in power. Some Arab countries, not unlike Iraq, are a confederation of ethnic and religious groups (Lebanon) or include large and restive minorities (the blacks in Sudan, the Berbers in Algeria, the Kurds and Alawites in Syria) in conflict with the Arab-Sunni majority whose leaders promote a jumbled Arab or Pan Arabist nationalism, which, in some cases, is combined with Islamic identity. Even Egypt, which for years was considered the leader of the Pan Arabist movement and the "largest Arab country," has yet to adopt a clear national identity that mingles its Arab, African, Moslem, Mediterranean, and Coptic and ancient Egyptian roots.

Under conditions in which Arab governments have failed to develop a sense of national identity among their citizens or acquire any degree of political legitimacy, the only way for the ruling elites to maintain their power and secure the existing status quo governments is through the control over military power and natural resources, by juggling domestic and local interests and allying with regional and global players. From that perspective, Saddam Hussein's domestic and foreign policies followed the Arab leaders' modus operandi of crushing and co-opting tribal, ethnic, and religious groups; accentuating foreign threats; burnishing Arab, Moslem, and Babylonian credentials; and trying to win the support of outside powers, including the Russians, the Europeans, and the Americans. Like other Arab leaders, Saddam recognized that when another player tries to tip the kaleidoscope—Iran tries to rally the Shiites in Iraq or Kuwait challenges Iraq's oil policies; the Kurds try to secede—you have to react, or you would find yourself in a new configuration that threatens your survival.

THE "NEW" IRAQ

Indeed, one could argue that in the context of the kaleidoscopic Middle East, Saddam Hussein was more of a pro–status quo player committed to nation-building in Iraq than a revolutionary figure, and that it was the United States, with its policies in the Middle East from the 1991 Gulf War to the 2004 war against Iraq, that has served as a radical agent for change. These U.S. policies were aimed at retarding and eventually ending the efforts of Saddam Hussein and the Baath party at creating an "Iraqi nation" and at setting the conditions—not for a democratic or liberal change in Iraq—but for ethnic and religious separatism. Kurdish nationalism and Shiite and Sunni religious identity are bound to replace the secular Arab character of Iraq. As former U.S. ambassador to Croatia Peter Galbraith notes, "the fundamental problem of Iraq is an absence of Iraqis," and the American policy insured that such an Iraqi nation would not emerge any time soon. Since the Gulf War in 1991, the Kurds in Northern Iraq, backed by the United States, have developed a de facto independent state, established a regional government, held semidemocratic elections, and are clearly interested in moving toward full independence. Hence "for an older generation of Kurds in the North, Iraq is a bad memory, while a younger generation, which largely does not speak Arabic, has no sense of being Iraqi."[48] The best-case scenario that one could envision with regard to the Kurds in Iraq is that they would be willing to continue to live under the rule of the Kurdistan regional government as part of an autonomous region protected by American troops. More likely, most of them would back the establishment of an independent Kurdish state in the north, with the more nationalist elements regarding such an action as the first step for the creation of a Greater Kurdistan that would include the Kurdish areas in Turkey, Iran, and Syria. If the North remains part of Iraq as a loose federation or confederation, the Kurds would demand that they maintain control over their security forces and that Iraq become bilingual and secular.

The Shiites in the south have been mobilized through political and religious groups that have accentuated the religious identity of the community and their ties with other Shiites communities in the region, including in Iran and Lebanon. While the American media highlights the views of secular Shiites in Iraq, very few experts doubt that an election taking place in the south would bring to power Shiite religious parties that will advocate establishing close ties with Iran and back Shiite groups such as the Hizbollah in Lebanon. Applying a best-case scenario to the Iraqi Shiites, one could assume that even a "moderate" Shiite leadership would demand that Islam become the source of law in Iraq and reject the idea of Kurdish autonomy. More likely, a Shiite-ruled government would adopt an anti-Western domestic and foreign agenda and establish close links to Teheran, and perhaps even supply assistance to Shiite secessionist movements in the Persian Gulf and the Levant.[49]

Reacting to the rise of the separate identities of Kurds and Shiites, the Sunnis are stressing their religious links to other Sunnis in the Arab world, a move that plays into the hands of radical Sunni movements, such as Al Qaeda. In that sense, the American invasion has helped also to weaken the foundations of whatever remained of secular Pan Arabism in Mesopotamia and in the region, which is going to have a major impact on other Arab states. At a minimum, the Sunni Arabs would be opposed to Kurdish autonomy or independence and could be expected to reject Kurdish efforts to reverse the process of Arabization in the north, including in oil-rich Kirkuk, that Saddam Hussein launched. Additionally, the Sunni Arabs would not accept a Shiite-controlled government that would turn them into second-class citizens. As noted earlier, the worst-case scenario with regard to the "Sunni Triangle" is that it could become a magnet to Islamic terrorist groups from all around the region who would try to spread their influence and violence to other Arab-Sunni countries, such as neighboring Syria, Jordan, and Saudi Arabia.[50]

Adding to this explosive mix is the fate of ethnic and religious groups, including the Christian communities and the Turkomans; the expected struggle over the control of the oil resources; and the impact that the disintegration of Iraq would have on other major players in the region. Taking this reality into consideration, it makes no sense at all why an American administration would decide to tilt the kaleidoscope in Mesopotamia, and in doing so raise the costs of its policies in lives and treasure to the stratosphere as it tries to juggle its conflicting commitments to the various ethnic, religious, and tribal groups as well as to regional players, especially as it also attempts to promote an ambitious Wilsonian project of democratizing Iraq and the Greater Middle East. Indeed, as legal scholars Amy Chua and Jed Rubenfeld have suggested, "It is impossible to predict who would win free and fair elections in Iraq, but given the demographic and economic conditions, it is extremely unlikely that such elections in the near future would produce a secular, pro-American outcome."[51] That would leave the United States no choice but to adopt the kind of repressive imperial policies that Ferguson and many neoconservatives have recommended—which supposedly should help Americans install democratic and liberal institutions in Iraq sometime in the distant future.[52]

Indeed, the expectation that the United States is going to have to maintain a large occupying force in Iraq in the foreseeable future reflects the reality as it is in Iraq, and not the way neoconservatives imagined it to be. Hence the failure to create a unified and legitimate Iraqi military force is not a result of inadequate training by the Americans, but a metaphor for the core predicament facing any power attempting to impose law and order in Iraq. You cannot form an effective national military without a sense of coherent national identity among the troops. The only options in the case of Iraq, and for that matter other Arab countries in the region, is either to permit the various ethnic, religious, or tribal groups to maintain security in their areas of control; to allow one group to impose its power on the country; or to use an outside power to provide security (or to apply of mix of all the above). Similarly, the goal of drawing up a constitution for Iraq and establishing a democratic government there faces the same kind of obstacles inherent in the political nature of Iraq, with its clash between the nationalist Kurds, the religious Shiite majority, and the Sunni losers. As much as the neoconservatives and other fellow travelers do not want to admit it, Iraq has neither a sense of national identity nor the kind of political culture that would allow for the creation of institutions to mediate and resolve tensions between the various communities of Iraq. As conservative columnist George Will concluded, the realities in Iraq have challenged the central neoconservative thesis about "our ability to wield political power to produce the requisite cultural change in a place such as Iraq."[53] Unfortunately, officials in Washington were not able to recognize those realities before they decided to tilt the kaleidoscope and create a new configuration in which America finds itself in a no-win situation.

BUSH OF ARABIA?

"Our armies do not come to your cities and lands as conquerors or enemies, but as liberators," General F. S. Maud, the British commander who occupied Baghdad in 1917, pledged to the people of Mesopotamia at that time.[54] As the post–Gulf War II realities in Iraq have demonstrated, the Americans, as film critic Frank Rich put it, "are playing the British in Mesopotamia," suggesting that David Lean's film "Lawrence of Arabia" had prefigured much of the current chaos in that country.[55] The United States in the early twenty-first century, like Great Britain in the early twentieth century, is now playing the leading role of a powerful outsider who enters the picture, hoping to impose its agenda. But that only produces counter-efforts by unsatisfied players to form opposing regional alliances and secure the support of other local and international powers. The outside power tilted the Middle East kaleidoscope. But the many tiny pieces of colored glass move to form a new configuration that looks very different from what was expected, just as the ousting of Saddam Hussein from power in Iraq in 2003 is creating an environment in the Middle East in which nationalism, religious extremism, and tribal warfare are becoming the central driving force more conducive to anti-American violence.

After all, it was easier to deal with one threatening player—in the form of Saddam Hussein's Iraq—than to confront a complex web of players, such as Shiites, Sunnis, and Kurds, fighting with each other in their attempts to win American support and ending up resenting Washington for siding with the other side. Consider the dilemmas the United States faces in finding the right balance in its relations with Israelis and Palestinians and multiply that again and again and again, and you will get a sense of the enormous problems Washington will be facing in Iraq and its peripheries in the coming years. Neoconservatives may welcome such an outcome of "creative destruction" in the Middle East, as the American Enterprise Institute's scholar Michael Ledeen has described it.[56] Such sentiments, which promote a U.S.–led revolutionary process in the Middle East—and tomorrow in the rest of the world?—may delight the ideological successors to Trotsky or Mussolini. But do these calls for global crusade represent the kind of legacy that a self-described "compassionate conservative" like George W. Bush, who once preached "humility" in the conduct of American relationship with the world, wants?

The war in Iraq did produce a change in Mesopotamia and the Middle East, a movement of the kaleidoscope. But that should not be equated with progress, with imperial fantasies or Wilsonian pipe-dreams, or a mixture of the two. A foreign policy establishment that remains committed to the MEP will only be able to choose between two strategies to deal with this change. They are: a relatively short, low-cost process of U.S. adjustment that would probably be pursued by liberal internationalist or conservative realist policymakers if and when the neoconservative agenda would prove to be a disaster and force Washington to adopt a less costly approach; or Washington could continue following the neoconservative policy, that of a longer and more costly process of adjustment that would end up resembling that of Britain's Middle East experience in the last century. But there is another alternative—breaking up with the old and costly MEP.

3

BREAKING UP
IS HARD TO DO

AMERICA'S FIXATION WITH
THE MIDDLE EAST'S "RIVAL TWINS"

Consider the following two scenes in the 2003 America-in-the-Middle-East movie: In the first scene, Prince Bandar bin Sultan, the Saudi ambassador to the United States, is being told by President Bush of his decision to go to war against Iraq. Prince Bandar learned of this even before President Bush informed his own Secretary of State Colin Powell. Prince Bandar bin Sultan is the Ambassador who represents a nation whose citizens constituted the majority of the terrorists who attacked the United States in 9/11; its state religion, Wahabbism, is spreading anti-Americanism and anti-Semitism—not only in Saudi Arabia but in the entire Moslem world. At the same time, the United States supports this corrupt regime, a theocracy, whose values run contrary to everything most Americans believe in terms of religious freedom, women's rights, and freedom of the press. The teachings of its religious leaders have been responsible for much of the anti-Americanism prevalent among Saudis—former citizen of the kingdom, Osama bin Ladin, being one example.[1]

In the second scene of the America-in-the-Middle-East movie we see the American president, the leader of the most powerful nation on the earth, rejecting the advice of the entire international community, including America's allies in Europe and the Middle East, and agreeing that Israel should keep big Jewish settlements in the West Bank. These were the same settlements that at one time were characterized by Washington as "illegal" and that were seen as the products of a drive by a group of Israeli nationalist-religious zealots. At the same time, as in the case of the Saudis, the American attitude of benign neglect toward the Greater Israel project—and support for it among neoconservatives—helps inflame the kind of anti-American attitudes in the Arab and Moslem world that eventually weakens the U.S. position in the Middle East.[2]

Perhaps some of the mystery in the movie we encounter will be resolved after we learn that Bandar had promised Bush to "fine-tune" oil prices for Bush's benefit in the 2004 presidential campaign, and that the endorsement of the Israeli policies was aimed at shoring up support for Bush among members of the Christian Right and the Jewish community in 2004 election.

Bush II's action vis-à-vis Saudi Arabia recalls a similar move by Bush I. While serving as vice president, he requested that the Saudis reduce production and increase the price of oil to help the recovery of the U.S. domestic oil business, and indirectly, the political fortune of the Republicans in the 1986 Senate races, especially in the farm belt and oil-producing states. Bush I's request produced for the Saudis "an incentive to restore the stability of prices."[3] By trying to win the support of Israel's backers in the 2004 presidential elections by accentuating his support for the Jewish state, the son was trying not to repeat the political sins of his father whose criticism of Israel's settlement policies may have contributed to his defeat in the 1992 race for the White House.

But domestic political and economic considerations are only part of the America-in-the-Middle East movie script being drawn up in Washington. Saudi Arabia and Israel and their respective allies in Washington can be compared to "rival twins." Despite their rivalry, they share a common interest in drawing the United States into the region; and in that context, the Arab-Israeli conflict has created an environment conducive for such intervention. Washington maintains a "special relationship" with both Riyadh and Jerusalem. With the Saudis, it was sealed when King Abdul Ibn Saud, the founder of the Saudi Kingdom, shook hands with President Franklin D. Roosevelt aboard a U.S. destroyer 60 years ago. With Israel it started when President Harry Truman became the first world leader to recognize the new Jewish state in 1948. Since then the United States has continued to face the problems of juggling its interests in the Arab-Israeli arena and in the oil-rich Persian Gulf. But the fact that the United States continued to engage in that complex and costly balancing act is a testimony to the combined power of the Saudis and the Israelis in Washington.

THE EXPENSIVE MIDDLE EAST MOVIE TICKET

While Saudi Arabia and Israel play leading roles in the Middle East movie produced by Washington, it is important to remember that the tickets for this movie are very expensive—and that they are being paid for by American taxpayers and American soldiers. According to reliable figures, since 1949 Israel has received more aid than any other foreign recipient during that period, a total of $94 billion in U.S. aid. Of the nearly $4 billion awarded to Israel annually, some $3 billion goes to Israel's military, including money for Israel's purchase of weaponry for use in the occupied territories.[4] At the same time, as one economist calculated, it probably cost the United States $30-$60 billion a year to safeguard oil supplies from Saudi Arabia and the rest of the Persian Gulf, a figure that does not take into consideration the costs of the war against Iraq and the continuing occupation of that country.[5] These numbers do not include the high costs America is paying for the support for Israel and Saudi Arabia in the form of anti-American sentiments among Arabs and Moslems that breed terrorism. They also do not factor in the costs that America has incurred in trying to juggle its commitments to Israel and its relationship with the Arab oil states— the most dramatic one being the Arab oil embargoes that followed the 1967 and 1973 Middle East wars—including the efforts to make peace between Arabs and Israelis.

U.S. presidents and lawmakers have maintained America's Middle East Paradigm (MEP) and pursued U.S. interests in the Middle East during the Cold War—and later from the 1991 Gulf War to the 2003 war in Iraq—as part of a hegemonic strategy in the region. American policy has been based on strengthening ties with its key allies or "strategic assets" in the Middle East—Israel and Egypt in the eastern Mediterranean and Saudi Arabia and the Shah's Iran in the Persian Gulf. These strategic alliances were supposed not only to help preserve U.S. strategic interests in the region but they were also expected to enhance the status of these so-called allies as viable pro-American and Western-oriented outposts in the region and to create the conditions for the comprehensive resolution of the Arab-Israeli conflict.

It seems that the price of the tickets is increasing, while the main actors' performances are not improving. The deadliest attack on the American homeland was carried out by a group of Saudi and Egyptian terrorists, members of an organization with links to the Saudis. The 9/11 attacks were aimed at punishing the United States for its support for Saudi Arabia, Egypt, and Israel and for its military presence in the region. Currently the House of Saud seems to be facing the greatest threat to its survival while the Egyptian military dictatorship is sitting on a political, economic, and demographic volcano that could explode any day. Similarly, Israel is confronting terrorist attacks on its civilians and its future as a Jewish state while being challenged by the demographic realities of a growing Palestinian population. And of course, an anti-American Shiite theocracy has been in place in Iran since 1979, and it is quite conceivable that as a result of the ouster of Saddam Hussein another Shiite theocracy could be established in Baghdad in the near future.

Indeed, America's designated allies have not been helping the United States to secure its stated goals in the region. More important from an American perspective, the United States is now having to pay more in terms of blood and dollars to deal with the anti-American violence that its support for the authoritarian Arab regimes and Israel's occupation of Palestine have triggered—leading to the Gulf war, the Iraq war, and to the military quagmire that the United States is sinking into in Mesopotamia. On top of all the dilemmas facing U.S. policy in the Middle East as a result of supporting Saudi Arabia, Israel, and the other pro-American regimes in the region, the beneficiaries of the astounding levels of U.S. support are confronting the greatest threats to their survival since they emerged as independent political entities.

One would assume that the outcome of such American policies would, at a minimum, result in some sort of reassessment and perhaps even bring about a change in the U.S. approach toward its friends in the Middle East. Instead, America has been expanding its presence in the region as well as its political support and military commitments to the Saudis, Egyptians, and Israelis, and in the process, invading Iraq and Afghanistan. The Bush administration's neoconservative ideologues have proposed that America launch a campaign to introduce a system of one man-one vote to Saudi Arabia, Egypt, and Palestine which would probably ensure the coming to power in Riyadh, Cairo, and East Jerusalem of political groups that would be opposed to stated American goals of establishing hegemony in the region and of protecting the pro-American regimes in Egypt, the Persian Gulf, and Israel.

One would also expect that the current violence in the Holy Land and Mesopotamia and the related bloody television images would put pressure on Capitol Hill and the media to reconsider American involvement in the Middle East. Instead, American lawmakers and columnists insist that America "do something" to end the conflict between Israelis and Palestinians and make sure that the Shiites, Sunnis, and Kurds in Iraq do not kill each other. There is very little debate about the sources of American involvement in the Middle East—about why America is expanding its military presence and diplomatic engagement in that region. As noted in the previous chapters, much of the criticism of Washington's policies in the Middle East has to do with the way they have been pursued. If only America had been more active in pursuing an Israeli-Palestinian peace, if only it had dispatched more troops to Iraq or adopted a more effective occupation strategy, well, things would have looked quite different. Or so argue those in Washington who have challenged the Bush administration's Middle East policy.

In the previous chapter, I tried to explain why the political realities of the Middle East have forced the United States into never-ending entanglements by focusing on the role of the United States' MEP in shaping American policy in that part of the world with the kaleidoscopic nature of its regional politics and its complex interactions with the international system. This chapter follows that discussion with a few observations about the way the costs produced by U.S. intervention in the Middle East are affected through the influence of American domestic political factors representing Middle East interests. Such domestic political pressures make it more difficult for the United States to disengage from the region despite the fact that American involvement seems to create more instability and chaos there. In particular, I am focusing on American fixation with the notion that the American economy is "dependent" on Middle Eastern oil— and that Washington has "to do something" in order to resolve the Israel/Palestine conflict. As I stressed in the first two chapters, I am not arguing that American policy in the Middle East has been "hijacked" by Zionist and Arabists in Washington. I am suggesting, however, that these political, institutional, and bureaucratic forces have helped provide political support as well as rationales for protecting the MEP despite the many challenges it has been facing.

THE BUTTERFLY EFFECT

Integrate the kaleidoscope model into the science of chaos theory, and some interesting applications could be drawn into the analysis of the Middle Eastern system and the American posture there. Chaos theory offers a way of seeing order and pattern where formerly only the random, the erratic, the unpredictable—in short, the chaotic—were observed. Despite its chaotic tendencies—social upheavals, political revolutions, regional wars, and global entanglements—there are certain elements of order, stability, and continuity that have characterized the Middle East system since the fall of the Ottoman Empire. The main features of the region are the ruling political, social, ethnic, and religious elites who fight for their survival by creating and dissolving shifting alliances with domestic, regional, and external players. Each move by a regional or an external player, like the famous Butterfly Effect, tends to produce new alliances and configurations and certain stability ensues as long as the various ruling elites sense that their interests are being maintained—at least for a while.[6]

The imposition after World War I of a nation-state system on the Middle East and the institutionalization of that system after World War II by the granting of political independence to new states did not bring lasting order. Instead, the nation-state system provided a new arena in which ruling elites, especially the proponents of Zionism and Pan Arabism, attempted to advance their interests. As Middle East historian David Fromkin puts it, the Middle East's unwillingness to adopt a more stable structure is explained by the fact that "in the Middle East there is no sense of legitimacy—no agreement on rules of the game—and no belief, universally shared in the region, that within whatever boundaries, the entities that call themselves countries and the men who claim to be rulers are entitled to recognition as such."[7] Most of the region's states are superficial entities that were created by British and French imperialism. Those states, in addition to lacking political legitimacy, have had neither economic viability nor experience with liberal or democratic traditions. In those societies, various ethnic and religious groups are engaged in fierce competition for power. That competition is typically won by whichever military clique controls the national television system and usually spills over into other states in the region in the form of secessionist or irredentist movements.

The previous chapters emphasized the failure of the United States and other external players to impose their will on the Middle East. In the long run, the costs of intervention and alliances with the region's ruling elites have usually increased in direct proportion to the external power's attempts to increase the power of one regional player at the expense of other players—or to dominate the region by excluding competing external players. Much of the discussion by pundits about the American invasion of Iraq and U.S. policy in the Middle East are based on the assumption that the right mix of American policies could produce "better" outcomes. But from my realpolitik perspective, it is difficult, if not impossible—and probably unnecessary—to determine whether the intervention of external power in the Middle East or elsewhere could even lead to "better" outcomes. The notion that such "better" outcomes are achievable and that their pursuit is legitimate, if not necessary, in terms of the national interest of the United States or other powers, is predicated on a progressive view of the world that runs contrary to the realist school of international relations whose view I share. This progressive, or Wilsonian, vision is based on what amounts to religious faith in the will and the ability of political leaders to do good at home and abroad and on a wishful reading of human nature. And while this progressive or "idealist" vision has dominated the analysis and rhetoric of American foreign policy, in reality, most of the major foreign policy decisions made in the Middle East and elsewhere by the United States, like those of other great powers, were based on the consideration of power politics as measured by geo-strategic and geo-economic interests as well as political pressures at home exerted by interest groups, opinion makers, the media, and other powerful institutions.[8] And the duty of the realist policymaker and policy analyst is to "exhibit things as they are, not as they ought to be" based on an ideal vision of reality.[9]

That American policy in the Middle East after World War II, not unlike that of Great Britain in the aftermath of World War II, promoted the interests of two national movements, Zionism and Arab nationalism, should not be seen as part of an effort to "do the right thing," to make the Middle East safe for self-determination and political freedom and to promote just causes that reflect progressive Western values. Based on such considerations, the Kurds, a national group with a common language, culture, and history that developed in a defined geographical area, should have won political independence and a state before such political status was granted to the 600,000 Jews in Palestine or to the Saudis, or, for that matter, to the Iraqi "nation." The fact is that the Kurds, the Berbers of North Africa, the non-Arab blacks in Sudan, the Armenians, and the Druze in Syria have not enjoyed the support of the United States or Great Britain, while the Arabs and the Zionists have. Such political outcomes reflected the reality of power politics—the success of Zionist and Arab elites to use their power to draw external powers into the Middle East and help them advance their interests.

PRE-WESTPHALIA MIDDLE EAST

Hence when we conclude a discussion of this or that U.S. move in the Middle East by stating "and the rest is history," we mean that, like the Butterfly Effect, those interactions between local, regional, and global powers that have led to the military and diplomatic intervention of the United States in the region, ended up producing new, different, and unpredictable outcomes. Those outcomes are pregnant with opportunities; but whether they are seized to advance productive or destructive ends depends on the players themselves and their interests. And in any case, unlike the market that provides a basis for making rational choices that are based on the price system, the arena of politics forces players to accept outcomes that run contrary to their interests. Under a constitutional-liberal political system with its checks and balances, we could strive to achieve more optimal policy outcomes than in authoritarian systems. But we cannot achieve that in the context of an anarchic international system.[10] The system of nation-states that emerged after the Peace of Westphalia provides us with ways to create some order in the international system. But it assumes, as in the case of the European state-system since the nineteenth century, that the governments that rule those states enjoy some level of domestic political legitimacy and that they are committed to some rules of the game to manage their relations.[11]

Such legitimacy has not been the case in the Middle East since the collapse of the Ottoman Empire. Until states in the Middle East solve the problem of legitimacy, reach the stage of their own Peace of Westphalia—the central political issue—and accept some rules of their regional game, the dominant political elites in the Middle East as well as those who challenge them will be engaged in continuous, bloody struggles for power over ethnic, religious, and national issues. In fact, foreign intervention has a tendency to aggravate the situation by creating inducements in the form of military and economic aid and diplomatic support. Such aid and support encourages the regional elites to hold on to their power and refrain from reforming their systems and from reaching agreement with their rivals. As a result, they establish neither political legitimacy nor a regional order under a set of accepted rules. It was the Cold War competition between the two superpowers that helped keep in place and consolidate the power of the military dictatorships and autocratic monarchies in the Arab world (and Iran until 1979) and which provided those Middle Eastern regimes with the resources and the incentives to use their military power at home and abroad as part of intra- and inter-Arab conflicts as well as against Israel.

Similarly, Israeli policies were based on the need to secure the support of global players—the Soviet Union and the United States in 1947–48, the French during the 1950s, and the Americans for most of the Cold War—as a way of compensating Israel for its diplomatic and military disadvantages vis-à-vis the Arab world and sustaining the Zionist elites in power. But since the 1967 war, the U.S. support has helped Israel maintain its control over the West Bank and Gaza and played into the hands of the proponents of the Greater Israel project as well as postponing economic reforms.

THE "RIVAL TWINS"

Imagine that we are present at the creation of the interventionist American MEP. It is 1945 and we are listening to the conversation taking place in Washington, D.C., at the home of Sumner Welles, a respected American diplomat who had served as undersecretary of state (1937–43). Welles, under the influence of his anti-imperialist hostility toward Britain, was one of the few supporters of Zionism in the foreign policy establishment at that time. Against the backdrop of the reports about the fate of European Jewry under the Nazis, those pro-Zionist Americans were critical of what they saw as London's abandonment of its 1917 commitment stipulated in the Balfour Declaration to establish a "Jewish Homeland" in Palestine. Welles was meeting then with Eliahu (Epstein) Elath, at the time the senior representative of the Zionist movement in Washington who later became the first Israeli ambassador to the United States. Elath complained about the growing political influence of the oil companies in Washington and their efforts to weaken support for the establishment of a Jewish state. He was worried that a coalition that included the oil companies, the State Department, and the Pentagon, which were at that time committed to the anti-Soviet containment strategy (later they would be known as the "Arabists") would emerge as Zionism's main opponents in Washington.[12]

To Elath's surprise, Welles suggested that one of the potential sources of Zionist success would be actually the power of those pro-Arab oil companies and the administration's Cold War proponents. The members of the oil companies and the new national security establishment had been instrumental in drawing attention to American strategic and economic interests in the Middle East and in expanding U.S. military and diplomatic involvement in the area. Otherwise, explained Welles, the Middle East would not have figured at the top of the American foreign policy agenda, since most Americans in the aftermath of World War II were drifting back into the nation's traditional isolationism. Welles's conclusion was that the interests of the Zionists and the Arabists were compatible on one level. The efforts of the anti-Zionists and the Cold Warriors in the administration and the Oil Lobby would in the long run work to the advantage of a Jewish state. Support for that state would be rooted primarily in moral and historical reasons. But Israel would later be able to position itself as operating in the interests of Washington in the Middle East, a region that was becoming more and more critical to the United States as part of its Cold War geo-strategic and geo-economic calculations. At the same time, a Jewish state in the Middle East could benefit the Cold War strategists and their allies in the oil companies, since it would provide moral and cultural justification for American involvement in a region populated by Arabs and other exotic people whose history was so alien to most Americans.

Welles's insights into the historical sources of U.S. intervention in the Middle East suggest that, contrary to conventional wisdom, the relationship between Zionists and Arabists, between "pro-Israelis" and "pro-Arabs" in

Washington and within the bureaucratic and interest groups that represent them, should not be regarded as purely a zero-sum game. Arabists and Zionists have both supported increasing American involvement in the Middle East—while disagreeing over the distribution of U.S. benefits in that region. But Welles could not have predicted that the Cold War (which was only starting to take shape when he met with Elath; the term "Cold War" was not being used at that point) would last for close to a half-century. He also underestimated the ability of policy elites and interest groups to advance and maintain a U.S. presence in the Middle East, and to mobilize the support of the White House and Congress for the policy, despite the end of the Cold War.

WASHINGTON'S INSIDE-THE-BELTWAY GAMES AND THE MEP

Public choice theory provides us with an original perspective on the way domestic interests affect U.S. foreign policy. As Nobel laureate James M. Buchanan and his co-author Gordon Tullock proposed, "Interest-group activity, measured in terms of organizational costs, is a direct function of the 'profits' expected from the political process by functional groups." Foreign policy decisions are "public goods" that provide such interest groups and their allies within the bureaucracy and Congress special "profits" and benefits. Those benefits take the form of growing presidential and public attention that in turn leads to expansion of the bureaucracy, to increases in budgets, and to the provisions of goods, such as economic aid and military assistance to foreign clients. Hence, foreign policy elites make "increased investment[s] in organization[s] aimed at securing differential gains by political means."

A spiral effect comes to play: The success of foreign policy elites in pushing for certain bureaucratic measures and Congressional legislation that protect and advance their interests and those of their clients increases total collective action in a given foreign policy "issue-area." That success, in turn, produces incentives for other functional or interest groups to invest resources in political organizations. The spiral effect is manifested in the rise of foreign policy "iron triangles," three-way interactions involving elected members of Congress, career bureaucrats, and special interest lobbies. From the close triad of interests "involving small circles of participants who [succeeded] in becoming largely autonomous," foreign policies emerge as Congress writes and passes favorable legislation, bureaucrats implement those Congressional mandates in return for big budgets, and special interest groups back with re-election money and other support the helpful members of Congress. Various conflicts and coalitions develop among members of the foreign policy triangle, but they all have an interest in preserving and expanding the issue-area in which they operate, to focus public attention on it, and to create an environment in which government is asked to "do something" to resolve the problems in the issue-area.[13]

The Middle East issue-area, that is, the MEP, has provided an opportunity for a foreign policy triangle to emerge. Washington's Middle Eastern professionals, both the "pro-Israelis" and the "pro-Arabs," derive obvious economic and political dividends from their services. Those dividends include decisions on oil prices, military procurements, elections to seats in Congress, professional advancement in the bureaucracy, and consulting jobs. Middle Eastern terrorism, for example, has become a full-time industry for many experts and consultants after 9/11.

One element of the Middle Eastern foreign policy triangle is the Israeli lobby that includes a network of American Jewish organizations headed by the American Israel Public Affairs Committee (AIPAC), which delivers votes and financial support to members of Congress in exchange for their securing votes for financial aid and other benefits for Israel. The Israeli lobby also mobilizes Congressional support for policies advanced by the bureaucracy in exchange for rewards, such as the transfer of sophisticated arms, to Israel from the executive branch.

Another component of the Middle Eastern triangle, the Arab oil lobby, is a unique constellation of corporate and bureaucratic supporters, lobbyists, and special interest groups that can be described as the "petro-military complex" that backs U.S. diplomatic, and military commitments to Saudi Arabia and the other Persian Gulf states and receives in exchange rewards such as expanded military budgets and high-powered jobs. As they become more and more dependent on Washington's assistance, the political elites in the Arab world and Israel, in turn, use that financial and military aid to perpetuate their political power and status in the Middle East.

This American support for the elites of Israel and the Arab countries tends to perpetuate their political and economic systems and produce disincentives for reform as well as create conditions conducive to continuing regional strife. That situation, of course, creates the need for more American aid and commitment to the Middle Eastern players.

KEEPING THE MEP ALIVE

Welles's forecast proved to be right on the money. The efforts of the Arabists in the late 1940s to focus American attention on the Middle East benefited Israel's long-term interests, and the Jewish state eventually succeeded, in the 1970s and

1980s, in selling itself as an effective American "unsinkable aircraft carrier" in the eastern Mediterranean. Similarly, Israeli efforts to draw the U.S. elite and public into more involvement in the area played into the hands of the Palestinians by helping them to elevate their concerns to the top of Washington's foreign policy agenda, as demonstrated by the frequent visits of the late Yasser Arafat to Washington in the 1990s. It is inconceivable that Washington would have offered the same kind of attention and largesse to the leaders of the Tamil separatists of Sri Lanka or even to the Albanians in Kosovo. By becoming the de facto patron of the Jewish state, Washington is being forced either to take action against or buy-off those who direct threats against Israel. When Washington succeeded in mediating the Egyptian-Israeli peace agreement in 1979, it had to pay for its services by providing new American aid to Egypt and adopting it as a permanent recipient of an annual American handout of economic and military aid. Similar aid packages were provided to Jordan and the Palestinians after they had signed peace accords with Israel.

It is not surprising, therefore, that Israeli and Arab oil lobbies and the Middle Eastern players they represent have had an interest in keeping public attention focused on the Middle East, in order to keep the MEP alive. Public attention has strengthened the ability of the members of the Middle Eastern foreign policy triangle to continue to provide public goods to their regional clients, including military and economic aid to Israel and military protection for Saudi Arabia and the Arab oil states. At some point, the various members of the triangle could lose their ability to provide those goods—if the American public loses interest in the Middle East or comes to the conclusion that the costs involved in maintaining U.S. commitments are too high. As economist Robert Higgs suggested, foreign policy elites are more successful than domestic policy elites in marketing ideologies and controlling information and, as a result, in manipulating public opinion, mainly because foreign policy issues are too distant and complex for the average citizen to comprehend. But Higgs argued that eventually "the burden of death and taxes" can constrain even the advancement of their agendas.[14]

But the Americans have been willing to carry the burden of death and taxes if foreign interventions are seen as part of a strategy to promote legitimate national interests or causes. The Cold War provided an ideological framework in which the intervention in the Middle East was justified until 1991. While Saddam Hussein and the Mullahs of Teheran were portrayed by George H. W. Bush and Bill Clinton as threats to U.S. national security, both presidents recognized that those two bogeymen could not serve as a basis for mobilizing public support for lengthy and costly intervention in the Middle East, as opposed to the more cost-free Pax Americana projects in the Middle East that were advanced for most of the 1990s. It was the attacks on the American homeland on 9/11 and the ensuing war on terrorism or Global Intifada that seemed to be providing an opportunity for establishing a new ideological frame for a major American intervention in the region.

SPLENDID LITTLE, AND COSTLY BIG, MIDDLE EASTERN WARS

Indeed, since 1945 the various Middle Eastern wars and crises—post–World War II instability and Soviet threats in the eastern Mediterranean (Turkey and Greece) and Iran; the 1956 Suez Campaign; the 1958 U.S. intervention in Lebanon; the 1967 Six-Day War; the 1973 Yom Kippur War; the 1982 Lebanon War; the Iran-Iraq War; the 1991 Gulf War; and the various Arab-Israel peace processes—have been used by the Middle Eastern foreign policy triangle to maintain or increase American involvement in the region. Two ideologies—the historical and moral commitment to Israel and the Cold War ideology—have been used to mobilize public support for expanded diplomatic and military interventionism. Each regional war and crisis has marked another step in the growing American involvement in the region. Wars and crises have helped to create new constituencies in the bureaucracy, Congress, and new interest groups that have acquired vested interests in American involvement in the region and joined the Middle Eastern foreign policy triangle. Hence, Arab-Israeli wars were an important turning point in the evolution of AIPAC, the pro-Israel lobby, as a political force in Washington. As each war increased Israel's dependence on the United States, the attendant increase in demand for AIPAC's successful lobbying was paralleled by an increase in the amount of aid and support Congress approved for the Jewish state.[15]

Regional wars and crises in the Middle East were usually followed by presidential doctrines. Those were supported by a bipartisan consensus in Congress and set new priorities for the U.S. foreign policy agenda and increased American diplomatic and military commitments to the Middle East—to the Arab states in the Persian Gulf after 1956, to Israel after the 1967 and 1973 wars, to the Arab oil states after the Iranian revolution and the Soviet invasion of Afghanistan, and to Egypt and Israel after the two had made peace. After each crisis, those doctrines, military commitments, and aid packages were institutionalized and became a permanent component of the American policy-making structure. There are few constituencies calling for their contraction, and members of the elite and the public seem to take them for granted, as though commitments of billions of dollars to sustain the bankrupted economy of Egypt or to subsidize Israeli prosperity were stipulated in the U.S. Bill of Rights.

OUR ALLIES, THE SAUDIS

In the previous chapters, I pointed to the way the American patron has been embroiled in costly entanglements in the Middle East with clients that have their own agendas that have not always corresponded to that of Washington. The U.S. relationship with Saudi Arabia and its policies in the Persian Gulf demonstrate that problem. Since the 1950s American policies there have revolved around one dilemma: which "regional policemen" will protect the regimes that control the oil resources of the area. Under the Shah, Iran had played that role throughout the 1950s, 1960s, and most of the 1970s. Until the 1979 Iranian Revolution, U.S. policy in the Persian Gulf was based on an attempt to establish a regional balance of power among Iran, Iraq, Saudi Arabia, and the other Arab oil states. In the early 1970s, when the United States was pursuing the Nixon Doctrine, American policy in the Persian Gulf rested on the twin pillars of Iran and Saudi Arabia. The Shah's Iran was expected to deter radical Iraq from realizing its aggressive intentions against Kuwait, a role played by Great Britain in the 1960s.

The costs to the United States and the American people were enormous. To help the Shah and the Saudis build their military might, the Nixon administration encouraged a spiraling rise in the price of Middle Eastern oil. Increased costs led to the emergence of an oil cartel as an international economic power, to the traumatic oil and economic crises of the 1970s (more on that in chapter 5), and to the rise of the petro-military states of the region that included Iraq and Libya in addition to Iran and Saudi Arabia. Those developments, in turn, helped bring about a major Middle Eastern crisis, the 1973 Yom Kippur War that produced new and very risky American military and diplomatic commitments. These international crises and wars created the conditions for the anti-Shah and anti-American backlash inside Iran that culminated in the 1979 revolution and the birth of the Iranian regional bully, whom Washington was asked to contain, leading eventually to the bloody Iran-Iraq war.[16] The decision to strengthen Iraq in order to deter Iran, and the policies that followed, especially the decision that U.S. naval vessels would escort reflagged Kuwaiti tankers during the Iran-Iraq war and provide American intelligence to the Iraqis, were examples of Washington's complex balance-of-power games in the region. Those policies were celebrated by the same analysts who later criticized the pro-Iraqi "tilt," who called for military action against Iraq, and who again advocated American restoration of regional balance. Hence Laurie Mylroie, one of the leading supporters of the Gulf War and the war against Iraq, had earlier been an advocate of strengthening U.S. ties with Saddam Hussein's Iraq.[17] The pro-Iraqi tilt, however, was a natural outcome of the balance-of-power policies. Trying to co-opt Iraq into the pro-American regional system and punishing Tehran made sense in the context of those Cold War policies.

But those Cold War policies may have encouraged Saddam Hussein to invade Kuwait in 1990 as part of his strategy to set up Iraq as a hegemon in the Persian Gulf, counter-balancing Iranian power. The Bush administration's decision to go to war against Iraq to liberate Kuwait did not reflect Cold War calculations but an interest in preventing Iraq from emerging as a regional hegemon—Clinton's policies vis-à-vis Iraq reflected similar concerns—and as part of a strategy to protect Kuwait and Saudi Arabia and maintain U.S. hegemony in the Persian Gulf and the Middle East in the aftermath of the Cold War. If Washington would have permitted Iran and Iraq to emerge as regional hegemons, Saudi Arabia and the rest of the oil-producing states in the region would have been transformed into political-military satellites of either Baghdad or Tehran—two governments that rejected the concept of Pax Americana in the Middle East. This was an outcome no U.S. administration committed to the traditional MEP could accept.

What is the end result of American policies pursued by several administrations? The United States has maintained in power a reactionary medieval theocracy in Saudi Arabia and a fascist military dictatorship in Iraq, encouraged the development of anti-Western Islamic guerrillas in Afghanistan, and ultimately created an environment conducive for anti-American terrorism. These policies help set the stage for the invasions of Afghanistan and Iraq, in which America finds itself even more committed to survival of the regimes in Saudi Arabia and to the creation of new political-military protectorates in Iraq and Afghanistan. This high-level of U.S. intervention and commitments in the Middle East end up providing short-term benefits to pro-American elites in the region and to their allies—but are harming the long-terms interests of the United States.

ARABIAN POLITICAL REALITIES

Saudi Arabia and its oil lobby in Washington, personified in the powerful Saudi ambassador, Prince Bandar, have been central and effective players in Washington, influencing policymaking and legislation behind the scenes. It would probably not be an exaggeration to suggest that Bandar and AIPAC are regarded as two of the most powerful players representing foreign interests in the

U.S. Capital.[18] There is no doubt that the Saudis have had to deal with growing criticism in Washington over the fact that 15 of the 19 hijackers in the Al Qaeda attacks in 9/11 were Saudi citizens and that Saudi money has been spreading the puritanical Sunni ideology, the official creed of the Saudi state, through mosques around the world. What is amazing is not the hostility toward the Saudis, which was reflected in opinion polls such as one conducted by *Time* magazine/CNN, which found that 72 percent of Americans would not trust Saudi Arabia as an ally, but the fact that the Bush administration continues to maintain the notion that Washington has a "special relationship" with Riyadh as demonstrated, among other things, by the decision of the White House to withhold from the public parts of a Congressional inquiry into 9/11, which lawmakers contend listed prominent Saudis under investigation for possible terrorist links.[19] While vocal members of Congress from both parties remain suspicious of the cozy relationship between Washington and Riyadh, it is not expected that any dramatic changes will take place in the strategic relationship between the two countries—as long as the United States continues to pursue its hegemonic policies in the region.

The move by the Bush Administration to end the deployment of U.S. troops in Saudi Arabia in August 2003 should not be regarded as part of an American strategy to disengage from Saudi Arabia, but as a way to relieve some of the political pressure exerted by the Saudi royal family by ending a deployment that dated to the Gulf War—and removing one of Osama bin Ladin's rallying cries. There were expectations in the aftermath of the invasion of Iraq that the United States would be able to use Iraq, whose oil reserves are second only to Saudi Arabia, as a springboard to democratize the Middle East and create the foundations for a Pax Americana based on an alliance with pro-American democratic oil producing countries. These schemes are proving to be nothing more than pipe-dreams.[20]

There is no doubt that the House of Saud that has ruled the Desert Kingdom since the country's foundation in 1932 faces an unprecedented threat to its survival and that "it is caught between the criticism from the United States— the kingdom's traditional ally that feels betrayed by Saudi's exporting of terrorism—and the pressures of a conservative religious establishment on whom it has long relies for its legitimacy."[21] But the response to this threat is not going to usher a new age of *glasnost* in Saudi Arabia. With the survival of the regime at stake, the members of the royal family, the el-Sauds, relying on their power base among the country's various tribes and religious authorities, will probably try to put personal rivalries aside and adopt a policy of both co-opting and repressing dissenters. The collapse of the royal family will certainly not lead to the emergence of a Saudi Gorbachev and an era of political reforms, but to the rise of a more radical Islamic regime, one that will most likely be based on an alliance between military figures and radical religious figures. Facing the threat of a military coup, one could expect the Saudis to preempt such a move by selecting a more conservative member of the dynasty to rule the country.

In any case, as long as Washington continues to cling to its MEP that assumes that the United States has to maintain its military supremacy in the Persian Gulf, it will not be able to resolve the dilemmas it is currently facing in the Middle East. The United States' alliance with the ruling Arab regimes and its military presence in the region will continue to foster anti-Americanism á la Al Qaeda and force the United States into more costly military engagements like the Gulf War and the Iraq War. Such a scenario will also involve the strengthening of ties with a theocracy like Saudi Arabia. At the same time, an effort to "democratize" these regimes would only bring to power more radical anti-American forces.

AND ARABIAN OIL FANTASIES

As this book suggests, the United States could and should disengage from the Middle East, since its presence there is not advancing U.S. interests; it is actually harming them. But one reason that America's MEP is alive and well is because the American people and their representatives in Washington seemed to have bought into the main "party line" that the proponents of this paradigm have been advancing—that American involvement in the Middle East is required in order to protect American economic interests by securing for the American people "access to cheap oil."

Contrary to the conventional wisdom accepted by many Americans—that "we are dependent on Saudi and Middle Eastern oil"—only 17 percent of oil imports to the United States in 2002 originated in Saudi Arabia and 6 percent came from Iraq. The largest source of foreign oil for Americans in 2002— more than 30 percent—was Latin America. Latin America's contribution was led by two countries with which the United States maintains an uneasy political relationship, Venezuela and Mexico.[22] Yet one hears or reads very little these days about American "dependency" on "Latin America oil" and the threats to American economic survival posed by Hugo Chavez, the anti-American and left-wing demagogue who rules Venezuela. After all, and contrary to the-American-economy-is-dependent-on-Middle-East-oil misconception, the United States was never dependent on oil from the Middle East. Even today it gets 70 percent of its crude oil supplies either from its own production or from neighboring countries in North and South America, according to oil expert Daniel Yergin, who calculated that with the addition of energy resources in West Africa and the North Sea, 90 percent of America's crude supplies do not originate in the Middle East.[23]

In a study that was written before the war against Iraq, economist Dan Losman blasted the myth of American "dependency" on Middle Eastern oil, or what he calls "America's oil paranoia." According to his calculations, safeguarding Middle East oil supplies has probably cost the United States $30-$60 billion a year. "That is outrageously high relative to the total value ($54 billion in 1999) of imported crude, of which only $15 billion came from the Persian Gulf," he noted.[24] As Losman and other economists argued, most of the economic damage from the 1973 oil embargo emanated from American policy blunders. Pre-embargo, poor U.S. policies made the American economy vulnerable, and post-embargo, continued price controls and misguided regulation magnified the damage. At the same time, U.S. foreign policy, including its alliance with the Iranian shah, Mohammed Reza Palhavi, who ruled the country until the 1979 revolution, and with Saudi Arabia, only helped increase the costs of safeguarding the access to the oil in the region: The shah was the leading hawk in the Organization of Petroleum Exporting Countries (OPEC) in moving the cartel to raise the price of oil. The Saudis were the driving force behind the oil embargo imposed on the United States in 1973 to punish it for supporting Israel during the Yom Kippur War. Oil prices leapt by more than 200 percent in the early 1970s and later quadrupled—as the United States and the rest of the industrialized world sank into a devastating economic recession. All this was taking place at a time when the United States was providing military assistance to both Iran and the Saudis—as well as to the Israelis who were embroiled in a war against the Egyptians and the Syrians, who were themselves backed financially and diplomatically by the Saudis. Such connections demonstrate another interesting point: One of the costs Washington has to pay in order to maintain its MEP involves making peace, or at least trying to end the fighting, between the rival twins, with the 1973 war and its aftermath being the most dramatic example.

Greater reliance on market-based resource allocations during the 1980s helped generate a substantial and sustained decline in oil prices and weaken the power of OPEC. Current prices, when adjusted for inflation, are lower than in all the years after the 1973 embargo price hikes. Currently, Saudi Arabia is only one of America's top crude oil suppliers, which include Venezuela, Canada, and Mexico. Additionally, the American economy is less energy dependent than it was years ago. Countries sell oil to United States because they need to do so in order to advance their economies and maintain control of the populations in their rapidly growing regions. They do not sell oil to reward the United States.

In fact, it is the costs of maintaining a U.S. military presence in the Middle East and of the resulting anti-American terrorism and not the economic realities of oil demand and supply that have increased the overall costs of oil consumption for the American people since 1991. No, Middle Eastern oil is not cheap for the American consumer if one takes into consideration the costs of those geo-political decisions that have been an integral part of America's Middle East paradigm, including the Gulf War and the dual containment of Iraq and Iran, and now the invasion of Afghanistan and Iraq and their aftermaths. A process of disengagement from the Middle East would have made the Gulf War and the dual containment strategy unnecessary and would have made it unlikely that 9/11 and the invasion of Iraq would have taken place. Such a policy would have not only provided the United States greater access to Iraqi and Iranian oil, but would have meant that Americans would not have had to pay the high costs in blood and treasure because of wars and terrorism in the Middle East. Just removing the embargo against Iraq would have been about $100 billion cheaper than going to war against that country in 2004, according to oil expert Jerry Taylor.[25] Yes, even under a process of U.S. disengagement from the Middle East, the American consumer would have to incur the costs of occasional bursts in oil prices. But compare that to the price it would have to pay for maintaining the occupation of Iraq in the aftermath of Gulf War. "Sir, let's go home. I'll pay five dollars a gallon!" said an army colonel to Losman when he landed in Saudi Arabia in preparation for Desert Storm.[26] That frames the moral question embedded in American national security strategy: Is it worth spilling American blood to keep import prices "acceptable?"

But what Americans are paying now is not for keeping oil prices "acceptable" or for having access to oil resources in the Persian Gulf. That is what they were doing during the Cold War as part of a strategy to insure that the members of its Western alliance in Europe and northeast Asia—and the United States—would have access to Middle Eastern oil. The American strategy of maintaining close ties with Saudi Arabia and Iran was not very cost-effective, since it may have actually encouraged those Middle Eastern producers to raise the price of oil. But the policy nevertheless made geo-strategic sense in terms of maintaining the unity of the Western alliance in opposition to the communist bloc and under American leadership. But since the end of the Cold War, the United States is using its military power in the Middle East to help the Europeans (and the Japanese) have access to affordable oil, which in turn encourages the free-riding of the Europeans (and Japanese) and creates disincentives for the Europeans (and the Japanese) to pay the costs of their own security.

All of that does not make a lot of sense if one considers core U.S. national interests. But as I argue in the following chapters, the members of the American foreign policy establishment, in alliance with the rival twins, the Arab oil producing states and Israel, see the control of the Middle East and its oil resources as part of a way to maintain a geo-political and geo-economic leverage over Europe (and Japan) and secure America's unipolar position. The control of the access to the energy resources in the Middle East provides the United States with such a leverage over the Europeans, the Japanese, and even the Chinese, whose economies are dependent on access to oil resources in the Middle East. From that perspective, Saudi Arabia and the other oil-producing states in the Persian Gulf are gas stations that America controls. If the Europeans want to fill the tanks of their cars with Saudi petrol they will need to deal with the American owners.

AMERICA'S PEACE-MAKING DILEMMA: THE NEED TO "DO SOMETHING"

One of the ways Washington was hoping to reduce the costs of protecting the MEP and maintaining its position in the Middle East during the Cold War had taken the form of trying to make peace between Israel and the Arabs. The Arab oil embargo and the nuclear face-off with the Soviet Union in 1973 were seen as direct outcomes of this dispute in the context of the Cold War and reflected the need for the United States to juggle its conflicting commitments to the two sides. Unless Washington was "doing something" to resolve the Arab-Israeli conflict, it would be antagonizing the Arabs and encouraging them to use their "oil weapon." It would be creating incentives for the Soviets to exploit and direct that Arab anger at the United States. Moreover, if and when the United States could make peace between Arabs and Israelis, the Middle Eastern twins would be rivals no more. Their common interest in helping the United States advance its interests in the Middle East would override any differences between them and create an environment conducive for the formation of a pro-American and anti-Soviet Arab-Israeli axis.

Hence in the 1970s and the 1980s the concerns over the Soviet role in the region and a possible Arab oil embargo as well as the need to protect Israel—demonstrated during the 1973 war—served as rationales for the enormous American political and economic commitments to peace. These American commitments to peace were embodied in the Egyptian-Israeli disengagement negotiations and the ensuing Camp David agreement. That accord was seen as a way to weaken Soviet influence in the region, placate the pro-American Arab oil regimes, and preserve Israel's security interests—while consolidating America's position in that area of the world.

That perspective tended to underestimate the role that self-interest played in Egyptian and Israeli calculations; they decided to make peace out of their respective national self-interest—and not Cold War calculations—as they recognized the growing human and economic costs of continuing the conflict. But both countries were able to draw Washington into a lengthy and complex negotiating process that required high-level U.S. involvement to win Israeli and Egyptian backing for American diplomacy. As a condition for signing the agreement, Cairo and Jerusalem were able to extract from the United States massive amounts of aid to help shore up public support for the American diplomatic arrangements and to pay the "costs of peace." In a way, the massive aid to the two countries signaled to the Middle Eastern players that peace was more important to the United States than to either Israel or the Arabs.

But in reality, both the Israelis and the Egyptians got exactly what they wanted from the accord: Egypt got back the Sinai Peninsula it had lost in the 1967 war and Israel detached Egypt from the anti-Israeli Arab front. In return, Israel gave back a piece of land that did not belong to it and Egypt made peace with Israel because it did not have the power or the will to make war against the Jewish state. The "concessions" they made were not very costly; but in return they won huge economic and military commitments from the United States, in addition to advancing their own interests. At the same time, Washington was now allied with an Egypt that was isolated in the Arab world and was facing growing anti-Americanism in the region for its failure to deliver Israeli concessions over the West Bank and Gaza. And after neutralizing the Egyptian military threat, Israel felt free to invade Lebanon in 1982 as part of an effort to destroy the Palestinian infrastructure there. That move led eventually to a costly and bloody U.S. military intervention in Lebanon that helped transform the Shiite community there into a major anti-American player. And the Israeli-Egyptian agreement certainly did not achieve the main goal that Washington's policymakers had in mind: to compensate the Americans for the "loss" of Iran as a result of the revolution there.

But advancing the Middle Eastern peace process—primarily by pressuring the Arabs to recognize Israel and trying to persuade Israel to give up the occupied territories—became an integral item on the foreign policy agenda of every American president after the Cold War. It became the model of an America-led "peace process." The Israelis and Arabs were expected to make concessions that were perceived as "favors" to America and its president; Washington, in turn, had to reciprocate with financial, diplomatic, or military aid and commitments.[27]

POST–COLD WAR REALITIES

In a way, the Cold War helped to "freeze" the Arab-Israeli conflict in place by creating expectations among both Arabs and Israelis that the two superpowers would always be ready to bail out their respective clients if they engaged in dangerous military adventures, and therefore encouraged irresponsible behavior on their part. Even the American willingness to mediate the conflict between "their" Arabs and Israel created incentives for intransigence on both sides; peace was perceived sometimes as being more in the interest of the United States than in that of the Israelis or Arabs. With the end of the Cold War, the status quo in the Middle East seemed to be changing and transforming Arab and Israeli calculations. The willingness of the Palestinians and the Syrians to engage with the Israelis in the Madrid Peace Conference was a direct result of their conclusion that the Soviet Union would not be there to help sustain them as clients and to back an uncompromising anti-Israeli policy. At the same time, as part of a post–Cold War drive toward hegemony in the Middle East, the Americans were more impatient with Israeli unwillingness to make concessions to the Arabs that seemed to be breeding anti-American radicalism in the region and endangering U.S. interests. The administration of Bush I made it clear to Israel that continuing to build Jewish settlements in the Palestinian territories would damage the Jewish state's diplomatic and economic ties with the United States and forced Jerusalem to change its policies. The conservative realist foreign policymakers in that Bush I administration assumed that sustaining the role of the United States as an Arab-Israeli mediator would help maintain America in its hegemonic role. It certainly seemed to be a cost-effective method at the time.

The end of the Cold War came in the aftermath of the Egyptian-Israeli accord and the weakening of the influence of the oil cartel; and the combined impact of those developments on the regional players was quite impressive. That Israeli and Palestinian negotiators quietly concluded the Oslo agreement with virtually no American diplomatic involvement in the process reflected the new post–Cold War realities in the Middle East. Put simply, the Arab-Israeli conflict had ceased to be at the center of Middle Eastern, much less global, politics. With the end of the superpower rivalry and the diminishing significance of the "oil weapon," the Arab-Israel conflict has been "de-internationalized," "regionalized," and "re-localized"—confined to the more limited dimensions of a Palestinian-Israeli struggle over territory, with little danger of escalating into a repetition of the 1973 war and the resulting conflict between great powers. The Palestinian-Israeli conflict was turning into another of the many "tribal" conflicts of the post–Cold War era—not unlike the struggles between Azeris and Armenians or between Iraqi Arabs and Kurds. While the United States continued to pursue efforts to get both sides to make peace as part of its deluxe Pax Americana, the perceptions in Middle Eastern capitals and in Washington was that the lack of progress in the negotiations would have less of an immediate and direct impact on vital U.S. interests—as it did during the Cold War. The Israelis and the Palestinians recognized that the Americans would be less inclined to commit the kind of diplomatic and military resources in getting them to make peace that they invested in achieving the accord between Israel and Egypt. At the end of the day, a collapse of the talks between Israelis and Palestinians would not have led to a regional Arab-Israeli war, to an Arab oil embargo, or to a nuclear confrontation with the Soviets. By pursuing Oslo in direct talks and not under an American framework of negotiations, the Israelis and the Palestinians were acknowledging that they were no longer doing a "favor" for Washington—but for themselves. They were also operating under the assumption that their ability to extract new aid and new commitments from the Americans—in return for doing what was anyway in their interest to do—had narrowed down.[28]

FROM OSLO TO CAMP DAVID: NO MORE COST-FREE HEGEMONY

Nothing symbolized more the role of the United States in the diplomatic efforts leading to the September 13, 1993, signing of the accord between Israel and the PLO than a cartoon that appeared in the *Times* of London. A photo-like drawing showed Israeli Prime Minister Yitzhak Rabin shaking hands with the PLO's Yasser Arafat, as President Clinton—fixing his tie, combing his hair, smiling to the camera—forced himself in front of the pair, trying to upstage them. Washington's role in the drama that brought about the Israeli-PLO detente was marginal and confined to stage-managing the signing ceremony. A skillful White House team helped prepare the script for the show and choreographed its several acts—climaxing in the historical Rabin-Arafat handshake—with Clinton serving as a well-rehearsed and quite effective master of ceremonies. Washington was a spectator to the Middle Eastern diplomatic drama while low-key Norwegian diplomats played the key supporting roles. The Clinton administration maintained major skepticism all along, of the attempts by Israeli Foreign Minister Shimon Peres to move toward direct PLO-Israeli negotiations. Only after it was faced with the fait accompli of the accord did the administration give its blessing. After the breakthrough in Oslo, which had caught President Clinton and his advisors off-guard, self-serving leaks by administration officials suggested that Washington was the driving force behind the secret negotiations. Similarly, the main goal of the September 13 media event at the White House was to signal to the world that the Clinton administration remained "in control" of the Middle Eastern peace process, that the handshake was indeed an integral part of the Pax Americana project in that region. To further accentuate its supposedly dominant role in the process, the administration followed up the White House ceremony by leading the effort to mobilize international support for a financial aid package of approximately $2 billion to build up the economic infrastructure of the Palestinian entity that was expected to emerge in the Gaza Strip and the West Bank town of Jericho. Those were relatively insignificant American commitments compared to those Washington had given to Egypt and Israel after they had signed their peace accord. [29]

In fact, it was Washington's benign neglect of the peace process that encouraged Israel and the PLO to talk directly to each other and eventually to reach an agreement.

One can imagine what would have happened if President Clinton and his advisers had tried to dominate those negotiations. Congress and the pro-Israel lobby would have made every effort to scuttle any dialogue with the PLO. Israel would have demanded increased aid or new diplomatic and military commitments from Washington in exchange for its willingness to talk with Arafat. The moderate Arab governments would have expressed anger and threatened retaliation if the administration failed to "deliver" Israeli concessions. The result probably would have been the collapse of the negotiations, with Washington being blamed by all sides for that disaster—which is exactly what happened when Washington adopted a more engaged diplomatic approach in 2000.

Indeed, the decision by the Clinton administration to upgrade the U.S. role in the Arab-Israeli peace process from damage controller, facilitator, and master of ceremonies to that of a hyper-active diplomat determined to resolve the Palestine-Israel conflict was a clear demonstration of the way American engagement could be counterproductive both for U.S. interests and that of peace in the Middle East. It was not surprising that the Clintonites were quite hesitant about getting involved in the Camp David negotiations and decided to move in that direction only after enormous pressure from the Israeli government, led by Prime Minister Ehud Barak. The Israeli prime minister lacked the public support at home to make dramatic concessions to the Palestinians and hoped that U.S. involvement in the negotiations in the form of "carrots" (economic and military assistance to compensate Israel for its expected concessions) and "sticks" ("President Clinton pressured me to make those painful concessions") would strengthen his domestic political position and help him win public support. And Barak counted on the Americans to side with the Israelis and help spin the possible collapse of the negotiations by blaming it on the Palestinians. It seemed to be a no-lose situation from Barak's point of view. But the costs involved in managing a resolution of the conflict were enormous. The costs included: more aid and commitments to both sides, possible risks for the Americans if the talks collapsed, a backlash in the Arab world, and criticism at home and by allies. At the same time, the gradual Oslo process had been actually quite successful. It was the continuing buildup of Jewish settlements in the West Bank and Gaza in violation of Oslo Accords and without strong U.S. opposition that were endangering the Israeli-Palestinian détente. Hence Barak's calculations that going "all the way" at Camp David with American backing could prove to be less politically costly for him than ending the settlement buildup.

There are many levels of analysis from which to approach the breakdown of the U.S-mediated Palestinian-Israeli negotiations at Camp David. Some analytic approaches include: the inability of the two sides to reach an agreement on two critical issues—the fate of the Palestinians refugees who fled Israel in 1947–48 (the Palestinians wanted Israel to recognize their "right of return") and the status of Jerusalem (how to divide the holy sites); the failure on the part of the Israelis, the Palestinians, and the Americans to do serious advance work before launching the talks; a lack of personal chemistry between Barak and Arafat; the timing of the meeting on the eve of the U.S. and Israeli elections; the management of the negotiations; the decision by Barak to focus his initial diplomatic efforts on reaching an agreement with Syria instead of investing all his energies in dealing with the Palestinian front; or alternatively, that he could have agreed to make more concessions in the negotiations with Syria, which could have placed more pressure on an isolated Arafat. These and other problems clearly contributed to what turned out to be a huge and costly diplomatic disaster for all the players involved. But perhaps the problem had to do with the fact that the expectations produced by Barak and the other Israeli negotiators and sustained by a sympathetic American administration were not compatible with the outlook on the Palestinian side. For the Israelis at Camp David, the negotiations were supposed to create the conditions for comprehensive peace, while for the Palestinian negotiators Camp David resembled nothing more than just another session in labor-dispute negotiations. In short, the Palestinians and the Israelis were dreaming different dreams before and during Camp David, and in order to continue sharing the same bed what was needed was some sort of interim agreement to deal with a series of manageable problems (an end of hostilities, security arrangements, improvement of economic conditions, ceasing buildup of Jewish settlements) and not a focus on large existential problems (refugees) and symbolic issues (Jerusalem).[30]

At the end, the Oslo peace process failed because of the American decision to back the Israeli "go all the way" approach, one that sought to reach a final and comprehensive solution to the Palestinian-Israeli conflict, instead of encouraging the Israelis to continue pursuing a set of interim agreements that could have led to a step-by-step Israeli withdrawal and an attempt to improve the economic conditions in the West Bank and Gaza while ending the settlements policy. President Clinton's decision to adopt a hyperactive U.S. diplomatic role in managing the Palestinian-Israeli negotiations helped trigger the Second Intifadah by creating undue expectations on both sides, especially among the Arabs and the Palestinians that Washington would "deliver" Israel, and by encouraging the Israelis and the Palestinians to try to raise their demands and get the Americans on their side.

The American failure at Camp David in 2000 seemed to disprove the arguments raised by most Middle East experts since the collapse of the Oslo Accords that the Americans needed to "do something" and adopt an activist diplomatic strategy in trying to end the Palestinian-Israeli violence. Those critics have yet to come up with a rationale for placing the Israel-Palestine conflict at the top of the U.S. foreign policy agenda and an explanation to the American people why a benign neglect approach toward that conflict would have an adverse affect on core U.S. national interests. In reality, raising the U.S. diplomatic and military role as part of a Palestinian-Israeli peacemaking strategy under Clinton not only harmed U.S. interests; it also failed to help resolve the bloody dispute and even made things worse. Those Americans who contend that the United States has the "moral obligation" to bring an end to the bloodbath should recognize that like many other national, religious, and ethnic conflicts around the world, both sides are willing to pay the costs of what they regard as a fight for their survival, and there is no reason why the Americans should "save them from themselves." Not unlike other civil wars, this one will end when both sides are exhausted and conclude that their interests would be served more effectively around the negotiating table than on the battlefield, with the outcome of the negotiations reflecting the existing balance of power.

Even during the Cold War, when Washington attempted to help mediate the conflict between Arabs and Israelis, its efforts proved successful during the 1979 Egyptian-Israeli peace talks only when the two sides agreed in advance to resolve their differences.[31] The U.S.-brokered Egyptian-Israeli peace treaty of 1979, regarded as a major American diplomatic achievement, has been frequently touted by analysts as a model that the American should apply in dealing with the Israel-Palestine conflict. But the accord should not be seen as a direct result of the effective use of American diplomatic power in the Middle East. In fact, the treaty was not the consequence of an American initiative but a response to a regional move on the part of Egyptian president Sadat, who was interested in reaching an accommodation with Israel based on consideration of Egypt's interests, which did not preclude a break with the Arab world. Cairo and Jerusalem acting in their own self-interest could have reached a similar formal or informal agreement without U.S. help—but both parties decided that bringing Washington into the negotiations would provide them with some diplomatic and economic rewards. U.S. policymakers initially regarded Washington's role as a major diplomatic victory, but it proved to be costly in both financial and diplomatic terms. Washington claimed exclusive sponsorship of the negotiations without having enough control over either Egypt or Israel to make the claim stick, thus ensuring that although the initiative would remain largely with the regional parties, the responsibility for any failure would be borne largely by the United States. Washington was unable to enlarge the scope of the peace process to include the Palestinian question. Differences between Cairo and Jerusalem on the Palestinian problem remained unbridgeable and Washington did not have the resources to pressure either of them to moderate their positions. That lack of progress on the Israeli-Palestinian front, which eventually brought about the 1982 war between Israel and the Palestinians in Lebanon, was perceived throughout the region as an American diplomatic failure. Consequently, Washington felt the need to project its leadership and political visibility in reaction to the Israeli invasion of Lebanon, which in turn led to a major and costly diplomatic debacle there, including anti-American terrorism and a growing conflict with the Shiites in that country. Washington's initial commitment to help solve the Palestinian problem at Camp David also encouraged the Palestinians to launch the First Intifada as part of a strategy to induce Washington to play a more active role in the area. Hence the real lessons of the Egyptian-Israeli accord suggest that the American diplomatic role can only be successful if it fits with the interests of the regional players. It also demonstrates the ability of other local and regional players, including those that benefited from American policy, to harm U.S. interests. That undertaking, however, made sense in the context of the Cold War. The American efforts to achieve détente between Israel and Egypt were nevertheless a reflection of U.S. interests in the Cold War—even if the benefits were limited.

From the perspective of the post–Cold War era, the urge that U.S. policy-makers and analysts project—that America needs to "do something" to resolve the Israel-Palestine conflict—is both futile and counterproductive if one takes into consideration core U.S. interests. However, if the assumption is that Washington needs to continue promoting its MEP, there is no other choice but to continue juggling the conflicting commitments to Israel and the Arabs, and in that context, to try to make peace between the two sides. Indeed, based on the assumption that the MEP needs to be protected, the United States could be in danger of losing its hegemonic position in the region if it fails to advance Israeli-Palestinian peace. Bill Clinton, at the end of his term in office, and later George W. Bush, both found to their chagrin that the American diplomatic balancing act in the Israel-Arab front can prove to be quite expensive. Clinton discovered those costs at Camp David and his successor continues to face the consequences of the Second Intifada and the never-ending violence in the Holy Land.

Bush II and his neoconservative advisors have pursued a policy with regard to the Israel-Palestine conflict that is based on the assumption that Washington could and should try to resolve it by siding with Israel and playing down Arab concerns. At the same time, critics from the liberal-internationalist and conservative-realist schools have argued that much of the costs involved in American intervention by the Middle East could be reduced through a comprehensive resolution of the Arab-Israeli conflict that would be based on reinstating the U.S. role as an "honest broker."

GOOD BYE TO ALL OF THAT?

Sumner Welles had predicted that American geo-strategic and geo-economic interests would help build up a powerful base in Washington for a U.S. commitment to both Zionism and Arab oil interests. But even he is probably turning in his grave now that the diplomatic and military engagement that was supposed to secure U.S. global interests during the Cold War has become the central focus of American foreign policy more than ten years after Americans and the Western alliance had won the war against the Soviet Union and its partners. The policy that he had originally advocated as a way to advance U.S. interests in the then-mounting Cold War is now igniting attacks on the homeland and consuming huge amounts of American human and financial resources. Welles assumed that the support for the Arabs and the Zionists would help protect U.S. interests. Even Welles did not expect that defending the interests of the corrupt Saudi royal family and those of a nationalist government in Israel would require the United States to lead two wars in the Middle East and to seriously consider establishing an American Empire a la Great Britain in the region.

But that is exactly what has been happening since the terrorist attacks on New York and Washington that demonstrated to Washington that the establishment of a Pax Americana in the region would force the United States to continue expanding its military presence in the region. Hence, the following is seen by many observers as a paradox but is in reality a direct outcome of U.S. policies: There is a direct correlation between the increase in U.S. commitments in the region and the growing inability of the Saudis and the Israelis to resolve their core existential problems. Or to put it differently, at a time when the United States is taking part in the largest and most costly intervention in the Middle East, the Saudis and the Israelis have been able to assert their influence in Washington—recall the two scenes described earlier in the chapter—while simultaneously facing the greatest threats to their survival.

THE NEOCONS TO THE RESCUE

Recall Welles's 1945 thesis: The Middle East and its oil reserves would acquire geo-strategic and geo-economic significance for the United States—a process that would also help the Jewish commonwealth located in that region to elevate its importance in America's Cold War agenda. Indeed, if Israel had been established in sub-Saharan Africa, it would have been very difficult for it to mobilize the kind of American economic and military assistance that is has received from the United States since 1948 and especially since 1967, when the support for Israel was integrated into U.S. Cold War strategy in the Middle East. Israel benefited therefore from the fact that American core interests were so tied to its presence in the Middle East. And while the United States was forced into risky and costly circumstances as it tried to juggle its conflicting (moral and historic) commitment to Israel and its ties with the pro-American Arab states that were based mostly on strategic and economic calculations—that was the price that Washington was willing to pay as part of proceeding with its MEP during the Cold War.

Now let's fast-forward to a half-century later, and Welles's analytical framework can be turned on its head. In fact, one could have made an argument that with the end of the Cold War and against the backdrop of the rising costs of American support for Saudi Arabia and the other Arab oil states, the 9/11 terrorist attacks could have been an opportunity to reassess American ties with Riyadh. At a minimum, the notion that the American people should shed their blood and spend their money to protect a medieval theocracy in the Arabian Peninsula could have been challenged if it were not seen as part of a strategy to advance American global interests. Members of the foreign policy establishment would have responded with their party line, "But what about the oil?" But it would have been difficult to expect the American people to accept the proposition that their sons and daughters would be deployed for decades in the Middle East—and that they will perhaps even have to reinstate the military draft and increase defense spending to the stratosphere—just in order to secure American access to "cheap oil." Bush II could not have succeeded in winning Congressional and public support for such an expansive strategy to establish American hegemony in the Middle East as part of an effort to protect the House of Saud. What made the difference in the early twenty-first century for Bush, and what allowed him to maintain the MEP, was the perception that American involvement in the Middle East was not only about "oil" but was part of new global commitments that Americans would have to bear. Hence, if the attraction to Saudi Arabia and Middle Eastern oil benefited a small and weak Jewish state in the middle of the twentieth century, the strong American ties to Israel and its supporters in Washington served the interests of the Saudis in the aftermath of the end of the Cold War, and especially after 9/11, when the ugly and costly reality of the American-Saudi "alliance" had become so obvious. In the early twenty-first century, the pro-Israeli neoconservatives performed the role that the "Arabists" played in the middle of the twentieth century—legitimizing U.S. engagement in the Middle East.

The most significant achievement of the neoconservative ideologues who have been the driving force behind post-9/11 American foreign policy was to exploit the terrorist attacks on the United States and the ensuing war on terrorism as ways of transforming a U.S. response to acts of terror and the subsequent extension of the MEP into part of a global existential conflict in which the United States, in alliance with Israel, was suddenly seen as leading a new world war against the forces of radical Islam and Arab nationalism, a terrorist–WMD Nexus of Evil in which Arab and Islamic fascism were symbolized respectively by Saddam Hussein and Osama bin Ladin. Expanding American engagement in the Middle East went beyond protecting oil interests and was now part of a struggle for the survival of America and the West—not unlike the earlier global clashes with the Nazis and the Communists. The notion advanced by the neocons and adopted by the administration of Bush II was that Americans were now engaged in a new world war in which they were standing up against the "evil ones" who threaten the American way of life, as opposed to just protecting a corrupt Saudi regime and solidifying access to an affordable supply of oil. By justifying continuing U.S. involvement in the Middle East, it was an argument that was clearly advancing the interests of the Saudis even if it was drawn by a group of pro-Israeli neoconservative intellectuals.

Like during the Cold War, the rival twins could reach—at least in the short-run—a certain level of détente that could help get the United States to use its diplomatic and military power to advance their respective interests and permit the American leaders to come up with a successful marketing formula for the MEP that could win the support of Congress and the American people. Indeed, as neoconservative intellectual Robert Kagan himself admitted, 9/11 "has paved the way for a neocon revolution in the same way that the Soviet-backed North Korean invasion of the south galvanized Washington into adopting the Truman Doctrine."[32]

THE TWINS—RIVALS AGAIN?

The neoconservative agenda seemed to dismiss the traditional notion that was adopted by previous U.S. administrations that American engagement in the Middle East required Washington to juggle Israeli and Arab interests in a balancing act of "even handed" policies. Instead, the neoconservative agenda promoted a strategy that assumed hegemonic U.S. goals and nationalist Israeli interests were identical. Such an assumption was bound to produce in the long-run growing tensions between the United States and the Saudis and other pro-American Arab players.

In a way, the neoconservatives were offering an updated version of a strategy they had tried to advance during the final stages of the Cold War. During the 1980s, the policies of the Reagan administration offered the then Likud government time to consolidate its hold on the West Bank and Gaza by advancing the proposition that Israel was a "strategic asset" in the global campaign against the Soviet Evil Empire and that Arafat and his PLO were Soviet stooges.[33] The neoconservatives who then occupied top positions on Reagan's foreign policy team encouraged Washington to view the Arab-Israeli conflict through these Cold War lenses, and to identify Palestinian nationalism as an extension of Soviet-induced terrorism. Washington could therefore view Israel's occupation of Palestinian lands with benign neglect.[34] Hence, the Reagan era's Arafat-is-a-Soviet-terrorist theme has served as a model for the lead into an Arafat-is-bin-Ladin strategy that the Likud and the neoconservatives successfully applied under George W. Bush, when Israeli occupation of the West Bank and Gaza was compared to America's invasion of Afghanistan and Iraq.

Many of the neoconservatives had hoped that the 1991 Gulf War would become an opportunity to re-establish the Israeli-American strategic alliance that seemed to be in decline with the collapse of the Soviet Union, and to redirect it against the new bogeyman, Saddam Hussein. But President Bush I not only forced Israel to refrain from responding to Iraqi missile attacks; he also pressed Israel to stop building new Jewish settlements in the occupied territories and negotiate with the PLO at the Madrid Peace Conference. For Bush I and his conservative realist advisors, the Gulf War was seen as part of an effort to maintain the MEP by applying the traditional Cold War-era policy of maintaining balanced relations between Israel and the Arabs and trying to resolve their conflict.

Bush II initially entered office determined to pursue a similar policy by assigning the conservative realist Secretary of State Colin Powell a leading role in the process. But in foreign policy, timing is everything. The terrorist attacks on New York and Washington took place only a few days before Powell was scheduled to deliver an "even-handed" Middle East policy address.[35] But after 9/11, Powell and the State Department lost ground to Secretary of Defense Donald Rumsfeld and Vice President Dick Cheney, who adopted a neoconservative position. The "green light" that the White House gave to Prime Minister Sharon to use military power to destroy the Palestinian political and military infrastructure, weaken the power of Yasser Arafat, and re-invade parts of the West Bank and Gaza from which Israeli forces had withdrawn during the implementation of the Oslo Accord, reflected the choice made by President Bush to place Palestinian independence on the backburner.[36] When it came to Israel, Bush II has chosen to turn the approach of Bush I on its head.[37] At the same time, the invasion of Iraq seemed to be part of a grand global imperial strategy concocted by the neoconservatives, aimed at redrawing the map of the Middle East to permit U.S. military and diplomatic hegemony in the region, including the "taming" of Iran and Syria and denying any power in the region, with the exception of Israel, access to nuclear weapons. Not surprisingly, the American strategy is seen in the Arab world and in Europe as part of an effort to allow the U.S.-Israel axis to dominate the Middle East, a sort of a neoconservative alliance between Imperial America and Greater Israel.[38]

Hence, in the long run, the rivalry between the interests of the Middle Eastern twins is bound to re-ignite. The ideological pro-Israeli component of the neoconservative storyline implies a willingness to accept Israeli mistreatment of the Palestinians—which runs contrary to U.S. interests in maintaining the support of Saudi Arabia and the other pro-American Arab regimes. An effort to resolve this inconsistency by making peace between the Israelis and the

Palestinians on Israel's term is not going to work. At the same time, an attempt to bring democracy and freedom to the entire Middle East—the Wilsonian side of the neoconservative agenda—is at odds with the U.S. interest in protecting the power of the Saudis. The attempt to resolve this inconsistency by "reforming" Saudi Arabia will prove to be unrealistic. The result is that U.S. decision makers will find themselves trapped in an intellectual and policy quagmire.

If Washington tries to modify the neoconservative agenda by rejecting the Wilsonian outline or by challenging Israeli policies, U.S. policy in the Middle East will be unmasked as a cynical strategy to defend Arab autocrats. And any U.S. president who, under the current conditions, would attempt to force Israel to make concessions on the Palestinian issue would be accused of adopting an "anti-Israeli" policy by supporters of Israel in Washington, whose views tend to be more hawkish than those of centrist Israeli politicians. But if Washington continues to pursue its original neoconservative scheme, the conditions for a clash between an American-Israeli bloc and the Arab and Moslem worlds that are being radicalized will be created, especially as anti-American sentiments threaten the regimes in Riyadh, Cairo, and Amman.

This neoconservative agenda is not only going to prove as contrary to the interests of most of the Arab regimes of the Middle East, including those of the Saudis that Washington is supposed to protect, it is also making it clear to France, Germany, and other European governments that the United States is now threatening their geo-strategic and geo-strategic interests in the region. The neoconservatives have succeeded in getting the Bush administration and large segments of the American foreign policy establishment to see this dispute between the United States and Europe over Iraq and Israel/Palestine as a clash between political cultures that will require America to use its unilateral military power and disregard the concerns of its former Cold War allies across the Atlantic. This neoconservative policy has created the environment in which the Americans and the Europeans are being driven into a geo-strategic and geo-economic confrontation over the Middle East.

IT'S INTERESTS—
NOT CULTURES, STUPID!

THE EURO-AMERICAN RIFT
OVER THE MIDDLE EAST

The war in Iraq has created tensions between the United States and some of its leading allies in Europe and exposed a deep diplomatic rift between the traditional transatlantic security partners. The controversy over Iraq has also ignited strong anti-American sentiments and threatened international cooperation in the war against Al Qaeda. Most observers agree that the transatlantic alliance, which has provided the basis for the security of the West for the last 50 years, is facing the most serious challenge to its existence in the aftermath of the war in Iraq.

Indeed, the rift between the United States and the leading members of the transatlantic alliance—in particular France and Germany—has exposed deep strategic differences between the traditional security partners. "For the first time since the Vietnam War," the *Financial Times* noted, "U.S. forces were engaged in a big military conflict without the support or even the acquiescence of several of America's most important European allies."[1]

Moreover, the tensions over Iraq have produced anti-American reactions in both the European elites and the general public, including in those European countries that supported the United States in Iraq, where the concern is that American policy in the Middle East could create political instability in the region and inflame anti-Western feelings in the Arab world, spurring more terrorism directed not just at the United States, but at all Western states. Under these circumstances, Europe, with its geographical proximity and close economic and demographic ties to the Middle East, could become the first victim of American policy. At the same time, the war in Iraq has also damaged international institutions, such as the United Nations (UN), the North Atlantic Treaty Organization (NATO), and the European Union (EU), which were conceived and nourished by the transatlantic allies.

WHAT A DIFFERENCE PRESIDENT GEORGE W. BUSH MAKES

President Bill Clinton faced serious challenges to U.S. policy in the Middle East as he tried to maintain a relatively cost-free U.S. hegemony in the Middle East. But both President Clinton and President George H. W. Bush, who shared the goal of establishing Pax Americana in the Middle East, succeeded in maintaining a sense of partnership with the Europeans in terms of a general approach toward the region. Those two White House occupants were willing to accommodate the concerns of their allies across the Atlantic, especially when it came to dealing with the Arab-Israeli conflict. Both of these Republican and Democratic administrations were able to sustain a general perception among Europeans that Washington was at least trying to "do something" about bringing an end to the Israeli-Palestinian conflict. Indeed, both Presidents Clinton and Bush I, in most of their terms, were dealing with moderate Israeli governments that were driven by their own interests and ideology to work with the Americans toward a political settlement with the Palestinians.

Moreover, while taking steps to promote U.S. interests in the Middle East, both Clinton and Bush I made an effort to frame their hegemonic policies as part of a multilateral strategy, with special emphasis on the relationship with the European allies. Those allies reluctantly backed the U.S. decision to go to war in Iraq in 1991, and contributed military and financial resources to the operation as well as to President Clinton's efforts to broker Israeli-Palestinian deals. If anything, the expectations in European capitals were that President George W. Bush's policy in the Middle East would resemble that of his father and be dominated by figures with ties to the conservative realist school of thought. These conservative realist thinkers included such luminaries as Henry Kissinger, Brent Scowcroft, and James Baker—with their bias toward Europe-centric policies and an "even-handed" approach towards Arab-Israeli issues.

European expectations that Bush II would primarily tow his father's line were reinforced by the statements made by Bush and his aides before the 2000 election. Candidate Bush preached the need for a sense of "humility" on the part of Washington, as it tried to shape the political-cultural values of other societies. His top foreign policy advisor, Condoleezza Rice, contrasted in *Foreign Affairs* magazine the global program of the new Republican White House with that of its predecessor by emphasizing the need to replace the excessive idealism of the Clinton era with a realistic policy aimed at "promoting the national interest" through a diplomacy that elevates the U.S. relationship with other great powers, including the EU, and a military force that "is most certainly not designed to build a civilian society."[2]

As the new President Bush took office, it was gradually becoming clear to the Europeans and to other allies of the United States that Bush II was different from Bush I. Some diplomatic tensions between the United States and the EU had already surfaced after President George W. Bush took office in 2001 and pulled out of the treaty forming an International Criminal Court and the Kyoto Treaty on global warming. Differences between the new Republican administration and the governments and publics across the Atlantic were highlighted during Bush's first official visit to Europe.[3] But Americans and Europeans, that is, the members of the Western alliance, including their common and powerful military instrument, NATO, seemed to be united as never before when Al Qaeda terrorists attacked New York and Washington on September 11, 2001.[4]

Growing disagreements between the EU and the United States over the strategy to contain terrorism became evident after President Bush's "Axis of Evil" speech in January 2002. The burgeoning rift was also reflected in their conflicting positions on the Israeli-Palestinian conflict, as increasing Palestinian terrorism and Israeli military retaliation seemed to be spilling over into Europe in the form of anti-Jewish violence. These differences produced a momentous split between the Europeans and the Americans when the Bush administration, backed by Britain's Prime Minister Tony Blair, indicated that it intended to use diplomatic and military means to get rid of Iraq's weapons of mass destruction (WMD).[5] The EU and the United States were able to forge a common diplomatic strategy on Iraq at the United Nations on the basis of Security Council resolution 1441. A growing diplomatic alienation developed, however, between an Anglo-American bloc, with some level of support from so-called New Europe countries, and the so-called Old Europe camp led by France and Germany.[6] The Bush administration made it clear that it intended to use military power against Iraq, and the French and the Germans, backed by the Russians and echoing the views of the majority of European publics and elites, insisted that they would oppose such a move. This split on the eve of the war with Iraq produced two dramatic developments in the history of the Western alliance. The first development involved the refusal by the Cold War-era allies, France and

Germany, to provide the United States with a UN Security Council resolution authorizing military action against Iraq. The active lobbying by the French, working together with Cold War-era adversary, Russia, aimed at sabotaging American efforts to win support for a second resolution.[7] The second development involved the resistance by France, supported by Germany and Belgium, to an American-backed request that NATO provide a package of defensive measures for Turkey. Approving the request would have implied that a war with Iraq was inevitable.

In the end, the Americans decided not to submit the second resolution for a vote at the Security Council, and, thus, avoided the specter of a French veto. At the same time, a deal was struck between the members of NATO to make the necessary decisions on protecting Turkey in the defense planning committee of which France is not a member.[8] There is no doubt that these episodes pointed to a major rupture among the Western powers and between NATO members, pitting the United States, Britain, and its "new" Europe partners, including Italy, Spain, Denmark, the Netherlands, Ireland, and the Central and Eastern European governments, against France, Germany, and Belgium, themselves backed by Greece, Finland, Sweden, and Austria. These developments led former Secretary of State Henry Kissinger to conclude that "the road to Iraqi disarmament has produced the gravest crisis within the Atlantic Alliance since its creation five decades ago."[9]

Explaining the growing divide in the transatlantic alliance has spurred an intellectual inquiry involving policymakers and analysts in Washington and many European capitals. In the debate over this issue, prominent neoconservative intellectuals and officials contend that the dispute between the United States and the EU over the war in Iraq, and the United States' broader strategy in the Middle East, reflects a clash of cultures. Such a perspective has become very popular. But this chapter explains it is European and American interests—not cultures—that produced the rift over war in Iraq; and that this split could only be mended—if at all—only by recognizing and dealing with these differing interests.

THE POLICY PITFALLS OF POLICY PARADIGMS

Placing this current Euro-American discord in context and trying to frame it is more than just an academic exercise. In fact, the way American government officials and media pundits assess an international crisis and market their conclusions to the elites and public in this country does not only shape the perceptions of the American people and their leaders. The way a particular international crisis is framed can also determine the kind of policy the U.S. government ends up adopting to deal with the crisis, producing a cycle of actions and reactions that can transform the initial frame into a self-fulfilling prophecy.[10]

The neoconservative intellectuals re-energized the MEP after 9/11 by suggesting that U.S. policy in the Middle East should be integrated into the global conflict against Middle East-based terrorism and into a campaign to transform the region and establish an American Democratic Empire there. From the neoconservative perspective, the member states of the EU, and in particular, France, are posing a peril to the American grand designs in the Middle East. According to this neoconservative interpretation, the divisions between the Europeans and the Americans go beyond specific policy differences over American policy toward Israel/Palestine and Iraq that could be managed through diplomatic bargaining. Instead, Europe is transformed into a civilizational challenge, if not an existential threat, to America and Israel.

Indeed, neoconservative foreign policy analysts in the United States have described the rift between the Americans and the Europeans over the war in Iraq and the transatlantic strains over the Middle East and other global policy issues as reflecting a major political-cultural split. Advancing the neoconservative view and adopting terms coined by self-help guru John Gray to describe the differences between men and women, Robert Kagan, director of the U.S. Leadership Project at the Carnegie Endowment for International Peace, argued that this transatlantic split demonstrated that "Americans are from Mars and Europeans from Venus: They agree on little and understand one another less and less." It is time to "stop pretending that Europeans and Americans share a common view of the world, or even that they occupy the same world," he concluded.[11]

According to this explanation by American intellectuals on the political right, the fact that the majority of Europeans opposed the Bush administration's decision to use military power as a way to oust Saddam Hussein and rid Iraq of its alleged WMD as well as the White House's alliance with Israeli Prime Minister Ariel Sharon[12] had very little to do with strategic considerations of national interests. Instead, the fact that even those nations that were members of the Coalition of the Willing disagreed with Bush—some 87 percent of Spaniards were against the Iraq war and a majority of Brits oppose U.S. policy towards Israel[13]—should be seen as a product of contrasting metacultural interpretations of politics and international relations, their approaches toward contemporary society and economics, and even their attitudes toward the environment and the death penalty, family and religion, Arabs and Jews, and, of course, Bush and Saddam Hussein.

Hence, the Euro-American discord over the Iraq war is seen not just as "one more episode in a long history of disagreements," as Harvard University's Stanley Hoffman put it, but as a rift that could not be resolved by applying the traditional tools of diplomacy as has been done in the past during earlier transatlantic tensions.[14] Instead, Americans should ask themselves whether the time has arrived to say "Goodbye to Europe?" as neoconservative military historian Victor Davis Hanson has proposed in an article in the leading neoconservative magazine *Commentary*. He suggests that Americans and Europeans should recognize that they are "coming to the end of a relationship" and are headed toward separation, if not geo-political divorce.[15]

MARS, VENUS, AND FOREIGN POLICY

If one utilizes the paradigm advanced by Kagan and other neoconservative commentators, Europeans live today in either a postmodern or "post-historical paradise," that is, a self-contained world based on transnational rules, negotiations, and cooperation.[16] At the same time, Americans are still mired in history, operating in a Hobbesian universe of political interests and conflicts, in which international law is disdained and only the fittest, that is, those with the necessary military power, survive. The Europeans are "idealists" who believe in the application of "soft power" to contain global challenges, and who want to apply their pacifist model worldwide and deal with international conflicts through reliance on multilateral institutions and international treaties. Americans, on the other hand, are "realists" who know that only the use of "hard power" can be effective in containing aggressors, and who blame the Europeans for trying to constrain their use of military power as they try to stand up against the Saddam Husseins and Osama bin Ladins of the world.

The Mars vs. Venus interpretation of the Euro-American split can be broadened and portrayed as a clash between Age (Europe) and Youth (America), Europe being a clapped-out old continent, "a wonderful place to visit but hardly the anvil of the future," as proposed by the *Economist* magazine.[17] America can be celebrated as the "virile" nation that as a result of higher birth rates and rising immigration will probably overtake "barren" Europe, with its lower fertility rates and barriers to immigration, in population and would look remarkably different from the Old World.[18] At the same time, there is the focus on the cultural split between the "vigorous and naïve" Americans who seem to be committed to traditional values of family, religion, and the flag, and the more "refined and unprincipled," if not "cynical and decadent" Europeans, who attend church services less frequently than Americans and are more tolerant of abortion, euthanasia, divorce, and suicide.[19] And of course, as many American (and European) free market proponents emphasized, especially during the booming economic years of the 1990s, the EU economies have failed to adopt the necessary reforms (cutting their governments' spending, restructuring their welfare systems, unlocking their immobile labor markets, removing barriers to trade) so as to compete with the Americans in the global economy.[20]

These are the kinds of comparisons between Europeans and Americans that neoconservative intellectuals like to draw as a way of explaining why Americans are ready to fight and protect their women against the barbarians at the gate, while the Europeans are not. British historian Timothy Garton Ash suggested in a *New York Review of Books* article that much of the neoconservative critique of Europe, in such American media outlets as the *Weekly Standard, National Review Online,* and the *Wall Street Journal* editorial page, has degenerated into an ugly anti-European caricature. "Pens are dipped in acid and lips curled to pillory 'the Europeans,' also known as 'the Euros,' 'the Euroids,' 'the peens,' or the 'Euroweenies,'" he wrote. According to Ash, Europeans are depicted as wimps. They are weak, hypocritical, disunited, duplicitous, and sometimes anti-American and anti-Semitic appeasers, whose "values and spines have dissolved in a lukewarm bath of multilateral, transnational, secular and postmodern fudge" as "they spend their euros on wine, holidays, bloated welfare states instead of defense," while Americans who are "strong, principled defenders of freedom" are standing tall and doing all the hard work and dirty business making the world safe for those "Euroweenies."

In fact, Ash and other analysts have pointed to the way sexual metaphors, an extension of Kagan's Mars vs. Venus imagery, have been used by these American critics. "The European is female, impotent, or castrated," who just "can't get it up," while the American is a virile, heterosexual male.[21] And in that context, the French seem to be the nation most despised by the American "Euronuchs"-haters, regarded as the "least manly" on the continent, and described by Jonah Goldberg of the *National Review* as "cheese-eating surrender monkeys." Whether one accepts such anti-European vilification or adopts the more sophisticated analysis provided by Kagan, the bottom line is that the failure by the Europeans to fall behind American policy regarding the Iraq war and the Israel-Palestine conflict is a clear indication that the Europeans have become, indeed, diplomatically and militarily impotent as a result of their Venus-like characteristics. They should be seen, as Goldberg puts it, as "a broad coalition of self-hating intellectuals and effete bureaucrats who have either abandoned their national identities out of embarrassment (as in Germany) or are using a new

European identity as a Trojan Horse for their own cultural ambitions (i.e., the French and Belgians)."[22]

Interestingly enough, some elements of anti-Americanism in France and elsewhere in Europe mirror the same kind of sexual imagery employed by American neoconservatives as a way of accentuating their metacultural interpretations of the Euro-American split over Iraq. Americans, and especially President Bush, have been depicted by European critics as gun-toting and bullying cowboys,[23] and as "a testosterone-driven adolescent[s] bereft of history and tradition."[24] It is revealing to contrast this European conception of America with American neoconservative Hanson's depiction of the Europeans as "geriatric teenagers."[25] The more intelligent critics of the Bush administration in Europe believe that the decision to use military power against Iraq reflected the "macho" inclinations of the president's supporters. These cowboys from Texas were supposedly committed to such "manly" values as militarism and a harsh form of capitalism. This "manly" approach is contrasted with the more "gentle" forms of peacemaking and social democracy practiced in Paris and Berlin. Some Europeans turned the Mars vs. Venus metaphor on its head and argue that the conflict between the Moslem world and America reflects a clash between a "feminist" American political culture and the masculine disposition of Arab warrior societies. In this confrontation between the Arabs, who are from Mars, and the Americans, who are from Venus, the Europeans, threatened by the "castrating" power of the American feminists, are apparently siding with the Arabs.[26]

Indeed, anti-American European intellectuals tend to reflect the cultural explanation proposed by the anti-European American political right. In their view, French opposition to providing UN legitimacy to the invasion of Iraq was much more than just a diplomatic crisis. It was culturally determined, another chapter in a clash of civilizations between Europe and America. Hence, the threat from the United States is not just economic or military. America poses a social and cultural danger to the civilization of Europe, an "American Peril." Some in the European anti-war movement "see the whole bundle of American values—consumer capitalism, a free market for information, an open electoral system—as having been imposed rather than chosen," according to historian Simon Schama.

SPRING TIME FOR HITLER IN EUROPE?

Very few observers would challenge the observation that the level of anti-American sentiments has reached an historic high during the war against Iraq. At the same time, the attitudes among Arabs toward the EU states, with the exception of Great Britain, and in particular, toward France, have been more favorable than in their attitudes towards the United States. Not surprisingly, neoconservative analysts have attributed changes in Arab and European opinion to the "pro-Arab" position held by the European governments, media, and public. This alleged sympathy toward the Arabs supposedly explains, in part, the refusal of France and other European countries to support the Bush administration's tough stand against terrorism and its military campaign against Iraq. At the same time, the American support for Israel illustrates identification with the democratic ideals of Israel and European sympathy toward Arab autocrats.

Moreover, the European "appeasement" of Saddam Hussein and the strong support in France and Europe for Palestinian independence was considered by American neoconservatives to be a reflection not only of anti-Israeli (and pro-Palestinian) attitudes in Europe, but as a sign that "anti-Semitism without Jews" is remerging in Europe, according to columnist George Will.[27] This rise in anti-Semitism, according to this argument, was dramatized by the attacks against synagogues and other Jewish property in France in the last two years. There is a growing danger that "the Arab style of Judeo-phobia, which is an anti-Semitism without the West's complexes," would be offering "a real redemptive project" to a growing number of French who are willing to embrace it, warned Christopher Caldwell, a columnist in the *Weekly Standard,* following a visit to Europe.[28] Again, French and European criticism of the policies of the Sharon government in Jerusalem was supposedly not based on a rational calculation of national interest as they are being affected by the Israel-Palestine conflict. Instead, "what we are seeing is pent-up anti-Semitism, the release— with Israel as the trigger—of a millennium-old urge that powerfully infected and shaped European history," observed leading neoconservative columnist Charles Krauthammer. Europeans have not been critical of Israel because of its policies toward the Palestinians. They hate the Jewish state because they are intolerant of "Jewish assertiveness, the Jewish refusal to accept victim-hood," which Israel embodies."[29]

Neoconservative intellectuals tend to disparage the "culture of victim-hood" practiced by leaders of racial minorities in the United States, which, they argue, perpetuates misconceptions that members of such groups are not responsible for their present conditions. But, ironically, these neoconservative intellectuals seem to apply that same faulty thinking when it comes to Israeli and American policies in the Middle East and the way such policies are viewed in Europe. Both Israel and the United States are perceived as somewhat passive actors who are hated by the Arabs and bashed by the Europeans not for what they do but for who they are. In an attempt to explain "why the Europeans and Arabs, each in their own way, hate America and Israel," neoconservative columnist David Brooks proposed that alleged anti-American and anti-Israeli sentiments in the Arab world and Europe are a projection of common resentment among "Europeans" and "Arabs" against "two peoples—the Americans and the Jews—[who] have emerged as the great exemplars of undeserved success."[30]

In this context, the neoconservative "civilizational" explanation becomes the basis for justifying Israeli and American policies while discrediting the European approach. After all, if you accept the notion that Israelis and Americans are victims of Euro-Arab hostility, these victims are doomed and will never be able to change those attitudes. Israel could withdraw tomorrow from the 1967 lines, dismantle the Jewish settlements in the West Bank and Gaza, and recognize an independent Palestinian state in those territories. The United States could drop its support for the autocratic regimes of Egypt and Saudi Arabia, cut its enormous aid package to Israel, and could have refrained from attacking Iraq or from imposing economic sanctions on it after the Gulf War. But even if all these radical policy adjustments were to happen, the Arabs and the Europeans would still hate the Americans and the Jews. Hence, there is no chain of causality linking European to American (and Israeli) policies in the Middle East. The neoconservative conception of the Euro-American divide is all about European multilateralism, wimpiness, appeasement, impotence, decadence, anti-Americanism, and anti-Semitism.

EUROPE: ANTI-SEMITIC OR ANTI-SHARON?

The view that Europe, and in particular France, have been experiencing a new wave of anti-Semitism, a revival of the European anti-Jewish disease that helped create the environment of the Holocaust, seems to have been adopted by serious American analysts who have accused contemporary Europe of offering "Christian anti-Semitism, without the Christianity," as the June 2002 edition of the *American Spectator* put it.[31] This "Europhobic Myth," disseminated by neoconservative writers in the United States promotes a claim that "Europe is awash in anti-Semitism, that the ghosts of Europe's Judeophobic past are rising again, and that this atavistic prejudice, Europe's original sin, explains widespread European criticism of Israel, sympathy for the Arab world, and even support for Iraq," according to New York University historian Tony Judt.[32] Much of this Springtime-for-Hitler-in-Europe assertion is based on reports of several attacks on Jews and Jewish property, including synagogues and cemeteries, in France and other European countries since the start of the Second Intifadah, and especially in the aftermath of 9/11. Most of those attacks were committed by Moslems, including members of France's community of 4–5 million Moslems.[33] That these attacks against Jewish targets in France were taking place at the same time that French populist Jean-Marie Le Pen rocketed to prominence by reaching the final round of France's presidential elections, and other far-right parties were doing well elsewhere in Europe, was an indication to American neocons that the genie of anti-Semitism was out of the bottle again in Europe.

But according to reliable opinion polls, anti-Semitism, defined as personal hostility against Jews based on religion or race, is neither widespread nor increasing in France, where 600,000 Jews have done well in politics, business, and academia since the end of World War II.[34] While Le Pen made some anti-Semitic statements in the past, his main target for bashing in the last election was the Moslems living in France; he has identified French interests with the American and Israeli war on terrorism. In fact, as the polls indicate, anti-Semitism has been in steep decline in most of Western Europe, including in Britain and Germany, especially among the young, and in particular among those on the political left. At the same time, there has been a backlash in many of these countries against Moslem immigrants, which explains the rise in support for anti-immigrant right-wing parties in Holland, Denmark, and Austria. In figures that are broadly comparable to results from similar polls taken in the United States, an overwhelming majority of young people questioned in France believe that French people and Europeans should speak more about the Holocaust and nearly nine out of ten agreed that attacks on synagogues were "scandalous."[35] At the same time, in countries like Holland and Germany where opinion polls detect the lowest level of anti-Semitism in Europe, the public also tends to be the most sympathetic toward the Palestinians.[36] Similarly, young people in Europe who describe themselves as leftists are both uncompromisingly anti-anti-Semitic and tough critics of Israeli policies towards the Palestinians—many of those who voted for Le Pen and other extreme right-wing political parties sympathize with Israeli policies.[37] In a way, today's mostly secular and liberal young generation of young Western Europeans, which was educated in the post-Holocaust era and in an open and pluralistic environment, is probably the most tolerant of Jews (and other ethnic and religious minorities) that Europe has ever known in its long and very anti-Semitic history.

Indeed, contrary to the neoconservative framework, what the European public is projecting is not a new or old form of anti-Semitism, but a more critical approach toward the policies of the State of Israel, especially in its treatment of the Palestinians.[38] Describing the attitudes toward Israel in Europe as "anti-Israeli" would be as misleading as suggesting that the American policies in the

Middle East are "anti-Arab" or "anti-Palestinian." Nor is the recent criticism of Israel, as reflected in opinion polls and the policies of EU governments, directed against Israel as a Jewish state and as part of an effort to delegitimize Zionism. After all, the EU is Israel's largest trading partner, and Germany, its second-largest supplier of arms (after the United States), is considered one of Israel's most important allies in the world. France was a military and diplomatic ally of Israel during most of the 1950s and early 1960s during the civil war in Algeria, when both countries regarded Egypt under Arab nationalist leader Gamal Abdel Nasser a common threat to their national interests. Israel and France (together with Britain) collaborated in a military invasion of Egypt in 1956 (condemned by the Americans); and the French provided Israel with military equipment, including advanced fighter jets, and helped the Jewish state develop its nuclear military capability at a time when Washington had imposed a military embargo against Israel.[39] In fact, Israeli leaders in the early 1960s were toying with the idea of adopting a "European Orientation" based on an alliance with the French-German bloc, which brought together strands of French Gaullism and muted German nationalism, and which, not unlike the current Paris-Berlin partnership, assumed an anti-American course. At the time, officials in Bonn, Paris, and Jerusalem concluded that President Kennedy was striving to reach a deal with Moscow based on an American-Soviet "condominium" in Europe and elsewhere that would secure the superpowers' nuclear supremacy. The French and the Israelis assumed that Kennedy was not only supporting Algerian independence but was moving toward closer ties with Egypt's President Nasser.[40]

French policy, together with those of other European countries, tilted more to the Arab and Palestinian side after Israel's military victory in 1967, when Jerusalem was strengthening its relationship with Washington and adopting an "American Orientation" and France was displaying Gaullist ambitions of challenging the United States. But the European policies in the Middle East have been dynamic and responded to changes in Israeli, Arab, and American policies. Hence, while the EU was critical of Israeli policies in the West Bank during the nationalist-religious Likud government,[41] it adopted a more sympathetic position toward Israel when Labor leader Ehud Barak came to power and took steps to make peace with the Palestinians. Indeed, some Palestinians had accused the EU at that time of adopting an "anti-Palestinian" approach.[42] And as much as the neoconservative Euro-bashers seem to direct their accusations of anti-Israeli attitudes against France and other "old" European countries, Britain and two "new" European nations, Spain and Italy—and not "old" Germany, which maintains close economic and military ties with the Jewish state—have been the leading promoters in the EU of the cause of Palestinian independence and of pressing Washington to force Israel to make concessions to the Palestinians.[43] With regard to Israel—and the United States—the EU and the European governments are mostly projecting not cultural values but national interests.

DECONSTRUCTING NEOCONSERVATIVE EUROPHOBIC MYTHS

The neoconservative civilizational interpretation of the Euro-American rift over the Middle East, advanced as the Mars vs. Venus clash, provides a larger policy frame in which alleged European anti-Semitism, anti-Israelism, appeasement, and Euro-Arabism are integrated. These attitudes are then depicted as part of an anti-American and anti-Israeli European sentiment driven by predetermined political-cultural variables and by concepts such as national identity, international relations, and, most important, power. Since history and culture make it impossible to bridge such a gap between Europeans and Americans as Kagan and other neoconservative explain it, we might as well accept this Euro-American disconnect and get used to it. We should refrain from trying to understand it as manageable policy differences. Americans should accept the notion of European "declinism" as a given and pursue their interests (global supremacy) and ideals (imperial democracy) as defined by the neocons and as applied to the MEP, and recognize that the Europeans will try to unsuccessfully challenge them from time to time. The Europeans are transformed from diplomatic allies to diplomatic pests, a nuisance that should be either treated with benign neglect or be dealt with in an imperial fashion, through the projection of military power and the methods of "divide and rule" (between "old" and "new" Europe).[44]

But the Euro-American clash is not civilizational; it's not about the definition of power. It's a political conflict; it's about power relations, not unlike the division between Europe and Israel. After all, in applying the Mars vs. Venus typology to analyze Japan's foreign policy, one is forced to conclude that Japan is indeed located somewhere on Venus. In a way, Japan is more related to Venus than are Germany and France. Japan is a pacifist country that, like the EU, identifies its foreign policy with the use of "soft power," and regards multilateral regimes as central to the advancement of its global interests. Unlike France, it has refrained from projecting an assertive nationalist posture in East Asia and worldwide. While Germany has even deployed troops to the Balkans and Afghanistan, Japan has been hesitant about making even such minimal security commitments. Yet, Japan was a member of the Coalition of the Willing in Iraq, has backed U.S. policy in the Middle East, and even deployed a small number of troops to Iraq; and neoconservatives urge that Washington recruit Tokyo as part of a strategy to "contain" China. In other words, political-strategic interests and not political-cultural values drive Japanese policy toward the United States.

Similarly, that European elites and the public regard a resolution of the Israel-Palestine conflict as a top priority reflects real political and geo-strategic interests. These attitudes are not a reflection of anti-Semitism, in the same way that the British-French alliance with Israel in the 1950s was not a result of pro-Zionist sentiments in London and Paris, but a product of geo-strategic considerations. Ironically, that British-French alliance with Israel had to do with the opposition that London, Paris, and Bonn shared with Jerusalem against the global and Middle Eastern policies of the United States in that period.

That there are political-cultural or civilizational components to relationships is not deniable. Foreign policymakers are political entrepreneurs who can advance and exploit the collective historical-political strains of their communities in support of "us" against the foreign "other" in order to mobilize elite and public support for certain diplomatic orientations. The more interesting phenomenon in the case of American and European Middle Eastern policies has been the way in which policymakers succeeded in overcoming some of the cultural or civilizational contradictions operating at the center of their diplomacy. During the 1960s, the support in France for a partnership with the Jewish State was promoted by right-wing forces with anti-Semitic leanings, who against the backdrop of the war of independence in Algeria regarded Israel as a strategic bastion against Pan Arabism in the Middle East and North Africa. One can also point to the more than 50-years-long diplomatic and military ties between Saudi Arabia and the United States, which had been quite stable until 9/11 despite the deep-rooted cultural gap between their two societies. If anything, one major reason that the Euro-American relationship could survive strategic tensions in the past has been the strong historical and cultural ties between the two central entities of the West.

In that context, there have certainly been political-cultural frictions in the relationship between the Europeans and the Americans; anti-American sentiments have been popular on both the political left and right in France and Germany. Nevertheless, those attitudes played a very marginal role during the Cold War era, when common political-strategic interests dominated the foreign policies of the members of the transatlantic alliance. It was those strategic ties that explained the U.S. alliance with Canada and Australia—and not the strong civilizational ties between the English-speaking peoples or the Anglo-Americans.

Another Europhopic myth that permits neoconservatives to spin political interests as cultural variables is the one that pits "new" Europe against "old" Europe. The neoconservatives propose that the support that Italy, Spain, Portugal, and Denmark and the Eastern European governments such Poland, Hungary, and the Czech Republic provided the Bush administration during the war in Iraq and in the diplomatic and military buildup to it, in contrast to the opposition from France, Germany, and Belgium, reflected deep political-cultural divisions between "new" and "old" Europe.[45] Other neoconservatives have argued that the British-American-Australian alliance during the war in Iraq helped revive Winston Churchill's old dream of establishing a union of the English-Speaking nations, or an "Anglosphere." Based on this term one could imagine Canada, New Zealand, Ireland, "and the other educated English-speaking populations of the Caribbean, Oceania, Africa and India" rising up to help defend the "Aglosphere's frontiers"[46] and confront a Francophone bloc or a Franco-German dominated EU.[47]

Ironically, some anti-American French intellectuals are pointing to the emergence of a unified Anglo-Saxon power that poses a threat to Europe. But has the Anglosphere really been energized during the Iran war? In fact, Canada refused to join the U.S.-Britain-Australia alliance on Iraq and India and South Africa opposed the Iraq war. Australian Prime Minister John Howard's Iraq policies were motivated, not so much by his country's cultural ties with America, but by the aspiration of turning his country into Washington's "deputy Sheriff" in Asia, as opposed to his predecessors in the Labor party who have promoted a more "Asian orientated" foreign policy.[48] Similarly, Tony Blair has been a long-time proponent of British integration into the EU, as opposed to many Euroskeptics in the British conservative party or on the far political left. If anything, Blair regarded the alliance with Washington during the war as a way of helping the Europeans restrain the Bush administration.[49]

Indeed, much of the distinction between "old" and "new" Europe remains fuzzy as cultural-political divisions are more evident inside each European country. Germany's Christian Democratic Union (CDU) party is generally pro-American; but it is also echoes "old" political-cultural sentiments in its opposition to liberalizing Germany's immigration policies. The Social Democrats opposed the Iraq war, yet they back liberalizing immigration rules.[50] Ironically, the pro-Bush policy on Iraq adopted by Romania and Poland was advanced by governments run by ex-Communist regimes, while French President Jacques Chirac is one of Europe's veteran anti-Communist and pro-free market figures.[51] And in any case, public opinion polls indicate that Europeans in both "old" and "new" Europe share similar views with regard to Iraq (opposing the war) and Israel/Palestine (critical of Israel).[52] On these issues "popular opinion in Eastern European nations eager to enter both NATO and the EU mirrors that of their Western brethren."[53]

Ironically, the leading "new" European nation Denmark spends less on defense than "old" and unmanly France.[54] In fact, the main reason for the pro-Bush posture on Iraq adopted by Italy and the government of Jose Maria Anzar in Spain had less to do with the pro-Americanism of the "new" Europeans and more with the interests of those governments in maintaining the American security umbrella so as not to be forced to pay for their own defense; in other words, old-fashioned free-riding. Similarly, the fact that the Romanian and Bulgarian governments exhibited such a staunch pro-Washington position is explained by the fact that they represent two of the poorest economies in Europe; they expected that their support for the Americans will be rewarded with economic assistance as well as with backing from Washington for NATO membership.

Some of the tensions over Iraq inside the EU reflected the challenge by European countries to prevent the emergence of a Franco-German "directorate" that might stitch up EU decisions to the exclusion of smaller EU countries. At the same time, Blair was hoping that asserting Britain's ties with Washington would help London strengthen its position vis-à-vis Paris and Berlin in the EU.[55] The Polish policy has probably less to do with Poland's support for U.S. policy in the Middle East and more with an attempt to counter Franco-German supremacy in the EU and to secure an American presence in NATO.[56] Similarly, the Aznar government in Spain had hoped that their pro-Iraq-war position would strengthen their position in the EU vis-à-vis France and Germany and allow them to act as "a bridge" between America and the EU.[57] On the other hand, the Franco-German opposition to the U.S. war in Iraq was clearly affected by the merging of the national interests of France in its Gaullist interpretation, and Germany, driven by post–Cold War efforts to "normalize" its world standing in the context of the EU and NATO.[58] At the same time, the intra-European rivalries and the Euro-American disputes over Iraq provided an opportunity for European leaders like French President Chirac,[59] German Chancellor Gerhard Schroeder [60]and Belgium's Prime Minister Guy Verhofstadt[61] to strengthen their position at home as they prepared or recovered from tough election campaigns. Spain's Prime Minister Anzar had expected that his pro-war position would win him U.S. support for his domestic war against Basque terrorism (it did) and help his party to win in the coming parliamentary election (it didn't).[62]

Interestingly enough, the outcome of the conflict over the Iraq war has produced in Europe a classic balance-of-power relationship between France and

Germany, on one hand, and Britain, on the other hand. Blair's Britain did not join the "new" Europeans to form a pro-American wing in the EU. Instead, "Blair seems to have thrown his lot with the Germans and the French," noted *Financial Times* columnist Gerard Baker, pointing to Blair's decision in 2003 to support the French-German model for EU defense cooperation.[63] The EU's Franco-German directorate has expanded to include Britain and such an inclusion could lead eventually to the formation of a Berlin-Paris-London triumvirate that will probably dominate Europe's and foreign policy in the coming years.[64] That creation of this new triumvirate would run contrary to the neoconservative fantasy of co-opting Britain as a leader of a "new" Europe. Instead, Britain, considering its long-term political and economic interests, is seeking "to make [the] France-German couple a threesome," according to the *Economist.*[65] That development might not fit into the Mars vs. Venus model of international relations; but it is a "realistic view of the world."[66]

THE MIDDLE EAST AND THE EURO-AMERICAN RIFT

While the examination of the current Euro-American rift by focusing on its intra-European aspects and domestic political considerations allows us to deconstruct the neoconservative Europhopic myths, it does not provide a complete explanation of why these developments brought about a crisis in the Western alliance over the Middle East. The main framework that one has to apply in order to understand the Euro-American division is through the geostrategic and geo-economic lenses that the Europeans and Americans have been using in order to configure their interests in the Middle East against the backdrop of the end of the Cold War. In that context, the French approach on Iraq, which echoed the views of the majority of elites and general public opinion in Europe was not a reflection of anti-Americanism rooted in cultural values or a manifestation of a declining entity committed to multilateralism and "soft power." Instead it reflected an opposition to the hegemonic Middle Eastern policies of the Bush administration as enunciated and implemented by the neoconservative intellectuals and policymakers. As French Middle East analyst Oliver Roy argued in the *New York Times,* the French and other Europeans believed that the U.S. Iraq war objectives stated by President Bush—destruction of Iraq's WMD, fighting against terrorism, ousting a tyrant—served as a smoke screen to hide the real strategic goals that the neoconservatives were able to get Bush to adopt after 9/11.[67]

All European governments and the majority of Europe stood unified behind the United States after the Al Qaeda terrorists launched their attacks on

New York and Washington. Americans and Europeans were never as united as when George Robertson, NATO's Secretary General, proposed that the organization invoke its Article Five authority to come to the defense of the United States. That provision states that an attack against one NATO nation is an attack against them all, which provided the binding glue of the alliance but had never before been used. Most European governments and the EU agreed to cooperate with the United Sates in fighting terrorism in Afghanistan and around the world; Germany sent thousands of peacekeeping troops to Afghanistan.[68]

It was Bush's "Axis of Evil" speech in January 2002 and the indication that the Bush administration was shifting the focus of the war on terrorism from pursuing members of the Al Qaeda network to Iraq that demonstrated to the Europeans that Washington was pursuing a policy that was "very risky and full of pitfalls"[69] and that ran contrary to their interests. Europeans like Roy were concerned that the fall of Saddam Hussein would lead to the disintegration of Iraq, to civil war between ethnic and religious groups, and that a free election in Iraq would lead to the emergence of an Iranian-style theocracy in Baghdad. By challenging the neoconservative "domino theory" of a democratic Iraq serving as a model for the entire Arab world, many Europeans warned of a destructive "spill-over" effect of an unstable Iraq on the Middle East—a process of "trickle-down radicalism."[70]

At the same time, while Bush's neoconservative advisors down-played the significance of the Israeli-Palestinian conflict to the stability in the region, arguing that a U.S. military victory in Iraq would create conditions for solving the Israel-Palestine crisis ("The road to Jerusalem leads through Baghdad"), the Europeans contended that resolution of the Israeli-Palestinian issues is central to establishing stability in the region and to mending relations with the Arabs. A war in Iraq would only aggravate anti-Western attitudes in the region, inflamed by Israel's treatment of the Palestinians, and should have been postponed until Washington succeeded in persuading Israel to make concessions to the Palestinians ("The road to Baghdad leads through Jerusalem"). The Europeans, whose policy in the Middle East is affected in part by the influence of a growing Moslem community in their respective countries, attributed the pro-Israeli direction of the Bush administration to the power of the pro-Israeli lobby and the American-Jewish community in Washington.[71]

However, for the Europeans, the Middle East is not a far-away region, such as Central America, where the EU and individual countries like France and Germany have limited economic and diplomatic interests today. For the Europeans, the Middle East is what Central America and the rest of Latin America is for the United States: its strategic backyard, or what the Moslem Central Asian republics are for Russia, its "near abroad." Geographical proximity, strategic-military interests, dependency on the oil resources of the region, and religious and historical bonds that go back to the Crusader era and to the struggle with the Arab-Islamic empires have been the driving forces behind the British and French efforts to penetrate the region through economic and military means. Those interests explain the Europeans' efforts to establish imperial outposts in the Middle East after the collapse of the Ottoman Empire in World War I. But their weakening economic and military status forced the British and the French to withdraw in stages from the Middle East in the aftermath of World War II and permitted the United States to replace them as the guarantor of Western interests in the Middle East, and contain the Soviet Union and other anti-Western threats in the region.[72]

THE MIDDLE EAST AND THE COLD WAR

From the perspective of the Europeans, and in particular, the French and the British, the relationship between Europe and the United States in the Middle East during the Cold War was marked by a combination of close cooperation and fierce rivalry, reflecting their Cold War convergence of interests and long-standing competition for preeminence in the region. After World War II, military and economic weakness caused Britain and France to pass the Middle Eastern torch to the United States. Washington hoped that its oil companies would capture the British-dominated Gulf oil markets and that the U.S. anti-imperialist image would help it replace the two former colonial powers, Britain and France, as a major player in the region. The Truman Doctrine, which sought to counter Soviet moves in the eastern Mediterranean that had threatened Western access to its oil, symbolized U.S. assertion of power in the region as the leader of the Western alliance.

In that context, the 1956 Suez campaign, in which the United States pressured France and Britain (and Israel) to withdraw from Egypt, highlighted to the Europeans the U.S. objective of undercutting Europe's status in the area.[73] Britain and France still saw themselves at that time as major world powers with special interests in the Middle East—Britain in Egypt and the Gulf, France in Syria and Lebanon. "As they became increasingly conscious of the lack of resources to sustain that role, they invited America to undertake a joint effort in the Middle East as it had with respect to Greece and Turkey when Britain was no longer able to hold that line," noted Henry Kissinger.[74] London and Paris regarded the nationalization of the Suez Canal by Egypt's President Gamal Abdel Nasser as a mortal threat to their lifeline to the Middle East and their influence there, and were ready to use power to force Nasser to reverse his decision. But the Eisenhower administration was not prepared to associate itself with British or French interests in the Middle East, and rejected their plans of using military power to force Egypt to open the Suez Canal. The Americans expected that postcolonial regimes like that of Egypt would then seize the opportunity to join the United States in the struggle against the Soviet Union. In exasperation and frustration, Britain and France went to war, only to face the opposition of the Americans, who, together with the Soviets, voted to condemn the Anglo-French war against Egypt, and threatened to withhold support for European currencies in financial markets.

For the British and the French as well as for other Europeans, the Suez crisis symbolized the decline of European power in the Middle East, marked by the ensuing British withdrawal from the Persian Gulf, the granting of independence to Algeria by France, and the rise to pre-eminence of the United States in the region, and, by extension, worldwide. The growing role of the United States in the Middle East was projected by the Eisenhower Doctrine of 1957, which committed the United States to defending the countries in the Middle East from external and internal threats, and was demonstrated by the decision to deploy American troops in Lebanon in 1958. The 1956 Suez debacle was also regarded as a possible precursor of a diplomacy in which Europe would be a bystander unless it organized itself for an independent course of action in the Middle East and elsewhere. According to then French Foreign Minister Christian Pineau, even the pro-American German Chancellor Konrad Adenauer said on the day that Britain and France accepted the American ultimatum to withdraw from Egypt that "There remained to [France and Britain] only one way of playing a decisive role in the world . . . We have not time to waste. [A united] Europe will be your revenge."[75]

The tight collaboration, and, at the same time rising conflict, that marked the U.S.-European relationship during the Cold War reflected also their different perspectives on the linkages between the Persian Gulf and the Arab-Israeli conflict. "Whereas the U.S. sees the problem of access to the Gulf in strategic terms, West Europeans see it primarily in political terms," explained a former State Department official in an attempt to analyze the fracturing of the Western alliance during the 1970s over Middle Eastern politics. The Europeans were "seeking to respond to the political and trade concerns of the nations of the Gulf region" and, motivated by their own economic interest in increasing trade, including arms sales to regional states, wanted to forge an unbreakable political linkage between the Palestinian-Israeli conflict and the security of the Persian Gulf. The Europeans argued that the U.S. refusal to accept such a linkage reflected the power of the Israeli lobby in Washington, while Americans interpreted Europe's commitment to that linkage as surrender to Arab oil blackmail.[76]

In the late 1960s and early 1970s, the transformation of the U.S. global and economic position and the emergence of the U.S. alliance with Israel encouraged the Europeans, who were moving toward closer economic and political integration, to begin competing again with Washington in the region. These tensions reached their painful climax in the 1973 Middle East War and the ensuing oil embargo. The European Community (EC) pressured Washington to make concessions to the Arabs and exploited a U.S. refusal to do so by concluding separate deals with the Arabs.[77] The post-1973 U.S.-sponsored Egyptian-Israeli peace process again seemed to enhance the U.S. position in the region, but the Europeans took advantage of the fact that the 1979 Camp David accords failed to resolve the Palestinian problem and in 1980 put forward the Venice Declaration, demanding that the Palestine Liberation Organization (PLO) be included in a Middle East peace conference. That initiative was aimed at tarnishing the U.S. diplomatic victory and at winning support from the Arab Gulf states opposed to the Camp David accords. Israeli and U.S. opposition helped to sink it.[78] At the same time, President Jimmy Carter's own doctrine for the Middle East, spelled out in 1980 following the revolution in Iran and the Soviet occupation of Afghanistan, helped to accentuate the cooperative elements in the American-European relationship in the Middle East. It served to highlight the American commitment to protect the oil resources in the Persian Gulf from an anti-Western threat, stressing that "[a]n attempt by an outside force to gain control of the Persian Gulf region will be regarded as an assault on the vital interests of the United States of America, and such an assault will be repelled by any means necessary, including military force."[79]

After the election of Ronald Reagan, Europe found itself paralyzed to some extent in the face of an increasingly assertive U.S. posture in the Middle East, which was based on close strategic cooperation with Israel, on one hand, and Saudi Arabia and Egypt, on the other hand. The U.S. policy was aimed at countering the power of the Soviet Union and of the Ayatollah Khomeini's revolutionary Iran. Feeling the consequences of the post-1973 oil shocks, unable to develop cohesive foreign and defense policies, and under the impact of the growing superpower tensions, Europe seemed to accept the U.S. leadership position in the region. However, U.S. policies in the Middle East deepened the desire among Europeans to maintain distance from the U.S. security posture and to emphasize measures to resolve conflicts before considering military options. Occasionally, the Europeans did clearly distance themselves from Washington—after the 1985 attack on Libya, for example. Meanwhile, the Europeans were suffering directly, in the form of terrorism, from the consequences of U.S. policies and its alliance with Israel that led to the 1982 invasion of Lebanon, and eventually to the rising Palestinian-Israeli violence in the West Bank and Gaza.

Already in the mid- and late-1980's the Europeans were starting to define a security role for themselves in the Middle East and the Persian Gulf. During this time what NATO called "out-of-area" questions had undergone subtle changes. The Suez crisis of 1956 was the most dramatic case of European intervention in the region and proved extremely divisive for the alliance. In addition to the differences between Europe and the United States over Middle Eastern issues, there were major disagreements on how and under what circumstances national defense resources should be utilized for non-NATO contingencies in the Middle East with their linkages to the East-West divide and the Arab-Israeli conflict. The Europeans, especially France and Italy, were becoming more assertive on out-of-area questions. There were projections of European military power in Lebanon from 1982 to 1984, and during the Iran-Iraq War in 1987–88; but even those actions were conducted only in coordination with the United States.[80]

The Europeans were aware that notwithstanding their rising economic power in the 1980s and early 1990s, only Washington had the military power to contain a Soviet threat in the Middle East and secure access for the EC and Japan to the oil resources in the Persian Gulf, on which they were more dependent than the United States. In the aftermath of the collapse of the Soviet Union and the end of the Cold War, including the vanishing of the Soviet threat in the Middle East, the United States pursued a hegemony-driven policy in the Middle East as demonstrated during the Gulf War. Operation Desert Storm and the Madrid Peace Conference permitted Washington to project its primacy in the Middle East as well as its role as the protector of the region's energy resources. In an international system that seemed to be more and more focused on geo-economic competition between economic blocs, the dominant U.S. position in the Middle East provided the United States with the power to secure its post–Cold War unipolar status.[81] Or so it seemed.

EUROPE PLAYS ROBIN TO THE AMERICAN BATMAN IN THE MIDDLE EAST

One way of making geo-political and geo-economic sense of the 1991 Gulf War, as opposed to just explaining it as a U.S.-led military response to the Iraqi aggression in Kuwait, is to consider it as an attempt by the first President Bush to assert a U.S. hegemonic role in the oil-rich Middle East and its peripheries during the immediate post–Cold War era. Critics argue that not only the first Gulf War, but also the late 1992 U.S. intervention in Somalia as well as the growing political-economic ties with the former Soviet Republics in Central Asia were all part of a common strategic axiom that was adopted by President George H. W. Bush and his foreign policy advisors: Whoever controls access to the oil resources in the Persian Gulf and Greater Middle East enjoys enormous political leverage over the major industrialized economies in Europe and East Asia.[82] Or as one political economist put it: "Controlling Iraq is about oil as power, rather than oil as fuel. Control over the Persian Gulf translates into control over Europe, Japan and China. It's having our hand on the spigot."[83]

The end of the Cold War could have been seen in the United States and in Europe as the beginning of a transition period in which the Americans could have been able to transfer some or most of their military responsibilities in the region to the Europeans. The latter received most of their energy supplies from the Middle East, and with their growing economic power had the capability to develop the needed military force to protect their interests in the region, especially at a time when most regional and global threats to stability there seemed containable. Here was an opportunity for the United States to re-define its goals in the Middle East and reduce its military commitments. But such a move would have brought an end to American hegemony in the Middle East and the replacement of its influence with that of the Europeans, with the result that their hands would have been "on the spigot." Such a development could have dealt a blow to the American MEP. That the Europeans could become the dominant power in the oil-rich Middle East had the potential to transform them into a central Euroasian rival to the United States, and could have created the conditions for what French President Chirac was calling for ten years later—the creation of a multipolar international system.

Indeed, strict geo-political reasons would have dictated that with the end of the Cold War and with no other global power threatening to establish hegemony in the Middle East, regional powers could be counterbalanced either by other regional powers or by players adjacent to the region, including Europe, whose interests in the area were more direct and immediate than those of the United States. Certainly with the end of the Cold War, the American people and their representatives were expected to question the wisdom of maintaining an American presence in the Persian Gulf. And an international system was emerging in which economic power seemed to be replacing military power—or at least modifying it—as the main source of influence in international competition. Under this new condition, Europe could assume a role equal to that of the

United States. Why should Americans have to continue paying the costs of defending access to the oil resources in the Persian Gulf for the Europeans who were trying to beat them in the global trade competition?

The reunification of Germany, the growing Franco-German military cooperation, and the development of the Western European Union (WEU) as an instrument of independent European security coordination suggested that Europe would be able to act independently in the Middle East and contemplate out-of-area responses there. The Europeans could then decide "whether to combine or integrate national rapid deployment forces and define what contingencies will require such responses."[84] At the same time, the Europeans were expected to translate their growing political unity and their economic power into diplomatic and military might and try to drive forth their own Middle East agenda, with an emphasis on diplomatic and economic rather than military power, and, especially, the need to link a Palestinian-Israeli solution with the security of the Gulf.

And then Saddam invaded Kuwait . . .

THE AMERICAN EMPIRE STRIKES BACK IN THE MIDDLE EAST

Interestingly enough, in testimony before the Senate Armed Services Committee following Saddam Hussein's invasion of Kuwait in 1991, former Secretary of State Henry Kissinger predicted that the U.S. leadership position in the Middle East might be coming to an end. "We are in a transitional period," he said. "I would think that over a period of 10 years, many of the security responsibilities that the United States is now shouldering in the [Persian] Gulf ought to be carried by the Europeans who receive a larger share of the oil from the region." But Saddam Hussein's invasion of Kuwait came while the United States was the hegemonic power in the Persian Gulf, explained Kissinger. The Americans "still have the post-war, global role and the military force capable of exercising it," he noted. At the same time, the Europeans lacked a security structure that would have enabled them to contain Iraq and play a role commensurate with their expanding political and economic power and their interests in the Middle East. "In the interim, the United States remains the key stabilizing factor in the region," said Kissinger, giving his blessing to the American military attack on Iraq. But he also cautioned American lawmakers and officials that in the long run, Washington would not be able to carry the Middle Eastern torch forever, and urged that America work with its allies to maintain a Western-dominant position in the region.[85]

Hence, geo-strategist Kissinger was proposing that Washington take advantage of the Iraqi aggression against Kuwait to try to reverse, or at least postpone, the Cold War trends that would have challenged U.S. hegemony in the Middle East, and by extension around the world. Since hegemonic powers tend to resist giving up their existing leadership prerogatives, and up-and-coming powers are often in no hurry to take on new responsibilities, the fact that the Gulf War was taking place at a time when the international system was in such a delicate transition period provided Washington with an opportunity to secure the status quo in the Middle East. It could establish American hegemony in the Middle East in the face of the collapse of the Soviet Union while continuing to maintain the kind of cooperative-competitive relationship that existed between the United States and Europe during the Cold War in the Middle East—in which the Americans emerged with the upper hand at the end of each crisis.

And that was exactly the kind of scenario that took place during and in the aftermath of Desert Storm. For President Bush and his advisors, the military victory of the U.S.-led coalition in the Persian Gulf suggested that the international system had entered a new period of Pax Americana, with an interventionist United States reigning supreme in the Middle East and in a unipolar world, in which Europe would continue to play a secondary role, like in the good old days of the Cold War.[86] The war with Iraq heralded a new division of labor in the Western alliance in which Europe would be expected to "deliver plenty of political support backed by hardware and a lot of money" while "leaving the driving to President Bush."[87] British Prime Minister Margaret Thatcher argued at that time that Europe should have abandoned the "romantic" and "dangerous" notions of a united and independent Europe capable of sharing international security responsibilities in the Middle East.[88] She made her comments before the American Enterprise Institute (AEI), a think tank that would provide an intellectual roof in the coming ten years to the group of neoconservative intellectuals who would later lead America in the next war against Iraq.

However, viewed from Paris and the then German capital, Bonn, American action in the Gulf War was an opportunity for the Americans to send an "I am back!" message to the world and put the Europeans, who had begun to challenge U.S. hegemony, in their place. Bush's aim, according to the French *Le Monde,* was to "drive a wedge between the Arab and European worlds, further slow down the creation of a grand European economic alliance, and set up a New World Order dominated by Washington."[89] The Europeans were far less enthusiastic about the prospects of a military action against Saddam. Not only was there little sympathy in Europe for the exiled leaders of Kuwait, but there was also a concern that a prolonged and bloody war with Iraq would produce chaos in the Middle East and harm the region's close economic and political relations with Europe. Responding to those sentiments, French President Francois Mitterrand tried on the eve of the war to lead an independent European effort based on a diplomatic linkage between an Iraqi withdrawal from Kuwait and Israeli withdrawal from the West Bank. Sounding a familiar Gaullist cry, he asserted France's independence from the United States: "I do not feel I am in a position of a second-class soldier who must obey his commanding general."[90]

Indeed, the success of the war in cutting Europe down to size was seen in Europe as evidence of an American grand design to weaken Europe's ability to project its power in the post–Cold War. The Gulf War was "America's War," stated then defense Minister Jean-Pierre Chevenement, who argued that by eventually sending troops to the Persian Gulf, "France attempted to help the United States restore world domination that its economic situation no longer assured." The fact that Washington set out to destroy Iraq, France's main and most powerful ally in the region and a counterweight to the more pro-American Saudi Arabia, was seen as part of an effort to erode Paris's interests in the region. Similarly, on the French political right, Jacques Chirac, who as president in 2003 led the European rebellion against Bush II, criticized Bush I in 1991 and suggested that the U.S. president had foreseen that Europe would be a great economic power in 20 years. Because Europe lacked independent sources of oil, Bush set out to make control of oil the United States' equalizer.[91]

PLAY IT AGAIN, BUSH: A TALE OF TWO WARS

The 1991 Gulf War exposed some major tensions between the Americans and the Europeans, in particular France and Germany, over U.S. policy toward Iraq and the Middle East that would re-emerge almost like scenes from a movie rerun ten years later. The movie features the Europeans, led by France and Germany and supported by the Russians, pushing for a diplomatic resolution to the Iraqi crisis and linking that to the need to deal with the Palestinian-Israeli conflict. Also starring are the British—led by Margaret Thatcher in 1991 and Tony Blair in 2003—determined to prevent the United States from "decoupling" from Europe, using the war to revive their "special relationship" with the United States. Indeed, the two Bushes made their decision to go to war only after receiving a green light from the respective British prime minister at the time. Twice in twelve years, the Anglo-American Island Power was marshalling its power to prevent the rise of a Euroasian challenger to Washington and London. The British interest in going to war with Iraq also stemmed from its historical ties with Kuwait as well as from the fact that Kuwaiti money helped prop up the British pound in world financial markets.[92]

Moreover, in both crises there was a lot of criticism in Europe of the alleged pro-Israeli bias in Washington, with one commentator suggesting in 1991 that there seemed to be a convergence of a "Washington-London-Tel Aviv axis" that would dominate the Middle East, a conspiracy-like perspective that would be echoed in Paris and Berlin ten years later.[93] And in 1992, not unlike in 2003, European governments resisted the efforts by Washington to win NATO's approval for using Turkey as a launching pad for an attack on Iraq. In both cases, there seemed to be a concern in Europe that Washington was trying to promote Turkey, its military ally and a close partner of Israel, as NATO's defense line in the Middle East, and to ensure that if and when Ankara joined the EU, it would help reorient Europe's diplomatic and military posture in the same direction— toward securing an American-led strategy in the Middle East.[94]

But there were also some major differences between the 1991 and 2003 crises and their effect on the Euro-American relationship. Even France, whose governments had in the past challenged U.S. policies in the region and advocated an independent European approach in the Middle East—and played a leading role in resisting U.S. policies in 2003—saw no alternative in 1991 but to play a silent partner to Washington during and following Desert Storm and the Madrid Peace Conference. In 1991, Italy and Spain joined France (and Greece) in adopting a common Euro-Mediterranean approach, reflecting those countries' apprehension that because of their large Moslem populations and ties with North Africa, they would be adversely affected by the war in the Middle East. A war with Iraq, warned then Spanish Foreign Minister Francisco Fernandes Ordonez, could lead to "a collision course between Islam and the West."[95] The Spaniards, like the French and Italians, were worried in 1991 that the war would fuel anti-European attitudes among Moslems in Europe and that support for Saddam Hussein in North Africa, manifested in several large pro-Iraqi demonstrations, would threaten the relatively moderate regimes there and create new waves of migrants to southern Europe with potentially explosive effects. In 2003, those concerns continued to influence the sentiments of the majority of the publics and elites in those countries; but unlike in 1991 when the governments in Paris, Madrid, and, Rome (and Athens) were controlled by socialist-leaning parties skeptical of American intentions, they were ruled in 2003 by conservative coalitions with relatively pro-American attitudes. The fact that Spain and Italy could exhibit such ambivalence, challenging U.S. policy in the Middle East as easily as they could back it, reflecting long-term concerns (geographical and demographic links to the Middle East) and ad hoc political interests (changes in governments, the need to balance between the ties with the Franco-German bloc and Washington) should certainly raise doubts about the "new" versus "old" Europe typology.

Germany drew strong criticism from the United States in 1991 for not contributing more directly to the war effort, reflecting the consensus at the time among Germans that their country should plan a peaceful international role with strict limits on the use of military force as embodied in the German Basic Law, which restricted the use of German forces to NATO territory in Europe. At the same time, many Germans also expressed concern that the war with Iraq would divert resources from the political and economic reconstruction of Eastern Europe.[96] But leading a pro-American Christian Democratic coalition, German Chancellor Helmut Kohl, who forged a solid political and personal friendship with President Bush during the dramatic collapse of the Communist Bloc and the moves to re-unify Germany, worked closely with Washington to manage the Euro-American relationship before and after Desert Storm. The pro-American orientation of the Kohl government could also be explained by the hostility projected by both the French and British government toward the post–Cold War resurgence of Germany. The reality of the German-American relationship went through a major transformation in 2003 as a result of growing Franco-German ties as well as tensions between the Social Democratic-Green government, led by Chancellor Gerhard Schroeder, and Bush II. Neoconservative spin doctors misinterpret that chapter in the German-American relationship by portraying Berlin and Schroeder as being "anti-American." But it was Schroeder and his Green foreign minister Joschka Fischer who presided over a major transformation of German foreign policy after 9/11 by winning support from the German parliament to deploy troops to Afghanistan as part of a common strategy with the United States.

But unlike in 2003, the Europeans ended up returning into the American strategic fold in the Middle East in 1991, as demonstrated by the French decision to deploy a few troops to Iraq and by the German financial backing of the U.S. military operations. The administration of Bush I, it seemed, succeeded in achieving its goal of preserving the U.S. leadership role in the Middle East, notwithstanding French anti-Washington rhetoric and German anti-American demonstrations. The Europeans "may be sidelined in the Middle East by Washington," admitted a French diplomat suggesting that a Pax Americana was established in the region.[97] In an extension of the unipolar international system, the United States was now in the same position that Great Britain found itself in after World War I—in control of the Middle East and with no serious regional or global challenger.[98]

But in the aftermath of the 1991 Gulf War, the Cold War–style acrimony was once again characterizing the relationship between Europe and the United States, with Americans accusing their allies across the Atlantic of free-riding in the Middle East while the Europeans were demanding more access to decision making in the region. Lawmakers in Washington were asserting that the Europeans were playing once again the role of free-riders, counting on the hegemon, the United States, to provide them with a cost-free defense of the region's oil. Americans, antagonized by the European behavior—German peace marches, ill-timed French diplomatic initiatives—believed that the Europeans should have contributed more militarily and financially to the American campaign. There was resentment in Washington at the reluctance of the Europeans, with the exception of Great Britain, to commit significant numbers of troops or provide large-scale support for the U.S. effort in the Persian Gulf. Former Democratic Senator David Boren of Oklahoma expressed the then prevailing U.S. view when he asked, "Is it going to be American taxpayers who are going to foot the bill [so] that when it's all over we end up with [the European] economies enhanced?"[99] The European approach seemed to reflect the free-rider problem: Europe wanted the benefits of a stable world order, including the security of the oil resources in the Persian Gulf, without bearing the costs.

At the same time, a European official told the British *Guardian* that the Euro-American relationship was "a classic case of taxation without representation." If Washington wanted them to cease being free-riders, argued the Europeans, it should allow them a place in the driver's seat of the Middle East policymaking. After all, if Europe had wielded significant influence over Middle East policies during the 1980s, it might have been able to prevent disasters like the 1982 Lebanon War or would have pushed more effectively for an Israeli-Palestinian peace. The outcome of more activist European policy in the Middle East would have strengthened the moderate Arab bloc and would have made the region less hospitable to Saddam's aggression. The message to Washington was that the United States could not have its cake (call the shots unilaterally in the Middle East) while eating it, too (expecting Europe to pay the costs).[100]

NEOCONSERVATIVES AT WAR . . . WITH CONSERVATIVES

That the tensions between the United States and Europe did not evolve into a full-blown confrontation in 1991 like they did in 2003, was not a twist of fate. It was a result of the competent policy management of diplomatic stars James Baker and Brent Scowcroft, who advised President Bush, and the methods they adopted to maintain U.S. hegemony in the Middle East. They were not proposing that the United States establish an American imperial system in the Middle East and launch a democratic crusade in the region. Instead, they devised a cost-effective strategy to expel Iraq out of Kuwait—but not to invade Iraq—in consultation with the pro-Western Arab partners and the European allies as part of a multilateral, UN-driven effort. The policy advanced by these conservative realist policymakers would provide international legitimacy to an American-led operation that would permit Washington to maintain its dominant position in the Middle East for a few more years.

At the same time, the Bush administration took action to provide Israel with Patriot missiles to help protect it from Iraqi Scud missiles and discourage it from attacking Iraq in response to such attacks. The White House also exerted pressure on the then Likud government to force it to end the building of Jewish settlements in the occupied West Bank and Gaza and reach a political settlement with the Palestinians. Bush I and his advisors ended up putting their money where their mouths were, by threatening to deny Israel $10 billion in loan guarantees to help absorb Russian immigrants if it continued to build Jewish settlements and by convening the Madrid peace conference immediately after the Gulf War.

These moves demonstrated that the Bush administration was promoting a Middle East agenda based on a consensus that took into consideration the concerns of America's Middle Eastern partners and the Europeans and created incentives for them to support American policy. In that way, it reduced the costs of maintaining the U.S.-dominant position in the region in the post–Cold War era. Bush II and his advisors, on the other hand, saw the war against Iraq as a prologue to the creation of an exclusive American protectorate in the Middle East that would deny regional players their voice and prevent other global players, like the Europeans, from participating in the decision making affecting policy in the Middle East. While Bush I and his advisors called for more political and economic freedom in Iraq and the Middle East, it was nothing more than "Idealism Lite," since they refrained from taking any major steps to achieve that. They ended up refusing to assist the Shiite rebellion, while agreeing to provide some limited protection to the Kurds in southern Iraq. They suggested they would be content to see the rise of a more compliant dictator in Iraq instead of taking steps that might lead to Kurdish and Shiite independence, which could have threatened Turkey and Saudi Arabia. Similarly, the efforts to promote an Arab-Israeli peace were not grounded in any idealistic notion of supporting self-determination for the Palestinians but simply to appease Arab concerns.

This conservative realist perspective was being challenged from within the ranks of the Bush administration by the rising neoconservative ideologues. In 1991, following the U.S. victory in the Persian Gulf, the neocons provided the foreign policy community at home and abroad with a first glance of their revolutionary orientation that would replace the methods of the Bush I team to maintain U.S. hegemony with an imperial approach toward reshaping the Middle East that would deny the Europeans any critical strategic role. The 1991 policy paper issued by a group of policymakers in the Defense Department stated that the mission of the United States in the post–Cold War era would be "convincing potential competitors that they need not aspire to a greater role or pursue a more aggressive posture to protect their legitimate interests." The 1991 Pentagon paper that was co-authored by Defense Department official Paul Wolfowitz, the neoconservative intellectual who would become a major driving force in persuading the President Bush II to oust Saddam Hussein from power, made the case for a world—and by extension, a Middle East—dominated by one superpower, the United States. American hegemony could be perpetuated by constructive behavior and sufficient military might so as to deter any nation or group of nations, including its Cold War allies in Europe, from disputing the U.S. position. In order to secure this leading role, suggested the 1991 paper, the United States "must sufficiently account for the interests of the advanced industrialized nations to discourage them from challenging our leadership or seeking to overturn the political and economic order." In the Middle East and the Persian Gulf, Washington should "remain the predominant outside power in the region and preserve U.S. and Western access to the region's oil." The United States, according to the authors of the Pentagon paper, was going to continue paying the costs of maintaining the order in the area. It would "seek to deter further aggression in the region, foster regional stability, protect U.S. nationals and property and safeguard our access to international air and seaways." As demonstrated by Iraq's invasion of Kuwait, it remained fundamentally important to prevent a hegemon or an alignment of powers from dominating the region. This pertains especially to the Arabian Peninsula, where the United States "must continue to play a strong role through enhanced deterrence and improved cooperative security is emphasized."[101]

In a way, Wolfowitz and his co-authors stressed in their paper what some realist conservative thinkers are not always willing to admit—that eventually any existing balance of power ends up being challenged by those players who think that they have the power and the legitimacy that are needed in order to gain more access to decision making and to political and economic resources. In fact, Kissinger, in an interview following Desert Storm, admitted that the Gulf

War was an "almost accidental combination of circumstances unlikely to be repeated."[102] But he and other realists inside and outside the administration of Bush I refrained from proposing ways to deal with the expected challenges to U.S. supremacy in the Middle East. They could have suggested, for example, a formation of a Euro-American strategic alliance that would co-opt post-Soviet Russia and other players into a new ensemble of great powers that would help contain threats to common Western interests in the Middle East. Instead, they permitted the neoconservative intellectuals to set the new agenda, to sketch the outlines of an alternative strategy aimed at dealing with potential threats to a U.S. position in the Middle East that would ensure American supremacy in the region by using American military force to emasculate those future competitors. Bush I, like his Democratic successor in the White House, distanced himself from the Wolfowitz memorandum. But another President Bush would hire the controversial thinker as a top defense department official and adopt most of the memo's ideas as the basis for his policy in the Middle East.

THE CLINTON INTERMEZZO: LOW-COST PAX AMERICANA

President Clinton and his liberal internationalist aides continued to pursue the relatively cost-free strategy of maintaining American hegemony in the Middle East; Clinton was engaged in the Middle East but not up to a point in which the political costs overran the benefits.[103] While previous American presidents, including Harry Truman, Dwight Eisenhower, Richard Nixon, and Jimmy Carter, had proclaimed their "doctrines" aimed at containing challengers in the Middle East in dramatic public addresses before Congress, President Clinton's Middle Eastern doctrine was set forth by a mid-level bureaucrat. Clinton's Middle East aide and the future U.S. ambassador to Israel, Martin Indyk, in a closed-door address before a small group of experts in Washington in May 1993, presented the Dual Containment doctrine that proclaimed that Washington would attempt to keep Iran and Iraq weak through a combination of American military power and international diplomatic and economic sanctions, and at the same time, the United States would continue to be a "full partner" in the peace process and a strategic partner of Israel and the pro-American Arab states.

Clinton ran his "It's the economy, stupid!" campaign against a U.S. president preoccupied with Middle Eastern policy. He then attempted to focus Washington's foreign policy on geo-economics as a way of supplanting traditional geo-politics. The emphasis of the new approach was on diverting resources from the military budget to revitalize the civilian economy and prepare the United States for the coming economic battles with the two other major global economic powers, the EU and Japan. This geo-economic orientation explained why for the Clintonites the strengthening of ties with the "emerging economies" of the Pacific Rim was seen as more essential to advancing American global interests in the era of globalization than maintaining a U.S. diplomatic-military position in the Middle East as part of the Atlantic-oriented strategy that developed during the Cold War. The Clintonites celebrated their aggressive "commercial diplomacy," with its focus on helping American companies expand their investment and trade ties, especially in East Asia, and stressed their commitment to managing relations with Japan and China. In the Clinton White House, officials seemed to be more interested in what was happening in APEC (Asian Pacific Economic Cooperation forum), the rising Pacific Rim economic powerhouse that Washington had joined as a leading member, than what AIPAC (American Israel Public Affairs Committee), the pro-Israeli lobby, was doing. Hence, it would not be surprising if history books would recall George H. W. Bush presiding over the Madrid Peace conference as his finest diplomatic moment, while Clinton will probably be remembered for convening the Leaders Meeting of APEC in Seattle in 1993, and certainly not for his failed Camp David Israeli-Palestinian peace summit in 2000.

In some respects the Clintonites' approach in the Middle East was characterized by a certain schizophrenia—a product of the tensions between the new geo-economic and old geo-strategic orientations of the administration. The perception in Washington was that the geo-strategic conflict between the old military superpowers was giving way to a geo-economic rivalry between the trade blocs, and that the Arab oil states had transformed from economic powers threatening U.S. interests into military midgets dependent on American armed might. President Clinton could begin reprioritizing U.S. foreign policy, concluding that the Middle East did not require his urgent and personal attention. But other political counter-pressures at home and abroad forced him to get re-engaged in the Middle East from time to time. The geo-economic logic would have certainly argued that investing too much of America's resources in maintaining security in the Persian Gulf would constitute a subsidy to its European (and Japanese) economic rivals, and that because those economic powers are the prime consumers of Persian Gulf energy resources, they should be the ones to make the sacrifices to keep the flow of oil from the region stable and at a low price. But the traditional geo-strategic view would determine that America continued to derive political leverage over Europe (and Japan) from its dominant position in the Persian Gulf and the entire Middle East and its peripheries, and that giving up such dominance would increase the geo-political power of an emerging and unified Europe. This geo-strategic perspective—and not humanitarian concerns—provides a more accurate explanation of the decision by the Clintonites to get Americans troops involved in the wars in the Balkans, one of the "soft" peripheries of the Middle East.

At the same time, the notion that Washington needed to respond to the concerns of the pro-American Arab states and "do something" to bring an end to Israeli-Palestinian tensions remained a central component of the MEP during the Clinton presidency. From this perspective, the best-case-scenario would have been to reach a comprehensive settlement to the Arab-Israeli problems that could lead to the integration of Israel in the Middle East and bring both Israeli and Egyptian-Saudi interests in line with those of the United States. Short of achieving that, Washington could only maintain its hegemony in the Middle East by juggling its commitments to Israel and to the pro-American Arab camp, while placating and antagonizing the lobbies that represented these two Middle Eastern players in Washington. But if the Clintonites had refrained from being engaged in that game, they would have only played into the hands of the Europeans who would exploit America's problems to win brownie points with the Arabs.

All these pressures resulted in a policy that might have seemed incoherent sometimes but had its own logic. Clinton's approach to Middle Eastern policy could be described as a "Bush-minus" approach, or the quest for a Pax Americana on the cheap: trying to secure America's control of the oil of the Persian Gulf and maintaining its dominant position in the Middle East by guaranteeing the security of the pro-American Arab states and the evolving Arab-Israeli peace process without investing major military, diplomatic, or domestic political resources. The administration's Dual Containment doctrine was based on such a low-cost strategy, since neither Iraq nor Iran was expected in the short- or medium-run to challenge the U.S. hegemon in the region. Periodic displays of military and diplomatic force, such as U.S. attacks on targets in Iraq in June 1993 and February 1998, the continuation of the U.S.-led embargo against Saddam Hussein, and the efforts to isolate Iran, including the May 1995 ban on U.S. trade with Iran, were expected to deter those countries from making aggressive moves against Saudi Arabia and the Arab oil states. And this low-cost element of the Clintonites' Middle East strategy could be seen in its involvement in the Arab-Israeli negotiations that, until the last part of President Clinton's second term, were not expected to progress to the point where major U.S. presidential engagement and leadership would be required. Sending diplomatic fire brigades to prevent potential crises from igniting and celebrating the finalization of Arab-Israeli negotiations in the form of televised White House events helped to produce the perception that Clinton was "in charge" of the peace process.

EURO-AMERICAN TENSIONS OVER LEBANON AND IRAN

Sustaining these policies in the Middle East did involve some costs and, as they became more evident, the Europeans started exploiting America's difficulties in the Middle East. That was clearly demonstrated during the tensions between the Clinton administration and its European allies over U.S. support for Israel's "Grapes of Wrath" operation in Lebanon in 1996. Under French inducement, the EU contested the U.S. position during the fighting between Israel and the Shiite Moslem guerrillas who were backed by Syria and Iran. While then Secretary of State Warren Christopher was trying to mediate an agreement between Israel and Syria, the EU and France, touting their "critical dialogue" with Teheran, were proposing an alternative route aimed at utilizing Iranian cooperation. The then French Foreign Minister Herve de Charette met in Damascus with Iran's Foreign Minister, Ali Akhbar Velayati, and proposed that Teheran persuade the Hezbollah guerillas to show restraint. The French countered the American proposal for a cease-fire with a plan for a comprehensive peace agreement between Israel and Lebanon, with the support of the EU members who "believe the United States should not monopolize the Middle East peace process." At a meeting of the European foreign ministers in Luxembourg on April 22, 1996, Italy's then Foreign Minister, Susan Angelli, who visited Syria and Lebanon as part of the EU diplomatic initiative, declared that "Europe should insist on playing a role in forging a settlement" in Lebanon and the entire Middle East. Israeli opposition to EU diplomacy allowed the United States to conclude a cease-fire agreement in Lebanon. But French and American officials ended up bickering over the paternity of the accord, with de Charette claiming that France was responsible for "80 percent of the ideas contained in the text."[104] French officials also argued that the delay in reaching the truce in Lebanon resulted from the tardiness of the U.S. government, noting that only after the bombing of the United Nations camp in Qana, Lebanon, which killed more than one hundred civilians, did Washington realize the dimensions of the crisis. An earlier move by the EU to reach an accord could have prevented the tragedy.[105]

The tensions between Washington and Europe over the crisis in Lebanon reflected serious differences over the long-term strategy in reaching a Middle East settlement, including whether to solicit Iran's cooperation, the extent of Israel's security guarantees, and a growing rivalry over arms sales to the region and on ways to divide up reconstruction of peace keeping duties. European diplomats said that the Lebanon crisis in 1996 confirmed that the United States remained jealous about letting go of its dominant role as the chief orchestrator of the Middle East peace process and complained that Washington allowed them in only when the time came to pay for the reconstruction costs and provide soldiers for peacekeeping—presaging some of the criticism they raised during the war on Iraq in 2003. "The United States cannot expect to call all the shots and then expect Europe to pay," concluded then President Jacques Chirac.[106] French officials said that they wanted to enlarge what they acknowledged was only a toehold in Middle East diplomacy into a wider political role for Europe as a whole, noting that countries in the region do not wish to rely solely on U.S. mediation and want other interlocutors as well.

The growing rift between the United States and Europe also manifested itself in the dispute over the Dual Containment strategy as it applied to Iran. The American policy on Iran was highlighted in the May 1995 ban on U.S. trade with that country. The portrayal of Teheran by U.S. officials and lawmakers as the instigator of an Islamic fundamentalist crusade against Israel, Egypt, Saudi Arabia, and Turkey was in line with the U.S. goal of accentuating its strategic significance. Bashing Iran produced minimal costs to U.S. businesses while providing politicians in Washington major political benefits. It was not surprising that Clinton announced his decision to impose trade sanctions against Iran during a World Jewish Congress conference or that former Senator Alfonse D'Amato, a Republican from New York, called for the tightening of the sanctions on Iran by punishing third parties who traded with Iran, in the form of a "secondary boycott."[107] D'Amato's 1995 legislation, backed by the pro-Israeli lobby, included threats to impose sanctions on foreign companies that assisted Iran in its efforts to develop oil and gas projects. The legislation targeted potential European suppliers of oil-drilling technologies with a series of sanctions. The measure called for a mandatory ban on U.S. government purchases from companies dealing with Iran, denial of export licenses to their regular subsidiaries, and a refusal of entry to the United States for their executives.[108] One target of the legislation was the French company Total SA, which took over a proposed $1 billion oil deal for Houston-based Conoco after Clinton blocked U.S. oil projects in Iraq. European officials led by then Italian Prime Minister Romano Prodi visited Washington in June 1996 to warn against punishing European companies who deal with Iran. Congress eventually passed the so-called Iran-Libya Sanctions Act, known also by its feminine acronym, ILSE, which required the administration to penalize the foreign companies investing in Iran's (and Libya's) oil and gas industry. President Clinton, despite his earlier opposition to the legislation, ended up signing it.

European opposition to Washington's approach toward Iran goes back to the era of Bush I, when their governments reestablished the diplomatic relations with Teheran that had been severed in the early 1980s. The Europeans were upset over the attempts by the Bush administration to restrict their trade with Teheran, and only at the beginning of 1992 were they able to settle a long-standing conflict with Washington, after the United States withdrew its objections to the sale to Iran of the European-made Airbus passenger jet that used U.S.-made engines. When then French Foreign Minister Ronald Dumas prepared in 1991 for a visit to Iran to settle some of the financial problems between Iran and France, he indicated that improving relations with Teheran was part of "France's determined effort to maintain an independent policy in the region despite increasing American predominance."[109] The Clintonites branded the French-led European opposition to its Dual Containment policy as cynical moves by greedy business executives and power-hungry officials who were willing to "appease" the religious fundamentalists in Teheran. The French were taken to task for chasing new oil and gas deals in Iran (and Iraq), but counter-charges of hypocrisy would not have been out of line, given the U.S. role as the leading arms supplier to the region, its strategic control of the oil resources in the region, and its alliance with the radical Likud government in Jerusalem that came to power after the Labor government led by Shimon Peres lost the 1996 parliamentary elections.

EXACTING THE "SUEZ REVENGE"

CAN EUROPE CHALLENGE U.S. HEGEMONY IN THE MIDDLE EAST?

Historians will continue to debate whether the 1991 Gulf War was inevitable or whether another set of U.S. policies could have prevented the invasion of Kuwait or forced Iraqi withdrawal from that country without American military action. But there is no doubt that President Bush I and members of his foreign policy team were willing to pay some costs for asserting U.S. primacy in the region in terms of the utilization of American military might. The Clintonites in the 1990s were less inclined to pay those costs and were searching for a best-of-all-possible-worlds strategy that would allow them to show who was the boss in the Middle East—and do so without investing a lot of military and diplomatic resources and by refraining from contesting powerful lawmakers and political constituencies.

AMERICA IN THE DRIVER'S SEAT

As suggested earlier in the book, Washington could have taken important steps in the post–Gulf War era that, in retrospect, could have reduced the probability of 9/11 happening and perhaps even prevented it. An example of such a possible step is the reaching of a deal with the Russians on establishing an American-Russian condominium in Afghanistan that would have permitted the Russian-appointed Najibullah to remain in power as head of state—or to be replaced by someone acceptable to the Americans and the Soviets—and would have prevented the Taliban from coming to power. Washington could have put pressure on Pakistan and Saudi Arabia to end their support for the Taliban before and after that group came to power in Kabul and to end Pakistani and Saudi links to anti-American radical Islamic groups like Al Qaeda. The Americans could have considered reducing or ending their military presence in Saudi Arabia and/or agreeing to phase out the sanctions against Iraq; these two policies only helped increase animosity for the United States in the Arab and Moslem worlds and played into the hands of Osama bin Ladin and his supporters. Washington could have also reassessed the other component of its Dual Containment policy—the attempts to isolate Iran—and commenced a policy of détente with Teheran in a way that would have strengthened Iran as a counter-weight to both Saddam's Iraq and the Taliban's Afghanistan, two sworn enemies of that government. Or the Clinton administration, like its predecessor, could have applied more pressure on the Likud government of Benjamin Netanyahu to end its annexionist policies in the West Bank.

In fact, those were exactly the kind of policies that had been proposed by the Europeans at the time. One could imagine several counter-factual "What if?" scenarios, speculations as to what would have happened if the Europeans were in the Middle East's driver's seat in the 1990's—or at least had had more input into policymaking in the region. More active engagement by the EU in the Middle East might have created more incentives for the Syrians and Lebanese to enter into peace talks with Israel and produced momentum for negotiations on the Palestinian-Israeli front. Shimon Peres would have been less inclined to mount the disastrous attack on Lebanon in 1996 that helped return the Likud to power and there would have been more opportunities for an orderly Israeli withdrawal from Southern Lebanon. Engagement with Iran would have created pressures on Iraq to adopt a more accommodating policy toward the West and would have strengthened the more moderate elements in Teheran. The end of the isolation of Iran and Iraq would have opened the door for the beginning of a U.S. military withdrawal from the Persian Gulf, while a clear and unified Western opposition to the Israeli policy of building settlements in the occupied Palestinian territories might have weakened the more messianic and nationalist forces in the Jewish state.

That none of these or similar scenarios happened reflects Washington's unwillingness to abandon its cherished Middle East Paradigm (MEP). That the Americans did not feel any pressure to consider their commitment to the MEP was made possible by the fact that the Europeans were not yet ready to challenge them in the Middle East. The result was that the Americans were even more content with maintaining the deluxe Pax America project in the region.

But the American position was not entirely secured, and as noted earlier, the status quo that was maintained after the Gulf War during the administrations of President Bush I and Clinton was facing some limited challenges from both regional states like Iraq and Iran as well as from more radical players like Osama bin Ladin's Al Qaeda network. While President Clinton faced some problems in maintaining U.S. leadership in the "soft" peripheries of the Middle East, the Horn of Africa, and in the Balkans, he continued to pursue the hegemonic policies of his predecessor through a low-cost Pax Americana project of committing limited resources to protect the security of pro-American Arab states and Israel, through unilateral dual containment of Iran and Iraq, and by sponsorship of the Arab-Israeli peace process. The Europeans, led by France, did challenge some U.S. policies, especially toward Iran and Iraq, pressing Washington to get more active in promoting an agreement between Israel and the Palestinians. Additionally, from time to time, the Europeans pursued independent diplomatic policies to deal with the Arab-Israeli issue. Hence, the French-led EU continued to press the Americans to energize the Israeli-Palestinian peace process, implying that unless Washington moved in that direction, the Europeans would take their own steps to launch peace negotiations. One could make the argument that the Oslo peace process itself was very much nourished by the Europeans directly—the negotiations took place in Oslo with the active support of Norway and other Scandinavian countries, and indirectly through many forms of private and public diplomatic channels that preceded it.[1]

Neither Bush I nor Clinton, nor any of their major advisors, was considering a more dynamic strategy aimed at drawing the Europeans into the decision making process in the Middle East and creating a new structure with a division of labor in which the Europeans might take turns with the United States in sitting in the driver's seat. One such proposal raised by British military analyst Brian Beedham envisioned the creation of a strategic entity of "Euro-America" that would operate together to contain new threats in the Middle East and its peripheries.[2] But like similar ideas floating around at that time, it assumed an American-British core of a revitalized Atlantic alliance, in which France and Germany would follow the lead of the Anglo-Americans and a nationalist Russia could still be considered a threat. A more radical plan was proposed by foreign affairs analyst Srdja Trifkovic, who called for a wider paradigm shift in U.S. foreign policy based on "the creation of a genuine Northern Alliance—that of Russia, Europe, and North America—that would be able to face the many threats (most notably that from militant Islam) our common civilization will experience in this century." Such a shift, he suggested, "should be coupled with either the abolition of NATO or Russia's inclusion in it as an equal and welcome partner."[3] But no new strategic paradigm based on genuine cooperation between the great powers in the Middle East and elsewhere succeeded in gaining the attention of decision makers and pundits in Washington, demonstrating once again that dramatic changes in the making of foreign policy in the United States and other democracies can take place only in times of international crisis during which the perceived costs of certain policies forces the elites and the public to re-examine their utility. That process did not take place until 9/11; and when the terrorist attacks occurred, the neoconservatives were ready with their own foreign policy methods to explain what happened and to propose how to keep the MEP in place.

As I noted, while neither president was willing to encourage the Europeans to share in the determination of Middle East policy, both President Bush I and Clinton and their top advisors refrained from portraying U.S. policy in the Middle East as part of a hegemonic American project and recognized the limits operating on U.S. policy in the Middle East; hence, the decision not to oust Saddam Hussein during the 1991 Gulf War and the resistance to "exporting" democracy to the region during both administrations. Both administrations framed U.S. involvement in the region in multilateral terms. Indeed, Bush I and Clinton rejected the ideas expressed in a policy paper drafted by neoconservative Pentagon official Paul Wolfowitz in 1991. That paper stated that the United States should "remain the predominant outside power in the [Middle East] and preserve U.S. and Western access to the region's oil," and that the Americans should continue paying the costs of maintaining order in the Middle East and use its power to deter any nations, including the European allies, from disputing U.S. primacy in the region. Wolfowitz and the other authors of the Pentagon paper stressed that Washington should "discourage [the Europeans and other potential rivals] from challenging our leadership or seeking to overturn the established political and economic order."[4]

It was Wolfowitz and other neoconservative policymakers who persuaded President Bush II to adopt an ambitious Middle East and global agenda after 9/11, stating these ideas in the official U.S. preemption strategy and using it as a basis for the war against Iraq and the project to create a hegemonic pesence in the Middle East.[5] The promotion of these policies under Bush II in turn created a diplomatic environment in which it became even more difficult to maintain cooperation between the EU and the United States over Iraq. Instead, these policies strengthened the position of those in Paris, Berlin, and elsewhere in Europe, who wanted to exploit the growing opposition to Bush's policy in the region in order to advance an independent European diplomatic and military strategy on the Middle East.

DAYDREAMING ABOUT "SUEZ IN REVERSE"

The 2003 Iraq War could be described as "Suez 1956 in Reverse," that is, an attempt by the French and the Germans to follow Konrad Adenauer's advice and try to use their growing diplomatic, economic, and military power to challenge U.S. policy in the Middle East and re-establish their status there.[6] Indeed, there were many similarities between Iraq 2003 and Suez 1956, with the two sides reproducing a movie in which they were principal actors once upon a time in the Middle East. But this time the roles were reversed, with the Europeans joining the majority of the Arab governments (and UN members) in opposing a military action by the United States, an ally with Israel, against an Arab nationalist, Saddam Hussein.[7]

In February 2003, a respected French intelligence-connected newsletter, *Intelligence Online,* described the outlines of the more assertive European approach, in an analysis: "The Strategy behind Paris-Berlin Moscow Ties." It suggested that the Europeans were ready to create a counter-power to that of the United States so as to prevent the Americans from establishing dominance in the Euroasian region. "A new logic, and even dynamic seems to have emerged," the newsletter suggested. "An alliance between Paris, Moscow and Berlin running from the Atlantic to Asia could foreshadow a limit to U.S. power. For the first time since the beginning of the 20th Century, the notion of a world heartland—the nightmare of British strategists—has crept back into international relations."[8] But these emerging European powers failed to counter the United States and the French and its European allies were not yet able to exact their "revenge" for Suez in 2003. They were, however, certainly in a better position to achieve their goals.

AMERICAN MIDDLE EAST HEGEMONY:
U.S. MILITARY AND U.S. DOLLAR

There is no doubt that France and Germany, two economically powerful nations representing the rising economic strength of the EU, were in 2003 in a stronger position to do battle with the United States in the Middle East than France and Britain had been in 1956. As some analysts suggested, it was the euro, and not France's veto power in the UN Security Council, that enabled France to oppose U.S. policy on Iraq in such an aggressive way and for such a long time. That the euro was turning into a political tool that could change the international balance of power became evident if one considered how, before the euro, it would have been "relatively easy for the U.S. to quietly bring the French into line." A "stealth U.S. attack on the French franc, and on French financial markets—more likely the hint of it—would do the job," suggested economist Stephen Cohen.[9] Indeed, in 1956 the United States utilized its power in the financial markets to put pressure on the French and British currencies and forced the two nations to withdraw from Suez.[10]

In the long run, as the euro becomes an alternative, or coreserve currency alongside the U.S. dollar, Washington could be deprived of its "soft power" in the financial markets and its ability to dominate the international economy. Economists and foreign policy analysts agree that the current powerful role of the U.S. dollar allows Washington to run widening trade deficits and escape the balance of payments discipline. That in turn boosts America's ability to finance its military and political power beyond its means and makes it possible for the neoconservatives to promote their costly imperial agenda. But the EU's "soft power" in the form of its own currency could eventually be translated into "hard power."[11] As historian Niall Ferguson points out, "U.S. reliance on foreign money can matter, strategically" for the United States as it tries to fulfill its imperial ambitions. America depends on foreign investors to maintain its global economic position, and by extension its military supremacy, which allows it to use its power unilaterally in the Middle East. "What happens if [foreign investors] trade dollars for euros?" asks Ferguson.[12] If that happens, Europe's "soft power" might not feel so soft anymore.

Indeed, if, from a geo-political perspective, America's current hegemony rests on its dominant military position in the Middle East and its control of access to oil resources as a way of containing a potential challenger in Euroasia, from a geo-economic standpoint, the U.S. dollar and the preservation of its role as the world reserve currency stands at the heart of the arrangements that created the basis for an American-led global economy. The overwhelming U.S. military superiority provides it with the geo-political edge. The United States today spends on defense more than three times the total for the entire EU, some $396 billion versus $118 billion in 2002, and more than the next 15 largest nations combined. Washington plans to spend an added $2.1 trillion over the coming five years on defense; no nation or group of nations come close in defense spending. Even China is at least 30 years away from becoming a serious military threat.

The second pillar of American superiority in the world is the dominant role of the U.S. dollar as a reserve currency. Until the advent of the euro in late 1999, there was no potential challenger to U.S. dollar hegemony in world trade. And since American global predominance is based on dollar hegemony, this geo-economic power is perhaps even more important than America's military power. As German historian F. William Engdahl argues, focusing on the war against Iraq in 2003 through geo-political and geo-economic lenses would suggest that American policies were driven by the need to preserve these two pillars of U.S. hegemony—military domination of Middle East and the use of the U.S. dollar as the world's reserve currency. In many respects, these two issues are intertwined with each other, and more important, with the role of oil in the form of the so-called petrodollar.[13] By weakening the relative importance of petrodollars, the petro-euro may enable Europe to challenge the United States in the Middle East.

The interaction between the geo-political and geo-economic aspects of a U.S. drive for dominance and the role U.S. currency has played in it, have been evident since the end of World War II and the start of the Cold War, when the United States emerged as the most powerful military power, with a huge industrial base and the largest gold reserves. Until the early 1970s and the shockwaves that the oil crisis sent through the global economy, the United States preserved its role as the leading Western power through a combination of its leadership role in NATO and the power it exerted in Euroasia, and its dominant position in the global economic system in which the stability of the Bretton Woods currency structure—itself an Anglo-American-made project—was sustained by an arrangement that tied the U.S. dollar to gold. This powerful geo-strategic and geo-economic status gave a clear advantage to the United States. The Americans provided dollar credits and aid to finance the rebuilding of Europe (and Japan). American business, including the big oil companies, dominated trade and investment in Western Europe (and Northeast Asia). American military power and the U.S. dollar, backed by gold and mighty industry, played a central role in maintaining the U.S. leadership position.

The soaring American deficits that resulted from U.S. defense spending in Vietnam, and the rise of Western Europe as an economic powerhouse, weakened some of the leverage America exerted on its European allies in the 1960s, which in turn produced growing pressure on the U.S. dollar. French and other central banks increased their call for U.S. gold in exchange for their dollar reserves, calculating that "with the soaring war deficits from Vietnam, it was only a matter of months before the United States itself would be forced to devalue against gold, so better to get their gold out at a high price," according to Engdahl.[14] By the early 1970s, the Nixon administration decided that rather than risk a collapse of the gold reserves of the United States it would opt to abandon gold entirely, going to a system of floating currencies in August 1971, and creating the conditions for the birth of the petrodollar.

THANK THE MIGHTY PETRO DOLLAR

The free floating of the dollar, combined with the 1973 raising of oil prices by the Organization of Petroleum Exporting Countries (OPEC) by 400 percent after the Yom Kippur War, led to the oil shocks that damaged the welfare of American consumers. But the major rise in the price of oil also ended up advancing the U.S. geo-economic and geo-strategic position. Oil importing countries needed the U.S. dollar to pay for their energy needs, and the OPEC economies were flooded with those new petrodollars, most of which ended up in American and British banks. These mostly American and British financial institutions, in turn, used these petrodollars to provide loans to Third-World countries who needed these dollars to finance their growing oil imports. Such a situation created the conditions for the Third-World crisis in the 1980s. Hence the process of "recycling petrodollars" was being shaped, as hundreds of billions of dollars were recycled among OPEC, international banks, and back to the Third-World borrowers who, in the aftermath of the debt crisis, found themselves under the management of the International Monetary Fund (IMF) and other international lending institutions controlled by Washington.[15] All these developments helped the U.S. dollar maintain its dominant position. The central bankers from the major industrialized and oil importing countries in Western Europe and Japan took steps to keep their economies in the U.S. dollar system, with occasional compromises being made to accommodate currency and trade imbalances. Implicit in this "grand bargain" between the United States and its Cold War allies and economic partners was American willingness to use its military power to protect the oil resources in the Middle East. While Western Europe and Japan benefited from this system, it was the United States that enjoyed the upper hand.

Indeed, the United States has benefited from this "petrodollar system" in which oil is traded in U.S. dollars. The system demands the buildup of huge trade surpluses in order to accumulate dollar surpluses for every country except the United States, which controls the dollars. Central banks around the world have to prevent speculative attacks on their currencies by holding huge dollar reserves, creating a built-in support for a strong U.S. dollar that in turn forces world central banks to acquire and hold more dollar reserves, making the U.S.

dollar even stronger. The fact that the central banks of Japan, China, and South Korea buy U.S. Treasury securities with their dollars permits the United States to have a stable dollar, low interest rates, and run a huge balance of payments deficit of about $500 billion a year with the rest of the world. By serving as an "importer of last resort," the United States helps to facilitate this complex financial system.

At the same time, the recycling of petro-dollars is the price that America has exacted on oil-producing countries for U.S. tolerance of the oil-exporting cartel since 1973 and in exchange for the security protection it provides to the Saudis and other Arab oil-producing states. Moreover, Washington's alliances with the oil-producing states, the Arab Gulf states, and Iran (until the 1979 revolution there) helped to form common interests and gave birth to an American petro-military complex, beginning with what Daniel Yergin describes as the "blank check" policy that Nixon and Kissinger established with the late Shah of Iran, which allowed him to spend billions of dollars on arms for his country. The American diplomatic-military and business establishments regarded the accumulation of wealth by the Middle Eastern oil states as an opportunity to cement strategic and economic ties with those countries that purchased huge quantities of American military equipment.[16] These transactions in arms became a huge business in the Middle East, while increasing the profits of the major American-controlled arms and oil companies. Weapons sales, aggressively pursued, were a way to enhance the security of the Arab oil states and maintain and gain influence, while "the countries in the region were just as eager to buy."[17]

Hence, American policies helped to promote the rise of OPEC and the political and economic power that led to the Arab oil embargo of 1973 and the international oil shocks of the 1970s. American taxpayers helped to support the petro-military complex through which the Middle Eastern oil-producing states, the oil companies, and the American banks were able to advance their respective interests. At the end of the day, the American people paid dearly to sustain the partnership with Arab oil-producing states in several ways. They bailed out the debt-ridden banks of the Third-World states devastated by the liquidity crisis of the 1980s, to the benefit of Arab creditors. Americans risked their lives and spent billions of dollars on the military to defend access for all oil-consuming states to the resources in the Middle East. Beyond these direct expenditures, higher oil prices were, in a way, a form of indirect taxation through which Americans, as well as energy consumers in other countries, funded the authoritarian Arab regimes in the Persian Gulf. These corrupt governments used their dollars, recycled into American and British banks, to buy American products and military hardware, but also to strengthen their hold on power at home. The rising power of these Arab regimes was, therefore, the inadvertent by-product of the American decision, crafted as part of the Cold War policies, to secure its MEP. Indeed, the American people and their representatives in Washington were willing to pay the high costs to maintain the U.S. geo-strategic and geo-economic position during the Cold War.

EUROS VS. DOLLARS AND THE MIDDLE EAST

But the end of the Cold War, the emergence of a new Europe, and the European Monetary Union in the early 1990s presented a new challenge to the American geo-economic position, although it would take a few more years, in the beginning of the new century, for the new challenge to become more obvious among U.S. policymakers. "Rather than work out areas of agreement with European partners, Washington increasingly sees Euro-land as the major strategic threat to American hegemony," notes Engdahl. "Just as Britain in decline after 1870 resorted to increasingly desperate imperial wars in South Africa and elsewhere, so the United States is using its military might to try to advance what it no longer can by economic means," he argues. But under the new geo-economic condition the U.S. dollar could become an Achilles heel, since "the dollar hegemony is strategic to the future of American global pre-dominance, in many respects as important if not more so, than the overwhelming military power."[18]

Interestingly, the notion of a United States experiencing an "imperial over-stretch" as a result of the growing costs, in the forms of rising military budgets and trade deficits, and of maintaining its hegemonic position, was very popular in the late 1980s when it was promoted by such strategic thinkers as Paul Kennedy. It seems to have lost its appeal during the American high-tech boom and subsequent stock market euphoria, at a time of reduced budget deficits and a growing sense that Americans would be able to secure their military pre-dominance without engaging in major wars. But following the bursting of the high-tech bubble and the arrival of the bear on Wall Street—coupled with the neoconservative hegemonic drive in the aftermath of 9/11—things are looking quite different. Kennedy's thesis of the "Rise and Fall of Great Powers" seems to have reignited new interest as the U.S. account deficit seems to be exploding, reflecting the growing defense spending and trade deficits, which are over 5 percent of the GDP.[19] These rising trade deficits mean that the United States needs to attract around a billion dollars a day so as to prevent a dollar collapse and keep interest rates low. Were foreigners to decide to shift a portion of their dollars reserves into euros, the United States could face a major economic crisis, a deadly combination of a weakening U.S. dollar and rising interest rates that could devastate its global position.

Such a scenario could evolve if and when the Arab oil producing states decide for political and economic reasons to switch from U.S. dollars to euros. Foreign policy analyst Trifkovic notes the benefits of a possible change from dollars to euros for the Middle Eastern oil producers: "The Euro-zone does not run a huge trade deficit like the United States. It is not heavily indebted to the rest of the world, and it is not subjected to the political will of a single national decision-making structure. Europe is the Middle East's biggest trading partner, it imports more oil and petroleum derivatives than the United States, and it has a bigger share of global trade."[20] The political argument for such a switch is even more compelling. If the Arab oil producing states and Iran see themselves as threatened by Washington's hegemonic project in the Middle East and its pro-Israeli stand, they may conclude that the monetary weapon is the only one that they can effectively use. In fact, when the war in Iraq was launched, many voices in the Arab world demanded that OPEC countries start selling oil for euros, not U.S. dollars. While this threat is currently regarded as remote because any significant decline in the value of the dollar would hurt major oil producers in the short run, it should not be discounted as a long-term scenario, especially if the hegemonic project in the Middle East is expanded to include Syria, Iran, and other countries, or if radical Islamic forces take control of Saudi Arabia and other Arab countries, or the U.S. deficit increases as a result of rising defense spending and the U.S. dollar continues to slide. Hence, the emergence of a Euro-Arab political and economic zone could prove to be a self-fulfilling prophecy, and the United States would be compelled to use its military power to take control of the oil resources in the region and prevent a devastating blow to its global economic security.

Some economic and political analysts have speculated that part of the euro's growing strength after the war in Iraq can be explained by geo-politics, including the events of the Iraq war, noting that Saudi investors who had poured billions of petro-dollars into the American economy are now concerned that their funds may be frozen at some point if tensions between the United States and Saudi Arabia increase. These concerns could lead Saudi investors to buy up euros.[21] Such a Saudi move is troubling as far as long-term U.S. interests are concerned, especially since the idea that the Saudis and other Arab oil states consider setting the price of oil in euros instead of dollars is now being raised by some leading figures in Arab politics and business. These commentators are also calling on the Arab oil producers to increase their economic and political leverage on the Americans by changing their pattern of trade and buying more goods from Europe instead of the United States—by strengthening their ties with China and other Asian economies that are becoming more dependent on Middle Eastern oil.[22] From an American point of view, a process that would create a world awash with petro-euros instead of petrodollars could spell the end of U.S. hegemony.

EUROPE AS A MILITARY MIDGET?

But the fact that the scenario of "Suez in Reverse" was not realized in 2003 points to the economic limits that operate on France and other European powers as they try to challenge the United States in the Middle East.[23] Even more problematic from the European perspective is the EU's relative political-military weakness. Much has been written before and after the U.S. military victory in Iraq about the extent of American military superiority that has become almost impossible to overstate. Many analysts noted that such a huge military lead is partly a result of American military spending that last year exceeded that of all the other NATO states, Russia, China, Japan, Iraq, and North Korea combined.[24] The reality of U.S. military supremacy makes it difficult for the EU to try to catch up with the Americans, assuming that its members had the resources, and more important, the political will to compete with the Americans in defense spending. The war in Iraq and the earlier impressive American military performances in the Balkans and Afghanistan suggests that while the EU has emerged as an economic giant, it still remains a political-military lightweight. The fact that the United States spent 3 percent of its GDP on defense in 2001, while the defense spending by individual European states was smaller (2.6 percent for France, 2.4 percent for Britain, 1.5 percent for Germany, 1.3 percent for Belgium, and 0.8 percent for Luxembourg), demonstrates that the Europeans together and separately need to increase their defense expenditures if they want to compete with the United States in the global security arena. In order to challenge U.S. policy, the EU needs also to strengthen its own foreign policy and defense structure as part of a Common Foreign and Security Policy (CFSP), an approach, according to a recent Eurobarometer opinion poll, that is supported by close to 75 percent of EU citizens.[25]

But as one analyst points out, "Europe's problem lies in its inability to define collectively its long-term foreign policy interests" and to respond with a clear policy challenge to the Bush administration's new national security strategy, especially as it applies to a region, the Middle East, that has a profound impact on Europe's security and prosperity.[26] There are growing indications that the American war in Iraq and the neoconservative strategy based on U.S. global supremacy and hegemony in the Middle East has been forcing EU members to accelerate their efforts toward strengthening their independent foreign policy and national security posture. France and Germany are certainly feeling the pressure to take steps in that direction after officials in Washington suggested the plan to "punish" the "old" Europeans by relocating U.S. military troops from Germany to Central and Eastern Europe.

At this stage, the new post-Iraq global reality ignited a debate among EU members, about whether, for example, the more activist European defense policy, especially in dealing with outside areas like the Balkans or the Middle East, should be projected through a European rapid reaction force (ERRF) that would be part of the EU and permit the Europeans more independence to pursue their policies—or through a NATO reaction force (NRF), which would still be under U.S. control.[27] As part of an effort to speed-up the creation of an independent EU military policy, Belgium, with the support of France, Germany, and Luxembourg, has initiated the formation of a "core" of countries, or a "pioneer group," to push forward defense cooperation in the EU.[28] Leaders of the four countries met in Brussels on April 29, 2003, and announced that they would set up a multinational headquarters by the end of the year and that the new partnership could deploy forces abroad for joint military operations.[29] As the plan called for the creation of a full-fledged European military headquarters separate from NATO, it was perceived by the Bush administration as a clear challenge to a U.S. military presence in Europe and its leadership position in NATO.[30]

POST–COLD WAR "NEW ATLANTICISM"

These developments should be placed in a historical context. Since the end of the Cold War and against the backdrop of the wars against Iraq in 1991 and 2003, the United States and its allies across the Atlantic have been engaging in a complex debate about the future of NATO and its response to "out-of-area" threats, that is, threats that emanate from outside the arenas the military alliance was supposed to protect during the Cold War. Even during the Cold War, the Europeans and the Americans clashed often on how to define NATO's out-of-area role, especially in the Middle East. American refusal to back Britain and France during the Suez Crisis of 1956 should be seen in that context, as a disagreement over whether Egypt under Nasser posed a threat to Western interests. On the other end, during the 1973 Middle East War, the Bonn government strongly objected to the movement of U.S. tanks from bases in West Germany to Israel because this seemed to overstep NATO's geographical mandate. In

1987, when the United States provided an escort to protect Kuwaiti tankers from Iranian gunboats, the European allies that participated in the mission carefully refrained from identifying it as a NATO operation.

The Gulf War, notwithstanding the short-term consensus that developed between the Europeans and the Americans, accentuated the tensions between them over the out-of-area entanglements and, in particular, the question of if and how the Middle East and the Persian Gulf should be integrated into the strategic structure of the Western alliance. For example, a controversy arose when the NATO Air Mobile Force, including 18 German aircraft, was sent to Turkey. Bonn insisted that these forces were to be used only in the defense of Turkish territory and not for attacks on Iraqi soil, rejecting Ankara's goal of expanding NATO's responsibility to the Gulf.

U.S. military planners downplayed the significance of such differences. The Gulf War, they argued, demonstrated that no individual European state or combination of states was able to raise the military forces required to contain the large armies, modern air forces, and WMD controlled by Saddam-like regimes in the Middle East. France and Britain might be able to tame a Middle Eastern military power for a short period by either bombing raids or gunboat diplomacy. However, only massive land power and large naval forces on the scale commanded by the United States were capable of containing threats to European security from its southern flank. It was essential, therefore, that as part of a new model of the transatlantic relationship dubbed the New Atlanticism, that the United States and Europe would coordinate their military policies in the Middle East. The sine qua non of Europe's security policy in the Persian Gulf would continue to be the large U.S. Navy, Marine Corps, and airborne divisions, which the New Atlanticism would provide.

The New Atlanticism envisioned a renewed U.S.-European partnership through an expanded NATO to contain security threats to the Western alliance, including out-of-area challenges emanating from the Middle East. U.S. military forces would remain in reduced numbers in Europe and would continue to provide the continent with a nuclear umbrella, while NATO could redefine its role to include out-of-area threats in regions such as the Middle East. Under this new security structure, whose outlines were drawn during the administrations of Presidents Bush I and Clinton, NATO was expected to have a stronger "European pillar." Europe could develop an independent military unit, but it would serve as a bridge between the EU and the United States, and the NATO commandership would alternate between the United States and Europe. Europe would enjoy a greater say in decision making while bearing a greater share of the defense burden, but would continue to rely on U.S. security leadership, especially outside Europe. Since the 1991 Gulf War, Washington promoted this vision of a New Atlanticism in several versions, stressing the need to create a large multinational rapid-deployment force under NATO auspices that could respond immediately to crises outside Europe. Hence, NATO commanders agreed in April 1992 to expand the alliance's European-staffed rapid-defense force to as many as 100,000 troops to deal with such eventualities.[31]

But as much as the Americans were trying to promote the New Atlanticism as a U.S.-Europe partnership, in reality it was based on the assumption that U.S. military power would continue to function as the ultimate arbiter of international conflicts, as the off-shore balancer in the Middle East and Persian Gulf, containing radical anti-status quo states there, while the Europeans would continue to play to role of Robin to the American Batman.

U.S. MILITARY POWER: PROTECTING EUROPE OR AMERICAN HEGEMONY?

While American rhetoric focused for much of the post–Gulf War period as well as during the eve of the 2003 war against Iraq on the nuclear threat posed by Saddam's Iraq, very few Americans posed the obvious questions: Even if Saddam Hussein had access to nuclear weapons, it was clear that Iraq did not have the capability to launch a nuclear attack on the United States the way the Soviet Union had such a potential. So in what way did Iraq's nuclear military build-up, assuming that one was taking place, threaten core U.S. national interests that required Americans to invest so much in protecting themselves from it? The response from policymakers in Washington was that the U.S. decision to challenge Iraq's (and Iran's) alleged access to nuclear weapons was meant to protect "our allies" in Europe and the Middle East to which Saddam Hussein's (and Iran's) nuclear military power did pose a direct threat. Even if Iraq (or Iran) posed a threat to European and Middle Eastern countries why couldn't the Europeans or the Middle Eastern powers threatened by Iraq (and Iran) protect their own interests without U.S. intervention? Europe certainly has the financial and military resources to deal with an Iraq (and Iran) armed with nuclear weapons as does Israel, itself a nuclear military power.

But the American concerns have less to do with the nuclear threat that Iraq or Iran is posing to the United States. What U.S. policymakers are worried about is that the rise of a nuclear Iraq or Iran would induce Middle Eastern powers and Europe to develop their own independent nuclear military strategy to deal with such threats. That, in turn, would make it unnecessary for them to rely on the United States for their protection. Indeed, the same kind of thinking explains American concerns over North Korea's nuclear military capability that could force Japan to develop nuclear military capability and loosen its reliance on American military protection. The New Atlanticism, like the policy of extending the Cold War–era military alliance with Japan (and South Korea) was intended to ensure that no independent security structure would emerge to compete with those controlled by the United States.

EUROPEAN SECURITY DILEMMAS

Hence the New Atlanticism promoted by Washington after the 1991 Gulf War was seen by the Europeans for what it was: a disguise for continuing U.S. hegemony. In fact, for the Europeans, the Gulf War was a wake-up call. It gradually became clear to many European officials that one of the major reasons for their inability to meet the U.S. challenge during the war was the lack of European institutions for developing independent political and security policies. The 1991 war was seen, therefore, as a reason to redouble efforts to more closely integrate the political and security policies of the European nations, reflecting a changed European perception of American military power. "From patronizing the United States as the country that can't-shoot-straight bumbledom, European elites have once more turned into envying and admiring it as the competent organizer of a dazzlingly smooth high-tech victory," commented one observer.[32] Although a lot of the media attention has been focused on the lack of a coordinated European approach toward Yugoslavia's wars of succession, the Europeans, under German-French leadership, since 1992 have been advancing plans for the creation of a "Euro-corps" that could become the nucleus of a future European army and that would handle defense responsibilities outside Europe and NATO's sphere of operation. These efforts led to the creation by the EU in 2000 of a rapid reaction force. The Europeans also took steps to expand a European defense pillar inside NATO that would be subservient to NATO in European military matters but free to act outside the NATO area.[33]

As noted earlier, many of the efforts that followed the 1991 Gulf War and that were later supported by British Prime Minister Tony Blair and resisted by the United States have been accelerated in the aftermath of the 2003 war against Iraq. The EU, with Britain playing an active role in the process, has drawn the outlines of an independent European security doctrine that challenges the Bush administration's National Security Strategy (NSS) document. Instead of Bush's emphasis on the need for preemptive military action to deal with emerging security threats, the EU promotes the idea of "preventive engagement," which emphasizes the need for multilateral action that combines diplomacy and the threat of the use of military force, through the EU, NATO, the UN, and other institutions to contain threats such as international terrorism, "rogue" states, and the proliferation of WMD. The EU security doctrine also referred to as the "Solana Doctrine," after Javier Solana, the EU Representative for Common Foreign and Security Policy, does not clarify when the EU would be ready and in what particular ways it would use military power to contain threats. Instead, the EU document calls for the use of "effective multilateralism," noting that "political, economic and other pressures" could be applied to contain WMD proliferation.

Even more critical, from the EU's perspective, is the need to provide the economic resources and institutional structure to permit the creation of a unified and effective military force. One institutional weakness is the current system in which the EU presidency is rotated every six months. A second institutional weakness is the lack of a foreign minister with real power to speak on the behalf of the entire EU. Additionally, the EU has yet to develop a coherent strategy that would lead to the creation of a military planning capability independent of NATO.[34] To put it differently, if the Europeans want to oppose U.S. policies in the Middle East, they need a security strategy that has coherence and "teeth," sustained by a unified diplomatic voice and a muscular military posture. It is important to remember that even the most impressive independent EU military unit, the Rapid Action Force, has no more than 60,000 troops.[35]

The evolving consensus on defense policy among France, Germany, and Britain has been evident since the war on Iraq despite American efforts to get the British to counter the Franco-German attempts to reassert European independence from Washington. At the end of 2003, the three European governments were able to strike a deal to set up an EU military planning cell. That move, and a decision by Paris and Berlin to dilute the earlier plan for a military headquarters for "core Europe" that excluded Britain, was also a sign that the French and the Germans have concluded that European foreign and defense policies cannot be built with the British. Defense analyst Charles Grant argues that there the Europeans had an opportunity to enhance their military capabilities and project it in out-of-area operations. France, Italy, and Spain have either switched or are switching to an all-professional force that can be more easily deployed overseas, and the EU has agreed to a British-French plan for an armaments agency that would monitor members' efforts to expand their military capabilities.[36] At the same time, Germany joined forces with Britain and France in early 2004 to create highly trained rapid deployment units, or "battle groups," for combat in jungle, desert, and mountain operations, in areas such as Afghanistan and Iraq.[37]

Indeed, the Europeans seem to have been taking baby steps in the direction of a more visible military involvement in the Middle East and its peripheries—but in coordination with NATO and the United States. In March 2003, as the debate among the EU members and between the Europeans and the Americans was continuing, EU peacekeeping troops, led by a French general, took over from NATO the responsibility for keeping peace in the protectorate of Macedonia, with American blessing. "The U.S., at the height of its bitter and continuing dispute over Iraq, approved the experiment and made it possible by agreeing to let the EU rely on NATO for support," suggested one report.[38] That Washington approved of the EU move in the Balkans was not very surprising, since such a limited EU military presence in tiny Macedonia fits very much with the minimal subservient role the Bush administration favors. Other U.S. plans, such as encouraging NATO to take over military operations in Afghanistan and assuming responsibility for a division of international troops in Iraq and Afghanistan, which were discussed during a meeting of NATO defense ministers in December 2003, assumed a leading American role. The Americans continued to resist, however, the plans to give the EU its own military planning cell and insert a provision of mutual defense into the EU's first constitution. Neoconservative critics have portrayed the initiatives as "a French-inspired drive to subvert NATO and curb U.S. influence."[39]

EUROPEANS REJECT "SECOND-CLASS" STATUS

Two years after the Americans and the Europeans split acrimoniously over whether to go to war in Iraq, there were only a few signs that the two sides have been able to put the rift behind them.[40] On the eve of three major international summits in June 2004—the meeting of the Group of Eight in Sea Island, Georgia; A European Union–United States summit in Ireland; and a NATO summit in Istanbul, Turkey—President Bush and his advisors were courting the Europeans and tried to create the impression that the transatlantic rancor on Iraq was "over"[41] and that the EU and NATO would join the United States in promoting its goals of stability and democracy in Iraq and the entire Middle East.[42]

As Dutchman Jaap de Hoop Scheffer took over as the new Secretary General of NATO in early 2004, President Bush and his aides were pressing the military group to deliver on an ambitious plan to extend its peacekeeping operations beyond Kabul and create links with the American-led offensive military operation in the south that was battling remnants of the Taliban. The Americans also wanted NATO to take command of the 9,000-member multinational brigade in central Iraq that has been run by Poland, and possibly the larger British-led operation in the south.[43]

At the same time, the Bush Administration was trying to enlist European support for a grand plan—the so-called Greater Middle East (GME) initiative—to reform the Arab and Islamic world and integrate it within a Western security umbrella.[44] Elements of the new initiative were introduced by Vice President Dick Cheney at the annual World Economic Conference in Davos, Switzerland, where he called on the Europeans to join the Americans in a "forward strategy for freedom" that "commits us to support those who work and sacrifice for reform across the greater Middle East."[45]

EU and NATO members, led by France and Germany, made it clear that they would be willing to expand their military presence in Afghanistan and play a substantive role in Iraq only if the Americans would permit them more say in policy regarding the Middle East. Otherwise, a European contribution to the American effort would have been seen as nothing more than helping the Bush administration, which had denied the Europeans a role in making policies but which wanted them to help it implement those policies when it was desperate to reduce its military presence in Afghanistan and Iraq. To put it differently, the Europeans did not have any incentive to increase their contribution to a NATO that was perceived as a political military club charged with promoting the American geo-strategic vision and through which wars were conducted by remote control from Washington. That could change if NATO, as its new secretary general suggested, could be transformed from "an instrument to serve our American friends" to an alliance whose job it is "to export security and stability, wholesale" under common Euro-American leadership.[46]

While the United States was trying to sell its grand Middle Eastern schemes to the Europeans, it seemed quite obvious that the Bush administration was unapologetic about its decision to go to war in Iraq. Additionally, the Europeans were unimpressed by what the war had produced in the Middle East. The Bush administration was floating through their GME initiative the idea of democratizing North Africa, the Near East, and South and Central Asia, bringing economic prosperity and establishing security in these areas that encompass close to a billion people—if one included Pakistan and the Moslems of India and Central Asia in the GME—and a mosaic of national, ethnic, and religious groups. But U.S. policy, driven by Washington's neoconservative policymakers, had yet to make even modest progress in democratizing Iraq and bringing an end to the conflict between Israelis and Palestinians.

Against this messy political backdrop in Iraq and Israel/Palestine, Washington continued to insist that it was not willing to give up its monopoly on

decision making not only in Iraq and Israel/Palestine but in the GME. That
Greater Middle East—renamed the Broader Middle East by U.S. policymakers
in 2004—as defined by President Bush and his aides, would not only include
the Eastern Mediterranean and the Gulf states, but would also encompass all
of Southwestern Asia, North Africa, and the Horn of Africa, extending from
the Balkans and Turkey, the old "Near East," to Afghanistan, and perhaps
even beyond the borders of the "Far East."[47] Members of the EU and NATO
were expected to follow American diplomatic and military leadership in this
part of the world, once controlled by the British and French empires, by taking up some "nation building" and security tasks in Iraq and Afghanistan—
and perhaps might even be permitted to bid on prime contracts for Iraq
reconstruction.[48]

Even among those Europeans who were sympathetic to the Bush administration, there was recognition that Washington did not really believe that it had
the will and the power to democratize the "stans" of Central Asia and plant the
seeds of political and economic freedom in the Arab Gulf states. The scheme
was seen in Europe as part of a U.S. attempt to create the perception that it was
involved in the process of mending the split with the Europeans, in particular
with the French and the Germans, and of inducing them to share in the costs
of the occupation of Iraq. British columnist Quentin Peel described the European sentiments regarding the American scheme there as "a suspicion that
Washington's Greater Middle East Initiative is more about public relations and
U.S. elections than it is about practical progress."[49] But it was not clear why the
Germans, French, and other Europeans who refused to give the Americans a
diplomatic green light to invade Iraq would be tempted to support with financial and military resources a plan aimed at providing Western legitimacy to the
U.S. strategy in Iraq and the entire Middle East. The Europeans were aware that
the Bush administration was not offering them a place in the Middle Eastern
driver's seat, in the sense of sharing as equals in the decision drawing the outlines for the policies on Iraq, Israel/Palestine, or Iran.

One interpretation of a proposed "division of labor" between the Europeans and the Americans in the Middle East suggested that the "real work" in
the region would be done by the "tough cop," that is by the United States, using
its military power to force governments to comply to Western demands. At the
same time, Europe, as the "soft cop," would be supplementing American military power with diplomatic action.[50] Based on this interpretation, American
military force in Iraq persuaded Teheran to halt a covert nuclear weapons work
and defused a potential confrontation with the United States. The British,

French, and German foreign ministers were able to point to that American military "stick" and put forth their own diplomatic "carrots" by offering Iran a trade-off in October 2003: agreeing to inspections and to suspending uranium enrichment in return for future access to civilian nuclear technology.[51] Indeed, some could argue that the effectiveness of such a new Euro-American strategy dependent on a muscular U.S. military looming offstage, combined with complementary European diplomatic efforts, was demonstrated by the decision by Col. Muhammad Qaddafi to rid Libya of its WMD and the European efforts to persuade Syria to take similar steps in return for a trade deal.[52]

The Europeans, however, could have made the argument that those examples—Iran, Libya, and Syria—demonstrated the kind of alliance-driven diplomacy they wanted to implement in Iraq after 9/11. A combined Euro-American military power (which included that of the United States, Britain, and the rest of NATO) could have been applied as part of a Euro-American diplomatic strategy in Mesopotamia and elsewhere in the Middle East, including as part of a continuing pressure on Saddam Hussein. This kind of alliance-driven diplomacy is what the EU described as "preventive engagement" in its new strategic doctrine which encompasses "political, diplomatic and military and civilian, trade and development activities" aimed at dealing with the threat of terrorism and proliferation of unconventional weapons. This European strategy was contrasted with the preemptive military approach favored by the Bush administration.[53] From the European perspective, a partnership meant the fashioning of a shared Western strategy for the region, which included the internationalization of the control of Iraq, a resolution to the Israel/Palestine conflict, and diplomatic engagement with Iran. Most important from the European perspective was the notion that change in the Middle East would not come through preemptive action and unilateral military action by the United States aimed at forced "regime change."[54] The European approach, however, was rejected by Washington in favor of a military attack on Iraq.

The Europeans were also advocating a greater sense of realism when it came to the U.S. neoconservative democratization schemes and they warned about the unintended consequences of hasty change in the region. Many Europeans officials regarded the American scheme for the broader Middle East as nothing more than a fantasy. "To think that from Morocco to Afghanistan we're going to have something which is structured is a bit of a chimera," cautioned EU foreign policy chief, Javier Solana.[55] The German government proposed that the United States and the EU form a new transatlantic initiative for the Middle East, while the French stressed that any effort to advance reforms should be confined to the Levant and North Africa and should focus on economic and social issues, as opposed to political change.[56] Still, a more cynical European interpretation of the GME initiative and the American call for exporting democracy to the Middle East saw these projects as deceptive devices to justify postponement of the Israeli-Palestinian peace process and as a means to divert attention from the messy problems the Americans were facing in Iraq.[57]

It was not surprising therefore that President Bush failed to win European backing for his Middle Eastern plans. The G–8 summit ended up endorsing a watered-down version of the ambitious GME initiative that would target the "broader Middle East and North Africa" and included, among other things, lending money to small businesses and establishing a task force to change the investment climate in the region. Most observers agreed that the initiative would probably produce nothing more than "high-profile 'talkathons' that shift away from substance towards process."[58] Bush and his Middle Eastern ideas also received a chilly reception from the Europeans at meetings in Ireland and Turkey. The allies agreed only to support a modest NATO program to train Iraqi police officers, and even that would have to take place outside of Iraq.[59]

While France agreed to support a UN Security Council resolution providing the framework for the hand-over of power to the new Iraqi interim government at the end of June 2004, French President Jacques Chirac stressed that neither the EU nor NATO would be willing to deploy troops in Iraq as long as U.S. military and diplomatic power continued to determine the future of that country.[60] He also opposed the American plan to use NATO's rapid-response force to help secure elections in Afghanistan. France, a major contributor to Western peacekeeping operations in the Balkans and Afghanistan, was reluctant to see NATO turn into a global cop, reflecting "suspicion in France that NATO is becoming an instrument of U.S. dominance."[61]

This opposition to Washington's policies is shared by most Europeans who are concerned that under President Bush the U.S. approach to managing the Euro-American relationship in the Middle East continues to be based on the principle that America leads diplomatically and militarily in the region and its peripheries and that the Europeans should follow and provide economic and military assistance. Even Jose Manuel Barroso, the former prime minister of Portugal who had backed the American invasion of Iraq and was considered one of Europe's leading Atlanticists, has played down his support for the United States after being nominated as president of the European Commission. He attacked Washington for its "arrogance" and "militarism" and insisted that he would ensure that the EU would not be treated as "second class" by the United States.[62]

THE "EUROPEAN CANDIDATE" LOSES
THE U.S. PRESIDENTIAL ELECTIONS

Many European officials and commentators, reflecting the views of the general public, were hoping that Democratic presidential candidate, Senator John Kerry of Massachusetts, would win the race to the White House in 2004. The assumption among Europeans was that, unlike Bush, Kerry would be willing to take steps to bridge the Euro-Americans rift over Iraq and Israel/Palestine and create the conditions for the revival of the transatlantic alliance. Mirror imaging these European view, American neoconservative analysts portrayed Kerry as the "European candidate" and warned that the Democrat would permit the French a greater role in influencing American policy in the Middle East.[63]

It was not surprising that the re-election of George W. Bush as president and the resignation of Secretary of State Colin Powell were greeted with anxiety among European observers. The death of Yasser Arafat and the agreement reached between the European triumvirate of Britain, France, and Germany, and Iranian officials to suspend Iran's uranium enrichment activities, two developments that took place a few days after the presidential elections, injected a sense of optimism on both sides of the Atlantic that the Americans and the Europeans would take steps to coordinate their policies in the Middle East. But the indications that Bush and his advisors are not willing to press Israel to make concessions to the Palestinians, and that they intend to adopt a tough approach toward Iran over its alleged nuclear military programs suggest that the transatlantic tensions over the Middle East will probably not be resolved during the second Bush term.

In fact, the selection of Condoleezza Rice, a staunch proponent of the scheme to democratize the Middle East, and the continuing influence of Vice President Dick Cheney and Donald Rumsfeld and their neoconservative advisors who seem determined to confront Iran as the new target for U.S. hegemonic strategy, is bound to widen the Euro-American split.[64] Interestingly enough, some Europeans seem to welcome the widening Euro-American rift in the expectation that it would help Europe assert its position vis à vis the United States and create the conditions for a multipolar international system.[65]

REPLACING THE MIDDLE EAST PARADIGM

A PAX AMERICANA— OR A NORTHERN ALLIANCE?

The time has come for Washington to reassess its commitment to its Cold War–era Middle East Paradigm (MEP) and the huge diplomatic, military, and economic engagement in the region that the MEP entails. During the superpower confrontation between the United States and the Soviet Union, America's intervention in the Middle East as a leader of the Western alliance involved costs that were offset by the benefits of containing a global threat. In addition, any temptation the United States might have had to establish hegemony in the Middle East was in many ways constrained by the challenge posed by the Soviet Union and its allies. To be sure, during the Cold War, the potential costs of conflict were very high and tangible—a nuclear confrontation between the two superpowers. But the real costs were more modest and derived from the nature of the kaleidoscope-like system of the Middle East, in which Washington found itself entangled in various intertwined commitments to local and regional players, led by the rival twins, Saudi Arabia and Israel. The mostly moral commitment to the Jewish state was integrated into the Cold War MEP, in which the geo-strategic and geo-economic interests of the United States were based on the following: preventing a global aggressor and its allies from taking control of a strategic region of the world and its energy resources on which the United States' European allies and Japan were dependent.

SAYING GOODBYE TO THE OLD MEP?

Instead of taking advantage of the end of the Cold War to reexamine U.S. policy in the Middle East and to set aside its obsolete MEP, the administrations of Bush I and then Clinton pursued a policy of winning and maintaining hegemony in the region, taking advantage of what seemed to be the post–Cold War unipolar international system in which other states had neither the power nor the will to challenge U.S. primacy in the Middle East. That quest for hegemony proved to be relatively cost-free during the administrations of Bush I and Clinton, but the 9/11 terrorist attacks on the American homeland demonstrated that the very real and long-term costs of maintaining the MEP would be actually higher than they were during the Cold War. And that it was a nonstate group that brought the costs home, literally and figuratively, starkly demonstrated a failure of imagination among the policy elites. These same elites would then unimaginatively pull from the script of traditional hegemonic behavior the invasion of first Afghanistan and then Iraq. Stuck in the MEP, policymakers could not see any alternative. The rising military and diplomatic commitments ended up igniting the kind of anti-Americanism that was displayed in 9/11. At the same time, the rising American commitments to Saudi Arabia and Israel not only increased each nation's dependency on Washington but also raised long-term threats to their survival.

The two central components of the MEP that became conventional wisdom among members of the foreign policy establishment and the American public are that the American economy is "dependent" on the energy resources in the Middle East and that Washington needs to "do something" to resolve the Israel-Palestine conflict. These two assumptions lead Americans to conclude that protecting access to Persian Gulf oil and engaging in the never ending Arab-Israel "peace processing" helps to advance core U.S. geo-economic and geo-strategic interests.

But the American economy is not dependent on Middle Eastern oil—70 percent of American energy supplies do not originate in the Middle East. The United States is actually more dependent on Latin American oil than it is on Saudi and other Persian Gulf oil. And the notion that American policy in the Middle East helps to provide Americans access to "cheap and affordable oil" makes little sense if one takes into consideration the military and other costs—including two Gulf Wars and the current Pax Americana in the Middle East—that are added to the price that the American consumer pays for driving his or her car. In fact, it is the economies of Europe and East Asia that are dependent on access to oil from the Middle East. The American military presence in the region encourages them to free-ride on U.S. protection which made sense during the Cold War but not in its aftermath. Control of the oil resources in the region provides Washington with geo-strategic and geo-economic leverage over the European and Asian governments, which they naturally resent and seek to counter.

Similarly, there is no reason why Washington should continue paying the huge costs involved in trying to resolve the Palestinian-Israeli conflict. During the Cold War, such a policy made sense because the Arab-Israeli conflict affected core U.S. interests in terms of American relations with the Arab states as the Soviet Union exploited anti-American sentiments in the region. Since the end of the Cold War, the Arab-Israeli conflict has been "de-internationalized" and "de-regionalized"; it is now a local conflict that should be resolved by those directly affected by it—the Israelis and the Palestinians, the regional players, and the Europeans. If anything, American diplomatic hyperactivity on the Israel-Palestine issue not only raises expectations that cannot be fulfilled, and as a result, ignites more anti-Americanism in the Arab world, but it also antagonizes the domestic political allies of the rival twins. This American approach also produces disincentives for the players involved to do what they need to do in order to advance their own self-interests. The Israelis and the Palestinians assume that they should be rewarded by Washington for making concessions that are perceived as "favors" for the Americans. At the same time, the Arab and European governments refrain from assuming responsibility for trying to help resolve the conflict.

THE OLD MEP ON LIFE SUPPORT: AMERICAN AND EUROPEAN DILEMMAS

Almost all members of the U.S. foreign policy establishment—liberal internationalists, conservative realists, and neoconservatives—want to make sure that the old MEP is alive and well. Maintaining access to Persian Gulf oil resources, engagement in the Israel-Palestine peace process, and containment of regional and local challenges, is seen by many American foreign policymakers and analysts as a way of securing U.S. hegemony in the Middle East and its peripheries. These Middle Eastern policies are regarded as crucial from a geo-strategic and geo-economic perspective if Washington wants to maintain its dominant position in the Euroasian World-Island and, by extension, over the entire international system. The control of the Middle East and its oil resources is seen not really about having access to "affordable and cheap oil" for Americans; that may be the formula Washington used in order to market its costly policies to the

American people. The policy is actually driven by the belief among adherents to the MEP that the control of the region and its energy resources provides Washington with geo-strategic and geo-economic leverage over the Europeans, Japan, South Korea, and eventually, China.

Liberal internationalists and conservative realists argue that the MEP can be kept alive by continuing a relatively low-cost strategy. They argue that the United States is able to secure its position through support from its European allies and regional partners. The American military presence in the Middle East and U.S. efforts to resolve the Israel-Palestine conflict are the international "public goods" that Washington provides to the Europeans and the Middle Eastern ruling elites. Neoconservatives reject these policy methods and concluded, in the aftermath of 9/11, that only direct U.S. military control over the Middle East, as part of an imperial strategy, would help the old MEP survive. They assume that American military power would be able to force the Europeans and the Arabs to accept U.S. dominance in the region and that there is no need to try to co-opt them by promises to "deliver" Israel as part of the Arab-Israeli peace process. In fact, the neoconservatives contend axiomatically that the Europeans will never have the power or the will to seriously challenge American power in the Middle East and that the United States and Europe will never be able to establish a collaborative approach toward the region because of structural political-cultural differences. The neoconservative strategy also helps Washington to market its MEP to the American public by depicting it as part of a new global confrontation between an American-Israeli bloc and a Euro-Arab axis.

The neoconservative strategy reflects a major dilemma facing American policy in the Middle East in what I believe to be a brief and passing unipolar "moment." On one hand, the United States needs to mobilize military and financial support from the Europeans in order to sustain and legitimize its hegemony in the Middle East. If the United States fails to so, it will find itself not only drawn into a long and costly quagmire in the Middle East but also into the position of "imperial overstretch." Its increasing military spending, coupled with growing budget and trade deficits, will make it more and more difficult to sustain its geo-strategic power (based on military strength and geo-economic position, sustained by its petro-dollar nexus) and will encourage the Europeans to challenge U.S. primacy in the Middle East by allying with local and regional challengers. But if the Americans respond to these pressures by permitting the Europeans an increasing role in decision making in the Middle East, they are at risk of losing their dominant position and the replacement of their hegemony with a Euro-American condominium. Either way, it would be impossible for the United States to maintain its old MEP based on a notion of an American monopoly in the Middle East.

The European dilemmas in the Middle East are mirror images of those of the Americans: they can continue to free-ride on the American military presence and assume a supporting role in the Middle East under policies advanced by liberal internationalists and conservative realists or they can submit to imperial American dictates under the neoconservative scenario. In either case, the Europeans do not need to direct more resources toward increasing their military power to allow them to challenge the United States in the Middle East as long as they accept the American hegemonic position there.

The problem is that out of their own self-interest, the Europeans cannot allow themselves to adopt such a secondary role because of their geo-strategic and geo-economic position. Unlike the Americans, their economy is dependent on access to the oil resources in the Middle East. The region is their strategic backyard and they have a growing population of immigrants from the Middle East. If they conclude that U.S. hegemonic policies in the region are harming their core interests in the Middle East, they will have no choice but to challenge them. Even if they reject the more assertive Gaullist position that Europe needs to counterbalance American hegemony in the Middle East and elsewhere, political, economic, and demographic interests would eventually force the Europeans to adopt such a role. Liberal internationalist and conservative realists in Washington and Atlanticists in Brussels hope to ensure that American and European interests in the Middle East become compatible and that there will be no need to adopt the neoconservative and Gaullist strategies, respectively.[1]

HELLO TO THE NEW MEP?

I am not very optimistic that Washington and Brussels will be able to agree on a process of managing the Euro-American relationship that would permit burden sharing under mutual agreement. From the American perspective under the current MEP, such a Euro-American agreement would have to be based on the European willingness to accept U.S. hegemony in the region. But from the European perspective, such a dominant American role is bound to run contrary to their interests, as the inability of the United States to resolve the Israel-Palestine conflict and its continuing links to Saudi Arabia and other autocratic Arab regimes ignite anti-American and anti-Western sentiments that spill over into Europe. I propose to bid farewell to the old MEP and try to draw the outlines of a new American policy in the Middle East. There is a need for a long-term policy of American "constructive disengagement" from the Middle East that will

encourage the Europeans to take upon themselves the responsibility of securing their interests in the region and while the regional actors solve the problems they have created.

What are the outlines of new American policy in the Middle East that will
bring an end to the American occupation of Iraq and the building of new foundations of a relationship with Israel? What is the essence of a new MEP that
would bring about a reduction of American military commitments and economic assistance to governments in the Middle East, help create new balance-
of-power systems in the Middle East, and force the Europeans to pay the costs
of containing threats to security and stability in the region, that is, to replace
the United States as the off-shore balancer or "balancer of last resort" in the
Middle East? What should be done?

Recall that in the first chapter I delineated the main tenets of the traditional MEP, derived from the Cold War environment. Corresponding to the
new environment, American policy should be based on the following tenets:

- *Geo-strategy:* The demise of Soviet threats to Western interests in the region
  means that the basic premise of the Cold War MEP has vanished. Continuing
  U.S. intervention helps ignite anti-Americanism in the region that takes the
  form of anti-American terrorism. The absence of an extra-regional threat
  (other than the United States) means that there is no reason why the balance
  of power in the Middle East could not be maintained through regional security arrangements and the assistance of the Europeans, the main outside
  players with direct interests in the region who have the capability to serve in
  the role of an off-shore balancer there. The EU should use its diplomatic and
  military power to deal with threats to stability and security in the Middle East
  that could affect it directly, including the dangers of rogue states, terrorism,
  and weapons of mass destruction (WMD) as well as the challenge that the
  Europeans face now in the form of the rising number of Arab immigrants
  from the Middle East and North Africa who are altering the demographic
  makeup of the continent.

- *Geo-economics:* Since the economies of the members of the EU and Japan, and
  not that of the United States, are dependent on access to oil resources from
  the Middle East, they—and not the Americans—should start paying most of
  the costs of protecting their economic interests in the region. Since the EU
  is becoming a major geo-economic competitor of the United States, there is
  no reason why America should continue to subsidize the Europeans by providing them with free security protection of these energy resources in the
  Persian Gulf through a costly partnership with the oil-producing states in the
  region. The time has come to reassess the U.S. commitment to these states,
  including Saudi Arabia, and bring an end to the European free-riding. This

new direction in American policy will create incentives for the Europeans to spend less money on wasteful welfare programs and more euros on their defense and to channel more diplomatic, military, and economic resources to dealing with threats to their interests in the Middle East.

- *Idealism:* American policy during the Cold War helped Israel maintain its margin of security in the context of the Arab-Israeli conflict and created the conditions for ending that conflict, starting with the Egyptian-Israeli disengagement and the peace agreements with Egypt in the 1970s and later with Jordan and other Arab governments. Israel is today a very strong regional military and economic power, with a nuclear military capability to protect itself against potential threats from states like Egypt and Iraq. The main threat to its survival as a democratic Jewish state is not the lack of U.S. assistance, but Israel's control over the West Bank and Gaza and the continuing conflict with the Palestinians. Hence, unconditional American support for Jerusalem is creating disincentives for changes in Israeli policies. Now that the Israeli-Palestinian dispute has been transformed into a local war between Jews and Arabs in the Holy Land, there should be less pressure on Washington to be drawn into a hyper-diplomatic engagement to resolve it. In fact, the prospects for American disengagement from the Middle East and for a lower diplomatic profile in the Palestinian-Israeli dispute should produce incentives for both sides, as well as for the Arab states and the EU, to deal with it.

This revision of American policy toward the Middle East flies full in the face of the conventional wisdom I have called the MEP. This is not a call for a revival of European imperialism in the region; rather it is a recognition that Europe has an interest in a stable and peaceful Middle East—not unlike America's approach toward Latin America. Neoconservative analysts such as Robert Kagan supported the deployment of EU troops to Macedonia and Kosovo, but they have opposed such a plan in Iraq or in Israel and the Palestinian territories. This inconsistency is explained away because, in the neoconservative view, only Israel or a large American military presence can contain threats in the Middle East.[2] The evidence does not support such a contention.

From the perspective of policymakers in the Bush administration, the long-term U.S. objective was to "make the Middle East a different place, and one safer for American interests" starting with Iraq, and to bring about an agreement between Israel and the Palestinians "that will come more on the terms of America's staunch ally in Israel."[3] But with over 100,000 American troops in the region, the Middle East is the same old same old, divided by factions of religious, tribal, and national character that use the United States for their own purposes. Meanwhile, peace between Israel and the Palestinians is no closer.

It's bad enough that American policies in the Middle East have failed on the very sands meant to bear the harvest of increased security. Even worse, America's hegemonic policy has set the stage for the current Euro-American rift. Policymakers in Washington should understand that at the center of the growing tensions between the Europeans and the Americans is not a civilizational Mars versus Venus clash, but serious policy differences over the Middle East.

THE EU: A MIDDLE EASTERN POWER?

In the United States public officials, journalists, and the general public seem to have bought into the neoconservative thesis that European attitudes toward the Middle East are a reflection of the Europeans' anti-American and anti-Israeli disposition. But as analysts Christina Balis and Simon Serfaty have suggested, to "all Europeans, the Middle East is as important as it is inescapable—disruptive (terrorism), dangerous (four wars), unstable (socioeconomic conditions), expensive (with even greater costs for peace than for war), and intrusive (because of the domestic dimensions of policy decisions in the area)." Even for the United Kingdom and the most pro-American governments in Rumsfeld's "new" Europe, Balis and Serfaty write, European "interests in the Middle East cannot be left to U.S. policies alone."[4]

It should not be surprising, therefore, if the Europeans react to America's Middle East policies by providing an alternative agenda, perhaps even by exploiting the growing anti-American sentiments in the region to their political and economic advantage. Indeed, the current U.S. policy plays directly into the hands of those forces in Europe—led by a Gaullist France—that are interested in establishing Europe as an ideological-cultural and strategic counterweight to America. In the short run, as the Europeans continue to move toward political and economic unification, but still lack diplomatic and military muscle, they will not be able to advance an ambitious strategy aimed at challenging U.S. preeminence in the Middle East. But the Europeans will probably also not wait for the American hegemon to throw them a few diplomatic and economic crumbs in the form of oil deals in Iraq or a marginal role in drawing the "road map" to Israeli-Palestinian peace. Instead, the Europeans could try pursuing a different and more activist and constructive path by using their "soft power" in dealing with the Middle East. More specifically, Europe could use its growing economic influence to maintain a more activist diplomatic relationship with the Middle East.

The Bush administration was promoting several ambitious plans to bring democracy and free markets to the broader Middle East and to establish free trade agreements between the economies in that region and the United States. But the Europeans have been advancing similar initiatives for years aimed at reforming the political and economic systems in the Eastern Mediterranean and linking them to the European markets.

Following the signing of the Helsinki Agreement in the mid-1970s, the southern European states, concerned about the potential for growing economic and demographic disparities between the northern and southern shores of the Mediterranean, began to discuss the need to create a Conference on Security and Cooperation in the Mediterranean (CSCM), modeled after the Conference and Security Cooperation in Europe. The idea reflected the interests of the southern European countries, led by France, to assert more diplomatic influence over the Middle East and North Africa by utilizing the economic might of the EU. They argued that the EU was putting too much emphasis on the relationship with Central and Eastern Europe, and should not ignore developments taking place in the "southern frontier" of North Africa and the eastern Mediterranean. Just as the wall had fallen between the eastern and western halves of Europe, "a bridge must be built across the Mediterranean," stressed French President Chirac.[5] First proposed by the Italians in 1989, the CSCM idea was formally introduced in the beginning of 1991 by France, Italy, Spain, and Portugal and then expanded beyond North Africa to include other regions and issues that affect Mediterranean security. The idea was received with enthusiasm by the North African countries, plus Turkey, Jordan, the Palestine Liberation Organization (PLO), and Israel.[6] Despite significant support for the CSCM, the movement for creating such a body was slowed by the continuing inability to resolve the Palestinian-Israeli issue and the lack of American support for the project.

The pressure by the southern European countries led to the convening of the Euro-Mediterranean conference in Barcelona, Spain, in November 1995, marking the EU's biggest effort to refocus its attention toward the Middle East. The conference, launching a partnership between the EU and 12 Middle Eastern and North African nations, pointed to the role that Europe could play in the Middle East and the potential for the formation of a Euro-Mediterranean bloc. The Barcelona Declaration launched the Euro-Mediterranean Partnership (EMP), which regionalized and tied together bilateral association agreements between the EU and individual states reached earlier with Tunisia, Israel, and Morocco; provided for a "Euro-Med" free trade area by the year 2010; increased U.S. aid and loans, worth $13 billion, to the region, targeted on infrastructure and the private sector; and offered incentives for the largely closed economies of North Africa and the Levant to integrate.[7]

In a way, the Euro-Med scheme is an intellectual successor to the CSCM plan. The idea is that free trade areas and more aid will enhance stability and prosperity on the southern and eastern Mediterranean rim, foster cross-border trade within that region, underpin the Middle East peace process, and help advance pluralism in a region where authoritarian government remained the norm. The Barcelona Declaration committed its signatories—Morocco, Algeria, Tunisia, Egypt, Jordan, Syria, Lebanon, Israel, Turkey, Cyprus, Malta and the Palestinian autonomous region (later to become the Palestinian Authority)—to "develop the rule of law and democracy" and guarantee human and minority rights as well as the freedoms of expression, association, thought, and belief.[8]

Hence, the EU has already formed its own version of the North American Free Trade Agreement (NAFTA) in the Middle East, in the form of the EMP, which in many respects resembles the broader Middle East initiative promoted by the Bush administration these days. Interestingly enough, two of the twelve governments that signed the Barcelona Declaration, Cyprus and Malta, have joined the EU as full members, which sends a positive message to the other members of the group, suggesting that association with the EU could lead eventually to membership. At the same time, the EU established cooperative economic arrangements with the six states of the Gulf Cooperation Council in 1989 and concluded a common external tariff arrangement in 2003.[9] More impressive, the EMP has become the only forum of its kind to have Israel and the Arab countries sitting around the same table, and the EU is also the major source of financial aid for the Palestinian Authority (PA). But the inclusion of Israel and the Arab states in the EMP also explains why the plan for Euro-Mediterranean integration has not gathered a lot of momentum. The Israeli-Palestinian conflict has made it impossible for the Europeans to get the Arabs and the Israelis to agree to establish the political and economic ties that are necessary for the creation of a free-trade area. There is no reason, therefore, to expect that the American initiatives of democracy building and economic development in the Middle East would get off the ground without some progress in resolving the conflict in the Holy Land.

Because of a disagreement with the EU over the creation of a development bank for the Middle East, the United States did not take part in the Euro-Med conference in Barcelona and organized almost at the same time the Middle East/North Africa economic summit in Amman, Jordan.[10] The United States has also helped to organize several other meetings that brought together industrialists, financiers, and officials from countries in the Middle East and North Africa. But with the exception of the energy supplies that America receives from the Persian Gulf, the United States regards the Middle East as an economic backwater. Billions of dollars of American aid have been squandered in financing statist economies and wasteful projects. The Free Trade Agreements (FTAs) that the United States signed with Israel and Jordan, and is planning to reach with Morocco, reflect political considerations, that is, the interest Washington has in strengthening politically those three important diplomatic partners. These FTAs certainly cannot be compared to the trade accords that the United States has concluded with the economies of the Pacific Rim, Western Europe, and Latin America, with which it has broad trade and investment ties—the kind that Europe has with the Middle East.

Indeed, figures published by the European Commission in 2003 point to the growing level of trade integration between the twelve Mediterranean countries and the fifteen EU members since 1980. In 2001, 53 percent of exports from Mediterranean economies went to the EU, and 62.9 percent of those economies' imports came from the EU. At the same time, all the Mediterranean countries, with the exception of Syria, have bilateral trade agreements with the EU. In that context, it is interesting to note that, notwithstanding the accusations that Europe is "anti-Israeli," EU-Israeli trade relations "reveal a striking pattern," according to Balis and Serfaty. "In the last decade alone, their bilateral trade volume has seen a threefold increase . . . confirming the EU as Israel's major trading partner and the number-one market for Israel's imports, surpassing even the United States in volume."[11]

The process of trade liberalization has not been perfect. European markets have remained closed to some of the Mediterranean countries' main products, especially agricultural goods. And the initiative was severely undermined as the Israeli-Palestinian peace process faltered. But the level of economic ties between the EU and the Mediterranean countries, including the growing dependency of Israel on trade with the EU, provides the Europeans with an opportunity to assert their diplomatic status in the region, preferably as part of a cooperative strategy with the United States.

EUROPEAN ROLE IN RESOLVING
THE ISRAEL-PALESTINE CONFLICT

To accelerate the process of linking the Middle East to the EU, European leaders should not block the entry of Turkey into the EU, provided Turkey ultimately meets all the criteria for EU membership. That act, combined with the entry of Cyprus and Malta, will confirm the EU's status as both an Eastern Mediterranean and a Middle Eastern power. An even more ambitious approach would be for the EU to announce its readiness to open negotiations with a free and democratic Iraq as well as with Israel and an independent Palestinian state. That could lead to the Palestinian state's gradual accession to the EU—a goal that would admittedly take many years to achieve.

By adopting a strategy of constructive engagement in the Middle East, the EU could try, through the use of both diplomatic and economic resources, to achieve the kind of goals that the Bush administration is trying to advance through the use of its military power: challenging the status quo in the Middle East while advancing the cause of peace and political and economic reform. Indeed, it is time for the Europeans to conclude that they cannot secure their interests in a region with which they maintain strategic, business, and demographic ties by burnishing their ties to corrupt political elites. That policy may have helped to protect short-term economic interests, while redirecting the hostility of the "Arab street" against the United States; however, perpetuating the rule of Arab autocrats has only helped turn the strategic and economic periphery of Europe into one of the least advanced and most unstable parts of the global economy. The Middle East exports not only oil to the EU but hundreds of thousands of poor and angry immigrants as well. Some Europeans look upon them as a demographic time bomb.

As long as both the Israelis and the Palestinians regard Washington as central to any resolution of their conflict, the EU will remain marginalized in the peace process. That is true despite the fact that Europe is the largest provider of aid to the Palestinian Authority and is Israel's most important trade partner. The EU has so far failed to translate that economic leverage into diplomatic influence. Signaling to the Israelis and the Palestinians that a peaceful resolution to their conflict could be a ticket for admission to the EU would be more than just enticing them with economic rewards. Conditioning Israel's entry into the EU on its agreement to withdraw from the occupied territories and dismantle the Jewish settlements there would strengthen the power of those Israelis who envision their state not as a militarized Jewish ghetto but as a Westernized liberal community.[12]

Indeed, the tragic fate of European Jewry served as the driving force for the creation of Israel, and welcoming the Jewish state into the European community makes historical and moral sense. Economic ties between the EU and the Mediterranean countries provide the Europeans with an opportunity to assert their diplomatic status in the region, preferably as part of a cooperative strategy with the United States. The prospect of joining the EU could even help launch a process of economic and political liberalization in an independent Palestine and an Iraqi federation. In the same way that the establishment of NAFTA produced pressure for democratic reform in Mexico, the evolution of trade and institutional ties among the EU, Palestine, and Iraq, and eventually Jordan, Syria, and Lebanon, could lay the foundations for a movement toward democracy in the entire Levant.

Hopes for EU membership have already played a critical role in accelerating democratic change in Turkey, leading to the collapse of the old political order and the election of a reform-minded democratic party. Putting Turkey's EU membership on hold only gives a boost to those in the military and nationalist Islamic groups who want to reorient Ankara's foreign policy away from the West and toward Iran and Russia. If anything, the recent tensions between Washington and Ankara over Iraq and the Kurds only demonstrate that anchoring Turkey in the EU is in the interest of both the Americans and the Europeans and could also help stabilize post-Saddam Iraq.

Moreover, the Americans and the Europeans have an opportunity now to try to draw a blueprint for Euro-American diplomatic and economic engagement in the Middle East that would bring together the ongoing Barcelona process with the elements proposed in the GME initiative. In fact, the former French Foreign Minister Dominique de Villepin, depicted by American neoconservatives as the leading "anti-American" figure in Europe, has proposed that the Barcelona and GME plans could be merged into a common Euro-American strategy. "We want to engage quickly a large debate over the Middle East," he said in February 2004. That engagement would take place with "our European partners first, then the concerned nations in the region with the Arab League as [prime mover] and other partners in the framework of the G–8," he pointed out, adding that "the important thing is that the Europeans and the Americans work together not only in good intelligence, but also in close cooperation with regional countries."[13]

Indeed, notwithstanding the rift between the EU and America over Iraq, it is possible to envision these two players working together to achieve some of their common goals in the Middle East, which include integrating Turkey into the West, resolving the Israeli-Palestinian conflict, and working together to liberalize the economic and political systems of the region. America should certainly provide incentives for the Europeans to devote more of their resources to creating a stable and prosperous Middle East, which would have a direct effect on European interests. Such a U.S. policy should replace the neoconservative approach highlighted by the cover story in the *Weekly Standard* on September 22, 2003, titled, "Against United Europe," with a policy that supports a stronger European entity under the leadership of Britain, France, and Germany. Such a Europe will not be as a neoconservative caricature proposes, a giant Switzerland, a prosperous, wimpy, and impotent global player, but the prime military and diplomatic partner of the United States in the early twenty-first century. The much-maligned Europe could end up providing the economic and diplomatic resources needed to help create a New Middle East.

THE GLOBAL "NORTHERN ALLIANCE"

It is difficult to predict whether the Americans and the Europeans would be able to prevent a "Suez in reverse" from taking place in the future. Great powers have rarely been able to adjust to changing power relations. But great powers in periods of uncertainty and following a major war have been able to agree on the formation of an oligopoly-type system in which they share power as part of a strategy of maintaining a status quo. One example of such an oligopolistic arrangement was the bi-polar system that emerged at the end of World War II, in the aftermath of the Yalta Summit under which the United States and the Soviet Union were able to maintain stability and peace in Europe by dividing it into respective spheres of influence. A second example of an oligopolistic arrangement is the multipolar structure that was formed in the Congress of Vienna following the Napoleonic Wars, under which the great powers of Europe co-opted defeated France and established a balance of power system to protect the existing status quo that could withstand the rising nationalism in the continent, including that of unified Italy and Germany.

Idealists decry these agreements as "cynical" and as reflections of the interests of ruling political and economic elites and the marginalization of the weaker powers in the system, such as the Serbs who were denied freedom under the Austro-Hungarian Empire or the Poles who remained under the Soviet sphere of influence. But both the Congress of Vienna system and the Yalta agreements made it possible for the international system to enjoy long and relatively peaceful periods and prevented large destruction and killings in the scale of the Napoleonic wars and the two world wars of the twentieth century. Moreover, the West in both the post-Napoleonic and post–World War II eras had enjoyed its "golden ages" of remarkable periods of economic growth and cultural renaissance.

Indeed, the Congress of Vienna system, which dealt with the complex relationship between the great European powers of the nineteenth century, provides a model for the United States and Europe to follow in working together on their strategic interests in the Middle East. The only realistic scenario aimed at advancing global U.S. interests will have to be based on cooperation with the

EU and Russia, an ensemble of great powers—a global Northern Alliance. As noted in earlier chapters, such a system, in addition to containing terrorism and dealing with instability in the Middle East and its periphery, would also help to bring China and India further into the international system as stable and pro-status-quo powers and might co-opt regional "influentials" like Brazil, Japan, South Africa, and Turkey.

The new system could evolve as a fusion of the Group of 7 (G–7) large industrialized nations (or G–8, if Russia is invited to the meetings) and a restructured UN Security Council that would include the United States, the EU, Russia, Japan, China, and India as its permanent members, as well as rotating members representing regional "influentials." They would coordinate both geo-strategic and geo-economic policies, whether currency exchange rates or the political future of Iraq and Israel/Palestine. This is the kind of geo-strategic/geo-economic directorate that would be more relevant today than ever in an international system in which the goal of combating terrorism is intertwined with the interests of maintaining political stability in the Middle East—which, in turn, affects access to and the price of oil in the Persian Gulf on which the economies of the EU, Japan, and China are so dependent.

It was the core of the Eurasian Island, the Middle East and its peripheries with their oil resources, that was the focus of the great geo-strategic conflicts of the twentieth century. The first moves in the Cold War were made in the Eastern Mediterranean (Turkey and Greece) and the Middle East (Iran) and its last chapter was the anti-Soviet insurgency in Afghanistan as part of an American effort to protect the Middle East. In a way, one could argue that the first post-post–Cold War and post-9/11 chapters were also written in the periphery of the Middle East, again in Afghanistan, where the United States, with the strong backing of the EU, and its former Cold War rivals, Russia and China, defeated a major threat to the new international status quo as dramatized by the terrorist attacks on the centers of Western economic and military power in New York and Washington. Indeed, the end of that war, like the conclusions of the Napoleonic Wars and World War II, should have provided an opportunity for the United States to bring together the EU and Russia, and other players like China and India, to establish new forms of geo-strategic cooperation in the Middle East and elsewhere. But as I have stressed in this book, instead of trying to build the foundations of a new global oligopoly in which American power would play a leading role, 9/11 and the military victory in Afghanistan were exploited by the Bush administration and its neoconservative ideologues to promote an American global monopoly.

THE MIDDLE EAST AND CHINA

Before 9/11, many of these same neoconservatives were toying with the idea of using the "threat" of an emerging China as a way of mobilizing domestic support for an assertive global American policy and of forming a new coalition (Japan, India, and Taiwan) to "contain" China. In the aftermath of 9/11 and the ensuing war on terrorism, Bush administration officials have emphasized the common interests that the United States and China share in combating Islamic terrorism and insurgency, including in China's Xingjiang region, where the government is facing a separatist challenge from a large Moslem Uighur minority.[14] But the approach adopted by the Bush administration should not be seen as part of a new détente policy toward Beijing. The neoconservatives recognize that with America preoccupied in Iraq and the Middle East, and taking into consideration its need for Chinese assistance in resolving the North Korean nuclear crisis, the United States is not in a position to launch a grand strategy to "contain" China.[15] Moreover, the central banks of China together with those of Japan are buying U.S. treasury bonds that help sustain America's huge current account deficit, and in turn help finance current U.S. hegemonic projects in the Middle East. In 2004, China had loans outstanding to the U.S. government for more than $120 billion, in the form of treasury debt. According to the *Wall Street Journal,* China holds probably that much again in Fannie Mae and other dollar-dominated securities.[16]

The neocons, however, also assume that American hegemony in the Middle East and Middle Eastern oil would provide Washington with a political-economic leverage over China. After all, China's booming economy is becoming increasingly dependent on the Middle Eastern oil controlled by the United States—in the same way that the United States tried to exploit Japan's dependency on energy imports to force it to make diplomatic concessions before World War II.[17] In such a future scenario when China's growing economy becomes dependent on energy imports, the United States could use its domination of the world's sea lanes to threaten China's oil lifeline unless Beijing bows to Washington's dictates on Taiwan and other issues, in the same way that post–World War II Japan, which receives much of its oil from the Middle East, has no choice but to back U.S. policies in Northeast Asia and the Middle East, including sending a small number of Japanese peacekeeping troops to Iraq.[18]

But a Northern Alliance system in which China would be co-opted would be based on the expectation that China, like the United States, the EU, and Russia, would have a common interest in ensuring a stable and reliable supply of oil from the Middle East as well as a shared interest in containing threats from anti-status-quo players in that region, including Islamic terrorist groups. In addition, the Chinese need to maintain peace and stability in East Asia and strengthen the foundations of an expanding global economy, including American exports markets, which are necessary in order to sustain the growth of its own economy.

Ironically, convincing the United States to accept collective decision making under such a framework could prove to be even more difficult than co-opting China. While one can expect President George W. Bush to try during his second term to mend the relationships with the Europeans and allow them to assume more responsibilities in the Middle East, it could prove much more difficult for an American administration to accept the idea of a multipolar international system in which the United States is a powerful player among other great powers.

COSTS OF AMERICAN RESISTANCE

But one cannot expect the EU or Russia, China, India, and other powers to be willing to finance and provide diplomatic and military support for a militarily and economically overstretched American empire. America is certainly a hegemon and may be occupying Iraq but, economically at least, it is doing the opposite of what Lenin expected of imperialist powers, according to British economist Angus Maddison. He noted that although America is often described as Britain's successor as the world's dominant power, it is behaving quite differently from the British, who had net foreign assets valued at 150 percent of their GDP during the height of the British Imperium before World War I. In 2002, at the height of the American Imperium, the foreign holdings of U.S. stocks, bonds, and other assets exceeded America's foreign assets to the tune of $2.3 trillion—or 22 percent of GDP.[19] Moreover, as historian Paul Kennedy suggests, while U.S. defense spending has been increasing over the past years, it is struggling to keep up with its overseas commitments. He estimates that by the end of 2003 the invasion of Iraq had already cost U.S. taxpayers $150 billion, in contrast to 1991 Gulf War, which cost only $7 billion, thanks to the extensive contributions of Arab and European allies and Japan.[20] Hence, rising American current account deficits and high defense spending make it less likely that the United States would be able to economically sustain its hegemony, especially if, as I suggested in earlier chapters, the U.S. dollar's position as the world's reserve currency is threatened as the result of a decision by European and Middle Eastern countries to set the price of oil in euros instead of dollars.

There is also every reason to expect that a hegemonic American approach would create countervailing coalitions of other players that resent U.S. supremacy. In that context, as this book argues, the Middle East may become a major arena for a geo-strategic competition between the Americans and the Europeans. It is quite mind boggling to read the comments by Bush administration officials, some of whom played a role in successfully managing the American balance of power competition with the Soviet Union, decrying the notion that we could be entering another period in which U.S. power is balanced by counterweights from other players. "Multi-polarity was never a unifying vision—it was a necessary evil," according to Condoleezza Rice.[21] But if anything, the fact that those great powers competing and cooperating as part of a new balance of power share common values would make it more likely that their relationship could be effectively managed in the new system, unlike that between the Western alliance and the communist bloc during the Cold War.

BYE BYE, PAN-ARABISM

Under such a system, the Middle East and its peripheries could become an arena in which the great powers maintain a division of labor in terms of dealing with threats to their common security, especially from terrorist groups and anti-status-quo powers or rogue regimes, with access to WMD. If the EU could emerge in the long run as the strategic player of last resort in the Middle East, Russia could play a similar role in parts of Central Asia, whereas India could become the central player in South Asia, especially in deterring the power of a potentially radical Pakistan. In the Middle East, an Iran that is co-opted into the system could help stabilize the Persian Gulf and Central Asia, while Turkey could continue to play its role as a strategic and cultural bridge between Europe and the Middle East and Central Asia, especially if the issue of Cyprus is resolved.

Much of the changes expected to take place in the Middle East would be dominated by nationalism and in a combining and unraveling of ethnic, religious, and tribal identities. On one hand, we are going to witness the decline of the two national movements that dominated the region during most of the last century, Pan-Arabism and Zionism. On the other hand, the rise of new ethnic and religious groups, like the Shiites and the Kurds, could give birth to new political entities, including new nation-states and mini-states. But contrary to the paradigm promoted by Samuel Huntington and others, the rise of political Islam in the Middle East is not the first stage in the creation of a unified Islamic community that would be engaged in a clash of civilizations scenario with the

West. As columnist William Pfaff put it, "Civilizations are not responsible political actors, having no government" and "to talk of 'wars' between them was like the nineteenth century provocative and prejudicial talk about wars between races."[22] Wars are made by nation-states and their governments, led by leaders that base their decisions on consideration of political, economic, and military interests. That we are not on the verge of a clash of civilizations was the point I had also made in an article published in *Foreign Affairs* magazine in 1993. In this article I argued that Islam, like any other religion, can be utilized by political figures and organizations as a way of mobilizing support for causes at home and abroad—to launch a mass revolution against the Shah in Iran; to help the United States and its allies Pakistan and Saudi Arabia win recruits for guerrilla forces in Afghanistan; to energize authentic national and ethnic insurgencies in Palestine, Bosnia, Kashmir, or Chechnya; or to advance peaceful political reform in Turkey.[23]

At the end of the day, a government ruled by an Islamic party, like one controlled by a Zionist or a Hindu-nationalist party, would probably pursue a foreign policy based more on core national interests than on religious agendas. For example, based on considerations of military power and national interests, Iran, under either a religious or secular government, would be inclined to develop or acquire nuclear weapons or tend to back the Armenian-Christians in their conflict with the Azeri-Moslems. In fact, the longest and bloodiest military conflict in the Middle East in the twentieth century was not between Arab-Moslems and Israeli-Jews, but between two Moslem nations, Iran and Iraq. Similarly, the possibility of Iraq remaining a unified state or breaking down into three mini-states depends very much on the mostly hostile relationship between three Moslem groups—Arab-Sunnis, Arab-Shiites, and Kurds. In any case, if the Arab people who share a common history, language, and culture can not achieve a political unity, there is no reason to expect that such a process of integration would take place between Moslems in the Middle East and Asia who are divided along deep national, ethnic, tribal, and sectarian lines.

Instead, with the Pan-Arabist dream of a unified Arab nation stretching from the Atlantic Ocean to the borders of Iraq losing its appeal, the Arab Middle East could gradually evolve in the long run into a nation-state system reflecting a mix of ethnic, religious, and cultural identities and divided into various sub-regional economic and political units. Some of the plausible scenarios could include a North African Maghreb who would bring together Algeria, Morocco, and Tunisia, a region where the Berbers (in particular in Algeria) and other minority groups could assert their influence. Egypt could become the leader of a Nile cooperative bloc that would include Sudan, or, instead, it could stress its Coptic identity and its links to the Eastern Mediterranean. In the Levant, Israel and a Palestinian entity, Jordan, together with Syria and Lebanon could establish a common market with links to the EU. Iraq could evolve into a loose confederation or into a centralized state under a "soft" authoritarian government or it could disintegrate into three separate mini-states.

In any case, one should expect a series of political earthquakes in the Middle East that would work the failure of the secular Arab nationalist movement to provide a sense of common identity to the Arab parts of the former Ottoman Empire. This crisis could re-energize political Islamic movements and lead to growing ethnic, tribal, and religious divisions. Continuing violence against ruling governments and elites, civil wars, and a process of fragmentation could lead not only to the breakup of Iraq, but also to those of Syria and even Iran and Turkey—especially if the Kurds were to launch a major campaign to win independence for Greater Kurdistan. In this context, the Palestinian-Israeli conflict should not be seen as a religious war between Moslems and Jews or as one of the waves in the clash between the Islam and the West. Hindu, Russian, and Serbian nationalists also like to spin their own armed conflicts with Moslem separatists, respectively, in Kashmir, Chechnya, and Bosnia along the same lines. The clash between Israelis and Palestinians is in essence a civil war between two national groups, products of secular nationalist movements—Zionism, which was founded by secular European Jews, and Pan-Arabism, whose ideological and political basis was created by Arab-Christian thinkers. This conflict is not very different from other civil wars that are taking place in Iraq, Sudan, Algeria (between Arab-Moslems and Berber-Moslems), Bosnia, and in other parts of the Balkans and in the Horn of Africa, in which religion is only one of the elements used to mobilize people to fight against the "other."

In Palestine/Israel, a failure to reach an agreement between Israel and a legitimate Palestinian leadership and a possible decision by the Israelis to withdraw unilaterally not only from the Gaza Strip but also from parts of the West Bank would leave Jordan no choice but to send its troops to the evacuated Palestinian territories if it wanted to prevent a large migration of Palestinians from there into the East Bank. In any case, growing radicalization among the Palestinian majority in Jordan could threaten the Hashemites, which could lead to a civil war between them and the Bedouins. Ironically, the new version of the old "Jordanian Option" in which a Palestinian state emerging in the East Bank would take over most of the West Bank and Gaza could actually become a way to resolve the Palestinian-Israeli conflict.

A post-Hashemite Jordan could also become a nucleus for the creation of a new Arab-Sunni state that would bring together the Arab-Sunni parts of what remains of Iraq and Syria. It certainly would be very difficult to predict the future political changes in Saudi Arabia and the rest of the Arab states in the Persian Gulf. The creation of a Shiite state in Iraq that would establish political links to Iran would probably strengthen the power of the Shiites in other parts of the region and help Teheran consolidate its power in the Persian Gulf, in which Saudi Arabia would become a sort of Moslem Vatican and the other mini-states there would become political satellites of Teheran.

ISRAELI DILEMMAS

Israel will also have to deal with the reality of a changing Middle East and make crucial choices that would determine its national identity and character. A unilateral Israeli withdrawal from the occupied Palestinian territories and a successful disengagement from the West Bank and Gaza—even without a comprehensive agreement with the Palestinians—together with an accession into the EU would allow Israel to "de-couple" itself from the Arab Middle East. Israel will become a "gated community" in the region by pursuing a similar strategy to that of Slovenia, with regard to the former Yugoslavia, or Greek Cyprus, in relation to the Turkish part. Under those circumstances, Israel would not enjoy all the possible benefits of peace with the Palestinians; but a lower level of military conflict could permit Israel to invest its human and economic resources in developing a modern society and a high-tech economy and to become one of the more advanced members of the EU.

However, a peace agreement between Israel and an independent Palestinian state could prove to be a win-win outcome for both sides. It could lead perhaps to the creation of an Israel-Palestine-Jordan economic market a la NAFTA that would make it possible for the Palestinians to join the EU and enjoy the rewards of its economic ties with Israel and membership in the EU. Under the most optimistic scenario, the Israelis and the Palestinians could then create the foundations for a very powerful economic entity. An Israel/Palestine federation could become a Middle Eastern Switzerland, a bridge between the Arab oil states and the EU and the global economy and a central trading and financial center that would serve as an engine for the economic and cultural renaissance of the entire Levant. Israel, Palestine, Jordan, Syria, and Lebanon could become a model for a new form of co-existence between national, ethnic, and religious groups with rich traditions and history, strong family ties, entrepreneurial success, and other ties to the West. Many Israelis, Palestinians, Lebanese, and Christians who have immigrated to Europe, North and South America, and Africa have excelled in commerce, banking, and other business and professional fields; there is no reason why, under conditions of relative peace and the creation of stable and open political and economic conditions, they would not do the same in their homelands, especially if they continue to maintain links to their communities in the diasporas.

But the continuing status quo in Israel/Palestine, the lack of a peace agreement between the two peoples, and the inability or unwillingness of the Israelis to disengage from the West Bank and Gaza may end up leaving the Israelis with two unpleasant options: Israel could grant the Palestinian Arabs in the West Bank and Gaza full civil rights, in which case Israel would cease to be an exclusive Jewish state and then be transformed into a binational state of Jews and Arabs and perhaps eventually into an Arab state with the Jews becoming a minority, not unlike the Maronite Christians of Lebanon. Or, Israel could choose to deny citizenship to the residents of the West Bank and Gaza and become a Middle Eastern version of South Africa, in which a Jewish minority controls an Arab majority that lacks basic political or civil rights. Under either of these two scenarios, Israel could start losing what remains of its commitment to European-style liberal and democratic traditions, suffer economic and cultural decline, cease to be a magnet to Jewish immigrants, and could experience a large emigration of its best and brightest to the West.

FAREWELL ZIONISM?

In any case, either as a result of a successful disengagement from the occupied Arab territories or following a peace accord that would lead to the establishment of an independent Palestinian state, Israel would need to face a reality in which the Zionist revolution would be over and it would be gradually transformed from a Jewish state into a state that belongs to all its citizens, Jews and non-Jews. Even after leaving the West Bank and Gaza, Israel would still have a large Arab minority of about 20 percent, plus other communities of non-Jews, including some of the immigrants from the former Soviet Union and families of guest workers from as far away as China who have settled in Israel. In recent years, Israelis have been debating their national identity and taking steps to liberalize their political and economic system as part of a process of Americanization. Pressure from secular Israelis, including many of the immigrants from Russia, is going to lead to more changes, including the drawing up of a constitution and slow moves toward the separation of religion and state. An Israel that would become more "normal" and integrated into the Eastern Mediterranean would reflect the rise of a more secular and commercialized nation. Oriented toward Tel Aviv, its business and secular cultural center, a confident

Israel entering a post-Zionist age could metamorphose from a militarized Jewish ghetto and socialized economy into a thriving and lively economic and cultural center.[24]

In the long run, only a process of "normalization" would ensure the survival of Israel and its chances of achieving some sense of security, the potential to maintain a Westernized society and grow its economy. An Israel that is oriented toward a Jerusalem that is dominated by the messianic and religious-nationalist proponents of Greater Israel will become a militarized Jewish ghetto that is dependent on the goodwill of a distant friend, the United States. Like the crusader states in the Levant, that kind of Israel would not be able to survive as an independent entity for more than a few generations and would be destined either to a slow decline or to a nuclear Masada-like fate.

The implied assumption in neoconservative thinking is that Israel can maintain its margin of security and economic standard of living as a political military outpost of the United States in the Middle East. According to this view, promoted by American pro-Likud thinkers such as Richard Perle, Douglas Feith, and David Wurmser, American support would allow Israel to protect itself against military threats from the Arab and Moslem worlds and contain diplomatic challenges from the Europeans. But this vision of an Israeli-American alliance confronting a Euro-Arab bloc is only creating expectations that would never be fulfilled.[25] Not only are geo-political considerations bound to force the United States to disengage from the Middle East sooner or later, but demographic changes in the American-Jewish community, including growing rates of intermarriage, would make it less likely that the pro-Israeli lobby in Washington would be able to maintain its influence on American politics and foreign policy for many years to come. There is no doubt that the memories of the Holocaust would help secure support for Israel in the United States even as Israel continues to repress the Palestinians in a Greater Israel and becomes more isolated in the international community as a pariah state. A shrinking American-Jewish community and changes in the international system would make it difficult to maintain this status quo for more than one or two decades.

ISRAEL: AMERICA'S WEAKEST LINK

At first blush, the grand strategic plan of an American Empire that was conceived by the neocons in the Bush administration seemed to be an attempt to lessen the costs of Israeli expansionist policies. After all, this U.S. strategy would create a regional environment in which U.S. hegemony and fractured and weakened Arab states would place no constraints on Israel's ability to pursue its most ambitious goals. In the same way that U.S. unilateralism—according to the new Bush doctrine—would make it impossible for any power to oppose U.S. global predominance, U.S. hegemony in the Middle East would protect Israel from challenges from regional players. In short, the American Empire could ultimately be designed to make the Middle East safe for Greater Israel.

But such a U.S. strategy should worry Israeli policymakers. It would make Israel a modern-day crusader state, an outlet of a global power whose political, economic, and military headquarters are on the other side of the world. America's commitment to the security of the Israeli "province" would always remain uncertain and fragile, reflecting changes in the balance of power in Washington and the shifting dynamics of U.S. politics and economics.

The current strength of the U.S.-Israeli connection is a product of unique conditions: America's post–Cold War unipolar moment, U.S. economic gains of the 1990s, the 9/11 terrorist attack, and the ensuing war on terrorism. Those developments have persuaded the U.S. president to align U.S. policy with a right-wing Israeli government.

But the values and long-term goals of a politically radical Israel run contrary to large segments of opinion makers and the public in the United States. The radical Zionist agenda is also weakening those forces in Israel that want to see their nation reach some sort of an accommodation with the Palestinians and build a modern Western society. Indeed, the policies pursued by nationalist Israeli governments, with strong support from Washington, will make it impossible for Israel to achieve those goals. It will also end up weakening its economy, dividing and corrupting its society, and eventually increasing its dependency on the United States.

For the Arab and Moslem nations—as well as for other powers, especially those challenging the international status quo—Israel would be perceived as the "weakest link" in the American Empire. Israel would thus become an ideal target for anti-American and anti-globalization forces. We are already seeing the shape of things to come in the growing sentiments in Europe and Asia, and in the way sentiments are starting to intertwine, in some cases, with dormant anti-Semitic attitudes.

In some respects, Israel's ties with the United States are starting to resemble the relationship between the old political and economic elites and the Jewish community in Europe during the nineteenth century. As Hannah Arendt pointed out in her classic study of European anti-Semitism, it was the erosion in the power of those elites—and their growing inability to protect the Jews of Europe—that sealed the fate of Jews.[26] The new and angry social classes and political players turned their frustration against the Jews they associated with the hated status quo—the group that was also very vulnerable. A similar scenario could take place on an international scale, when a weaker and less confident United States would be under pressure at home and abroad to reduce its global commitments. This would leave Israel—its weakest link—vulnerable to attacks not only from Arab and Moslem nations, but from other new anti-status quo powers.

Ironically, the original mission of classical Zionism was to release Europe's Jews from the trap that Hannah Arendt described, to turn them into a normal people, living in a normal state, able to protect themselves, not dependent on others for their survival. In the real world of nation states and power politics, and in the face of opposition from the surrounding Arab states, Israel has had to search for support from foreign powers, including the United States (and France in the 1950s and the Soviet Union in the late 1940s). But that support was seen by Israel's founders as a temporary measure to sustain its national security. The long-term goal was to use that outside support and combine it with Israel's military power as a way of pressing the Arabs to recognize that Israel was a permanent feature in the Middle East—and to make peace with it. Some of the Israeli policies that followed the 1967 Middle East War, especially those created by the Likud, violated those principles. U.S. support was utilized to fulfill a Messianic agenda of settling Judea and Samaria—and pursuing the creeping annexation of those territories. Ultimately, it was a policy that was never supported by the majority of the Israelis, but one that was promoted by nationalist and religious fanatics. And it only played into the hands of the extremists on the other side, helping to set off the vicious circle of Palestinian-Israeli violence that we are now witnessing.

Perhaps it's not too late for the Israelis to figure out how to take a path towards normalcy in the Middle East that leads to peaceful co-existence with the Palestinians and their other neighbors in the next generations. And, most important, Israel has to do so as an independent nation-state and not as a crusader state whose fate is determined by the decisions of a foreign and distant power.

"BUT WHAT ABOUT ISRAEL?"

It is appropriate perhaps that I would conclude this book by referring to the long-term dilemmas that are bound to affect the Israeli-American relationship. Even many of the readers who might be persuaded by my challenges to the American Middle East paradigm as it applies to the U.S. relationship with the Arab Middle East are expected to raise the predictable question: "But what about Israel?" Even if one agrees that "oil" should not force the United States into a costly involvement in the Middle East in the aftermath of the Cold War, America cannot disengage from the Middle East because of its moral and historic commitment to the Jewish state, these critics would argue.

Indeed, American support of the establishment of a Jewish state in the Middle East against the backdrop of the Holocaust, and reflecting a strong consensus among Western and American elites, ran very much contrary to realpolitik geo-strategic and geo-economic considerations that led to U.S. involvement in the Middle East after 1945 and during most of the Cold War. It was not surprising that many of the hard-core realists in the Truman administration, including then Secretary of State George Marshall, were opposed to the White House's decision to recognize the newly independent state. The fact that following the Six-Day War and especially under the influence of the neoconservative ideologues in the Reagan and Bush II administrations, Israel was transformed into an American "strategic asset"—first against Soviet expansionism in the Middle East, and then against Islamic radicalism—helped produce certain misperceptions about American and Israeli interests and policies.

The main reason that America was involved in such a major way in the Middle East had less to do with Israel and more to do with its core geo-strategic interests as perceived by the American leaders and the American public, although as I have pointed in this book, integrating the support for Israel into its Middle East policy did help foreign policymakers to win support for an ever wider and more expansive engagement in the region than would have otherwise been expected. But as a "strategic asset," Israel played a very minor role in helping the United States achieve its goals in the region, and if anything it ended up producing major costs in terms of igniting anti-American sentiments and leading to such dangerous developments as the 1973 Middle East War and the 1982 War in Lebanon.

The other side of the American-Israeli coin is that the existential threats that Israel has faced since 1948 had less to do with Soviet expansionism or radical Islam and more to do with the conflict between Zionism and Arab nationalism and its two products, Israel and the Palestinian national movement over the control of the Land of Israel/Palestine. The Soviets did provide support for Pan Arabists such as Egypt's Gamal Abdel Nasser and its allies in Syria, Iraq, and the Palestine Liberation Organization (PLO), but the Americans were allied with Saudi Arabia and supported Arab and Moslem states and movements whose animosity toward the Jewish state was even more intense than that of secular Arab nationalists such as Nasser. Moreover, it was the support that the Americans provided to the Mujaheddin in Afghanistan, as well as to Saudi Arabia and Pakistan, and that Egyptian President Anwar Sadat had given to the

Moslem Brotherhood in Egypt, which led to the rise of the current radical Islamic groups in the Middle East and the Moslem world. Israel's main challenge continues to be the need to find a way to divide the Land of Israel/Palestine in a way that would be acceptable to both sides and their regional and international supporters. As long as that does not happen, the Palestinians will be able to count on some outside support, for the Arab and Moslem worlds as well as from the EU in the coming years. The rise of radical Islamic groups just makes it more difficult, but not impossible, to resolve the conflict in the long run.

Before the Likud-neoconservative alliance became so powerful in Washington and Jerusalem, American support for Israel helped provide it with resources to protect its narrow margin of security. But U.S. support was not a substitute for what remained Israel's top national security goal: making peace with the Arabs and the Palestinians and becoming a recognized and legitimate part of the Middle East. If under Reagan, the Likud-neoconservative policies in the name of an anti-Soviet strategic alliance helped bring about the disastrous outcome of the 1982 Lebanon War and the ensuing American bloody intervention, similar policies under Bush II resulted in a new willingness on the part of Washington, in the name of fighting radical Islam, to back the Likud government's approach toward the Palestinians. But in the same way that Palestinian nationalism was not a puppet of Moscow during the Cold War, it has not been a stooge of Al Qaeda after 9/11.

Hence the current American policies are not providing Israel with a way to protect its security as much as they are creating incentives to adopt policies that would harm Israel's security and long-term survival. Indeed, one could make the argument that these policies are not in line with the American moral and historic commitment to the Jewish state since they are creating the conditions in which the existence of Israel as a Jewish state and as a Western democratic state would be threatened. In fact, a Middle-Eastern version of the old apartheid system of South Africa would not be able to count on the long-term moral and historic commitment that Israel has enjoyed in the United States since its establishment after World War II.

"A LOT OF PEOPLE WHO DON'T THINK LIKE US"

But even in the case of Israel, a Westernized, if not an Americanized, society with strong political, economic, cultural, and demographic ties to the United States, Washington's ability to influence the policy choices that its leaders and public make are limited under the best of circumstances. Israelis and American supporters of the Jewish state should recognize that moral concerns cannot serve as a basis for any long-term foreign policy, that idealistic commitments are historically bound, and that considerations of national interests determine the way nations behave. After all, very few observers would have predicted in the 1950s, at a time when American support for the Republic of China (Taiwan) in the United States was very strong and based on moral and historic commitments as well as on the support of a very powerful lobby in Washington, that one day the United States would abandon its ally in Taipei as part of a broader geo-strategic scheme to establish ties with the communist leaders in China.

Indeed, the American relationship with Israel as well as with the rest of the Middle East would and should be based mainly on realistic calculations of American interests in the region and the world. As I have argued in this book, the neoconservative program of bringing political and economic freedom to the Middle East is not only a fantasy, as the adventure in Iraq is demonstrating, but is also inconsistent with the neoconservative goal of achieving stability and advancing American hegemony in the region. Realists who adhere to a conservative view of the world that distrusts central governments and their power to change societies and human nature should be the first to recognize that an American Wilsonian project in the Middle East or in any part of the world is at best unlikely to succeed or be cost effective. And at worst, the policies promoted by the neoconservatives could produce outcomes that are even more destructive than the status quo they attempted to change.

By tilting the Middle East kaleidoscope, the ouster of Saddam Hussein has released new waves of national, ethnic, and religious forces that have very little to do with Western concepts of political freedom. Quite often, those involved in the formulation and implementation of U.S. policy in the Middle East assume that the people in Saudi Arabia, Iraq, and Afghanistan "think like you and want the same things as you." At a recent Pentagon meeting, a strategic thinker, Thomas Barnett, was trying to convince a group of military officers that American power could be applied to democratize the Middle East. "Everyone wants a better future for their kids," Barnett asserted. The comment drew a sharp rebuke from a U.S. army colonel who attended the briefing. "I've been around a lot of people who don't think like us," the officer replied.[27]

Indeed, in the Middle East, Americans are encountering a lot of people who "don't think like us" and who see U.S. power as either an obstacle to achieving their goals or as a tool to advance their interests. The time has come for Americans to start debating the rising costs of this engagement in the Middle East and whether it helps Americans achieve a better future for their kids.

Notes

PREFACE

1. Leon T. Hadar, *Quagmire: America in the Middle East* (Washington, D.C.: Cato Institute, 1992), p. 173.
2. Ibid., p. 173.
3. Ibid., p. 178.
3. Ibid., p. 178.
4. Ibid., p. 180–81.
5. Ibid., p. 179.
6. Ibid., p. 179–80.
8. Ibid., p. 191.
7. Ibid., p. 121.
8. Ibid., p. 119.
9. See Zbigniew Brzezinski, *The Choice: Global Domination or Global Leadership* (New York: Basic Books, 2004).
10. See Brent Scowcroft, "A Middle East Opening," *Washington Post,* November 12, 2004.

CHAPTER I

1. Thomas S. Kuhn, *The Structure of Scientific Revolutions* (Chicago: University of Chicago Press, 1996), p. viii.
2. These famous lines come from his 1919 book, *Democratic Ideals and Reality,* and are quoted in Paul Kennedy, "Mission Impossible," *The New York Review of Books,* June 10, 2004, p. 16.
3. Eric Hobsbawm, *The Age of Extremes: A History of the World, 1914–1991* (New York: Vintage, 1996).
4. Kuhn, *The Structure of Scientific Revolutions,* pp. 6–7.
5. David Frum and Richard Perle, *An End to Evil: How to Win the War on Terror* (New York: Random House, 2003).
6. On Clinton's policies in the Middle East, see Leon T. Hadar, "America's Moment in the Middle East," *Current History,* January 1996, Vol. 95, No. 597.
7. See Kenneth M. Pollack, "Securing the Gulf," *Foreign Affairs,* July/August 2003, Vo. 82, No. 4.
8. See Leon T. Hadar, "Letter From Washington: Pax Americana's Four Pillars of Folly," *Journal of Palestine Studies,* Spring 1998, Vol. XXVII, No. 3.
9. See Michael T. Klare, *Resource Wars: The New Landscape of Global Conflict* (New York: Owl Books, 2002).

10. See Steve Coll, *Ghost Wars: The Secret History of the CIA, Afghanistan, and Bin Laden, from the Soviet Invasion to September 10, 2001* (New York: The Penguin Press, 2004).

11. Chalmers Johnson, *Blowback: The Costs and Consequences of American Empire* (New York: Metropolitan Books, 2000).

12. Stefan Halper and Jonathan Clarke, *American Alone: The Neo-Conservatives and the Global Order* (Cambridge: Cambridge University Press, 2004).

13. See Warren Zimmermann, *First Great Triumph: How Five Americans Made Their Country a World Power* (New York: Farrar, Straus and Giroux, 2004).

14. John J. Mearsheimer, *The Tragedy of Great Power Politics* (New York: W. W. Norton & Company, 2001).

CHAPTER 2

1. Shimon Peres, *The New Middle East* (New York: Henry Holt & Company, 1995).

2. Thomas L. Friedman, *The Lexus and the Olive Tree: Understanding Globalization* (New York: Anchor, 2000).

3. See Gareth Smith, "Torch Bearer for Iran's Pragmatic Conservatives," *Financial Times,* January 24, 2004 and Guy Dinmore, "America's Neo-Conservative Lobbyists Tune in For Regime Change in Iran," *Financial Times,* December 6/7, 2003.

4. Elizabeth Rubin, "A Saudi Response on Reform: Round Up the Usual Dissidents," *New York Times,* April 2, 2004.

5. Roula Khalaf, "'There is a Dangerous Period Coming': Between Reform and Repression, the House of Saud Faces its Greatest Peril," *Financial Times,* November 18, 2003.

6. Quoted in "Freedom Calls, at Last," *The Economist,* April 3, 2004. p. 47

7. John F. Burns, "The Road Ahead May be Even Rougher," *New York Times,* April 7, 2004; and Thomas L. Friedman, "Kicking Over the Chessboard," *New York Times,* April 18, 2004.

8. See James Bennet, "The Parallels of Wars Past," *New York Times,* April 10, 2004.

9. James Bennet, "Sharon Coup: U.S. Go-Ahead," *New York Times,* April 15, 2004.

10. Jackson Diehl, "Foresight Was 20/20," *Washington Post,* January 5, 2004.

11. For the pre-war utopian blueprint for post-war Iraq, see George Packer, "Dreaming of Democracy," *New York Times Magazine,* March 2, 2003.

12. On Ahmed Chalabi, see Heidi Kingstone, "Man With a Mission," *Financial Times,* December 20/21, 2003.

13. See Rajiv Chandrasekaran and Karl Vick, "Revolts in Iraq Deepen Crisis in Occupation," *Washington Post,* April 17, 2004; James Risen, "Account of Shiite Revolt Contradicts White House Stand," *New York Times,* April 8, 2004; and Carla Ann Robbins and el., "As Insurgency in Iraq Rages, Bush Faces Unappealing Option," *Wall Street Journal,* April 9, 2004.

14. Edward Wong, "Once-Ruling Sunnis Unite To Regain Piece of the Pie," *New York Times,* January 12, 2004.

15. See David Gardner and el., "Ali Sistani: The Keeper of Iraq's Keys," *Financial Times,* November 15/16, 2003; and Vali Nasr, "Understanding Sistani's Role," *Washington Post,* April 19, 2004.

16. See Greg Jaffe and Christopher Cooper, "Shiite Militants Pose New Threat to U.S. in Iraq," *Wall Street Journal,* April 6, 2004; and Edward Wong, "Cleric's Militia Upend Shiite Power Balance," *New York Times,* April 21, 2004.

17. See Steven R. Weisman, "Kurdish Region in Northern Iraq Will Get to Keep Special Status," *New York Times,* January 5, 2004; Peter Spiegel, "Kurds Put Up Fresh Hurdle to Iraq Transition," *Financial Times,* January 1, 2004; and William Safire, "The Kurdish Question," *New York Times,* January 14, 2004.

18. See Neil MacFarquhar, "Gains by Kin in Iraq Inflame Anger at Syria," *New York Times,* March 24, 2004.

19. See Roula Khalaf, "Iraq: Will the County's Fragile Unity Survive the Handover of Sovereignty," *Financial Times,* June 28, 2004.

20. See Robin Wright, "U.S. Wary as Iran Works to Increase Influence in Iraq," *Washington Post,* June 12, 2004; and Jim Hoagland, "Obsessed with Iran," *Washington Post,* May 28, 2004.

21. See Sadi Baig, "A Clean Break for Israel, *Asia Times,* June 30, 2004. Available online at: http://www.atimes.com/atimes/Middle_East/FF30Ak07.html.

22. See Dexter Filkins, "Kurds Advancing to Reclaim Land in Northern Iraq," *New York Times,* June 20, 2004.

23. See Steven Weisman, "Kurds Find U.S. Alliance is Built on Shifting Sands," *New York Times,* June 11, 2003.

24. See Seymour M. Hersh, "Plan B: As June 30th Approaches, Israel Looks to the Kurds," *The New Yorker,* June 28, 2004.

25. See Edward Wong, "Uprising Has Increased the Influence of Sunni Clerics," *New York Times,* May 31, 2004.

26. See Karl Vick and Anthony Shadid, "Fallujah Gains Mythic Air," *Washington Post,* April 13, 2004; Jeffrey Gettleman, "Anti-U.S. Outrage United A Growing Iraqi Resistance," *New York Times,* April 11, 2004; Farnaz Fasshi, "Iraqis Increasingly Sympathize With Rebels," *Wall Street Journal,* April 12, 2004; and Edward Wong, "Iraqi Nationalism Takes Root, Sort of," *New York Times,* April 25, 2004.

27. See Stephen Fidler, "Focus Shift from Terrorism to Iraq Caused Problems," *Financial Times,* July 7, 2004.

28. The author quoted in Walter Pincus, "CIA Analyst Assails War on Terrorism," *Washington Post,* June 26, 2004.

29. See Jeffrey Gettleman, "The Baatihfication of Fallujah: Mohammad Latif's Troops—including the insurgents who had battling the Americans—are patrolling the streets and being paid in U.S. dollars," *The New York Times Magazine,* June 20, 2004.

30. Dexter Filkins and Robert F. Worth, "Armored Forces Blast Their Way Into Rebel Nest," *New York Times,* November 14, 2004.

31. L. Carl Brown, *International Politics and the Middle East: Old Rules, Dangerous Games* (Princeton, N.J.: Princeton University Press, 1984), p. 171.

32. Ibid., p. 16.

33. Guy Dinmore, "Washington Hardliners War of Engaging With Iran," *Financial Times,* March 17, 2004.

34. The references in this chapter dealing with U.S. policy in the Middle East are based in part of the following sources: Warren Bass, *Support Any Friend: Kennedy's Middle East and the Making of the U.S.-Israeli Alliance* (New York: Oxford University Press, 2003); Stephen Kizner: *All the Shah's Men: An American Coup and the Roots of Middle East Terror* (New York: John Wiley and Sons, 2003); Donald Neff, *Warriors for Jerusalem: The Six Days that Changed the Middle East* (New York: Simon & Schuster, 1984); Donald Neff, *Warriors at Suez: Eisenhower Takes America in the Middle East* (New York: Simon & Schuster, 1981); Donald Neff, *Warriors Against Israel:*

How Israel Won the Battle to Become America's Ally (Beltsville; Maryland: Amana Books, 1992); Michael B. Oren, *Six Days of War: June 1967 and the Making of the Modern Middle East* (New York: Presidio Press, 2003); Henry A. Kissinger, *Years of Upheaval* (New York: Random House, 1987); Henry A. Kissinger, *Years of Renewal* (New York: Simon & Schuster, 1999); Henry A. Kissinger, *The White House Years* (New York: Little Brown & Company, 1979); Steven L. Spiegel, *The Other Arab-Israeli Conflict: Making America's Middle East Policy from Truman to Reagan* (University of Chicago Press, 1986); William B. Quandt, *Peace Process: American Diplomacy and the Arab-Israeli Conflict since 1967* (University of California Press, 2001); William B. Quandt, *Camp David: Peacemaking and Politics* (Washington, D.C.: The Brookings Institution, 1986); Judith A. Klinghoffer, *Vietnam, Jews and the Middle East: Unintended Consequences* (Palgrave Macmillan, 1999).

35.   Quoted in George Crile, *Charlie Wilson's War: The Extraordinary Story of the Largest Covert Operation in History* (New York: Atlantic Monthly Press, 2003), p. 513.

36.   For a thorough analysis of American relationship with Pakistan and the development in Afghanistan, see Leon T. Hadar, *"Pakistan in America's War against Terrorism: Strategic Ally or Unreliable Client,"* Cato Policy Analysis, No. 43, May 8, 2002. Available online at: http://www.cato.org/pubs/pas/pa–436es.html.

37.   For a history of the British experience in the Middle East, see David Fromkin, *A Peace to End All Peace: The Fall of the Ottoman Empire and the Creation of the Modern Middle East* (New York: Avon Books, 1989).

38.   Roula Khalaf and Guy Dinmore, "Reforming the Arab World: The US is Serious—It wants to Change the Middle East but it Doesn't Know How," *Financial Times,* March 23, 2004.

39.   "On Prudence and Restraints in Foreign Policy," Susan Windybank talks to Owen Harris, *Policy,* Autumn 2002. Available online at: http://www.cis.org.au/Policy/aut2002/polaut02–6.htm.

40.   Niall Ferguson, *Colossus: The Price of America's Empire,* (New York: The Penguin Press, 2004).

41.   Michael Ignatieff, "The Burden," *New York Times Magazine,* January 7, 2003.

42.   Max Boot, *The Savage Wars of Peace: Small Wars and the Rise of American Power* (New York: Basic Books, 2002).

43.   Corey Robin, "Grand Designs: How 9/11 Unified Conservatives in Pursuit of Empire," *Washington Post,* May 2, 2004.

44.   See Leon Hadar, "U.S. Empire? Let's Get Real," *Los Angeles Times,* July 2, 2003.

45.   Peter Galbraith, "How to Get Out of Iraq," *The New York Review of Books,* May 13, 2004.

46.   Niall Ferguson, "The Last Insurgency," *New York Times,* April 18, 2004.

47.   On the political history of Iraq, see Sandra MacKey, *The Reckoning: Iraq and the Legacy of Saddam Hussein* (New York: W. W. Norton, 2003).

48.   Galbraith, "How to Get Out of Iraq," p. 44.

49.   See Jon Lee Anderson, "The Candidate: The Scion of a Famous Shiite Family Says that, If Elected, He Can Run Iraq," *The New Yorker,* February 2, 2004; and Anthony Shadid, "Call of History Draws Iraqi Cleric to the Political Fore," *Washington Post,* February 1, 2004.

50.   Jon Lee Anderson, "Letter From Baghdad: The Uprising," *The New Yorker,* May 3, 2004.

51.   Amy Chua and Jed Rubenfeld, "Never Underestimate the Power of Ethnicity in Iraq," *Washington Post,* January 4, 2004.

52. See Barbara Lerner, "Rumsfeld's War, Powell's Occupation: Rumsfeld wanted Iraqis in on the action—right from the beginning," *National Review Online* April 30, 2004. Available online at: http://www.nationalreview.com/comment/lerner 200404300929.asp.

53. George Will, "Time for Bush To See the Realities of Iraq," *Washington Post*, May 4, 2004.

54. Quoted in Frank Rich, "'Lawrence of Arabia' Redux," *New York Times*, April 18, 2004.

55. Ibid.

56. Michael Ledeen, "Creative Destruction: How to Wage a Revolutionary War," *National Review Online*, September 20, 2001. Available online at: http://www.nationalreview.com/contributors/ledeen092001.shtml.

CHAPTER 3

1. See Bob Woodward, *Plan of Attack* (New York: Simon & Schuster, 2004).

2. An April 14, 2004, agreement between Israeli Prime Minister Ariel Sharon and U.S. President George W. Bush, set out in an exchange of letters, rested on the understanding that within a framework of a final status agreement, Israel would keep big settlements in the West Bank. See Harvey Morris, "A Crushing Setback for Sharon: What Now for His Plan to Withdraw from Gaza After Rejection by His Own Party?," *Financial Times*, May 4, 2004.

3. Daniel Yergin, *The Prize: The Epic Quest for Oil, Money and Power* (New York: Simon & Schuster, 1991), p. 758.

4. Paul Starobin, "Rethinking Zionisn," *National Journal*, April 24, 2004.

5. Donald Losman, "Oil Denial: An Empty Fear," *Cato Institute Daily Commentary*, October 13, 2001. Available online at: http://www.cato.org/dailys/10-13-01.html. And see also "Economic Security: A National Security Folly?," *Cato Institute Policy Analysis*, no. 409, August 1, 2001.

6. See James Gleick, *Chaos: Making a New Science* (New York: Viking, 1987), and pp. 20–23 about the Butterfly Effect.

7. David Fromkin, *A Peace to End All Peace: The Fall of the Ottoman Empire and the Creation of the Modern Middle East* (New York: Avon Books, 1989), pp. 20–23.

8. On the debate between realism, idealism, and other schools of thoughts in U.S. foreign policy, see Walter Russell Mead, *Special Providence: American Foreign Policy and How It Changed the World* (New York: Routledge, 2002); and Walter McDougall, *Promised Land, Crusader State: The American Encounter with the World Since 1776* (New York: Houghton Mifflin, 1998). Also, for a general discussion on the philosophical sources of foreign policy schools of thoughts, see Michael W. Doyle, *Ways of War and Peace: Realism, Liberalism, and Socialism* (New York: W. W. Norton & Company, 1997).

9. Alexander Hamilton quoted in Ron Chernow, *Alexander Hamilton* (New York: The Penguin Press, 2004).

10. For a comparison of the market and politics, see Friedrich A. Hayek, *The Constitution of Liberty* (Chicago: The University of Chicago Press, 1960).

11. See Philip Bobbitt, *The Shield of Achilles: War, Peace, and the Course of History* (New York: Alfred A. Knopf, 2002).

12. The discussion between Welles and Elath is described in Eliahu Elath, *The Struggle for Statehood* (Hebrew) (Tel Aviv: Am Oved, 1983) Vol. 1, pp. 144–45.

13. James M. Buchanan and Gordon Tullock, *The Calculus of Consent: Logical Foundations of Constitutional Democracy* (Ann Arbor: University of Michigan Press, 1966), pp. 286–87.

14. Robert Higgs, "U.S. Military Spending in the Cold War Era: Opportunity Costs, Foreign Crises, and Domestic Constraints," *Cato Institute Policy Analysis*, no. 114, November 30, 1988, p. 17.

15. On AIPAC and other elements of the pro-Israel coalition in Washington, see J. J. Goldberg *Jewish Power: Inside the American Jewish Establishment* (New York: Perseus Publishing, 1997); and Paul Findley, *They Dare to Speak Out: People and Institutions Confront Israel's Lobby* (New York: Lawrence, 1985).

16. See Barry M. Rubin *Paved With Good Intentions: The American Experience and Iran* (New York: Oxford University Press, 1993).

17. See Laurie Mylroie, "The Baghdad Alternative," *Orbis* 32, no. 3, Summer 1988.

18. See Elsa Walsh, "The Prince: How the Saudi Ambassador became Washington's Indispensable Operator," *The New Yorker*, March 24, 2003; David Plotz, "Saudi Ambassador Prince Bandar: Why Washington's Smoothest Diplomat if Falling from Favor," *Slate*, October 24, 2001. Available online at: http://slate.msn.com/id/2057214/ and Michael Massing, "Deal Breakers," *The American Prospect*, March 11, 2002. Available online at: http://www.prospect.org/print/V13/5/massing-m.html.

19. Guy Dinmore and Roula Khalaf, "The U.S. National Interest is Caught Up with the Saudis in a Very Complex Way. They are More Than a Gas Pump," *Financial Times*, November 19, 2003.

20. Andrew Higgins, "In Quest for Energy Security, U.S. Makes Bet: On Democracy," *Wall Street Journal*, February 4, 2004.

21. In Roula Khalaf, "'There is a Dangerous Period Coming': Between reform and Repression, the House of Saud Faces Its Greatest Peril," *Financial Times*, November 18, 2003.

22. Figures in Tim Appenzeller, "The End of Cheap Oil," *National Geographic*, June 2004, pp. 88–89, Vol. 205, No. 6.

23. Daniel Yergin, "Gulf Oil: How Important Is It Anyway?" *Financial Times*, March 22/23, 2003.

24. Donald Losman, "Oil Denial: An Empty Fear," *Cato Institute Daily Commentary*, October 13, 2001. Available online at: http://www.cato.org/dailys/10–13–01.html. And see "Economic Security: A National Security Folly?," *Cato Institute Policy Analysis*, no. 409, August 1, 2001.

25. Jerry Taylor, "Blood for Oil," *Cato Institute Daily Commentary,*" March 13, 2003. Available online at: *http://www.cato.org/dailys/03–18–03.html.*

26. Quoted in Losman, "Oil Denial: An Empty Fear."

27. See Leon T. Hadar, "Creating a Policy of Constructive Disengagement in the Middle East," *Cato Institute Policy Analysis*, no. 125, December 29, 1989.

28. See Leon T. Hadar, "Reforming Israel Before It's Too Late," *Foreign Policy*, Winter 1990–91; and "Letter From Washington," in *Journal of Palestine Studies* XX no. 6, Summer 1991, and XXI no. 2, Winter 1992.

29. Leon T. Hadar, "America's Moment in the Middle East," *Current History*, January 1996; and "Letter From Washington," in *Journal of Palestine Studies* XXVII no. 3, Spring 1998 and XXXVIII no. 1, Spring 1998.

30. See Ehud Barak, "Camp David and After: An Exchange," *The New York Review of Books*, June 2002, Volume 49, No. 10. Robert Malley and Hussein Agha, "Camp

David: The Tragedy of Errors," *The New York Review of Books*, Volume 48, Number 13, August 9, 2001.

31. See Leon T. Hadar, "The Real Lesson of the Oslo Accord: 'Localize' the Arab-Israeli Conflict," *Cato Foreign Policy Briefing*, no. 31, May 9, 1994.

32. See Gerard Baker and Stephen Fidler, "America's democratic imperialists: How the neoconservatives Rose from Humility to Empire in Two years," *Financial Times*, March 6, 2003.

33. See Steven L. Spiegel, *The Other Arab-Israeli Conflict: Making America's Middle East Policy from Truman To Reagan* (Chicago: Chicago University Press, 1986).

34. For the neoconservatives' influence in the Reagan Administration, see Leon T. Hadar, "The 'Neocons'" From the Cold War to the 'Global Intifadah,'" *Washington Report on Middle East Affairs*, April 1991.

35. On the debate inside the Bush Administration, see Bob Woodward, *Bush At War* (New York: Simon & Schuster, 2002).

36. See Robert Kaiser, "Bush and Sharon Nearly Identical On Mideast Policy," *Washington Post*, February 9, 2003; and Arnaud de Borchgrave, "A Bush-Sharon Doctrine," *Washington Times*, February 14, 2003.

37. Aluf Benn, "Washington is Voting for Sharon," *Ha'aretz*, November 28, 2002, and Gideon Samet, "The American Obstacle to Peace, *Ha'aretz*, December 18, 2002.

38. See discussion of the role of the neoconservatives in Giles Kepel, *The War for Muslim Minds: Islam and the West* (Cambridge: Belknap Press, 2004).

CHAPTER 4

1. Gerard Baker, "The U.S. Has Come to See the Status Quo as Inherently Dangerous," *Financial Times*, May 30, 2003.

2. Condoleeza Rice, "Promoting the National Interest," *Foreign Affairs*, 79, no. I (January/February 2000), p. 53.

3. "George Bush's European Tour: A Bumpy Landing," *Economist*, March 16, 2001, p. 29.

4. Alan Cowell, "A Worried World Shows Discord," *New York Times*, March 1999, 2003; and Marc Champion, Charles Fleming, Ian Johnson, Carla Ann Robbins, "Behind the U.S., Rift with Europeans: Slights and Politics," *Wall Street Journal*, March 27, 2003.

5. Steven R. Weisman, "A Long Winding Road to a Diplomatic Dead End," *New York Times*, March 17, 2003.

6. "Outrage at 'Old Europe' Remarks," *BBC News*, 23 January, 2003. Available online at: http://news.bbc.co.uk/2/hi/europe/2687403.stm.

7. Felicity Barringer, "UN Split as Allies Dismiss Deadline on Iraq," *New York Times*, March 8, 2003.

8. "NATO Crisis Deepens Rift Between US and Europe," *Financial Times*, February 11, 2002; Judy Dempsey, "NATO Agrees to Strengthen Country's Border Defense," *Financial Times*, March 20, 2003.

9. Henry Kissinger, "The Atlantic Alliance in its Gravest Crisis," *Tribune Media Services International*, February 9, 2003. Available online through: http://www.tms-features.com/tmsfeatures/subcategory.jsp.

10. On the framing of political reality, including foreign policy, see David L. Altheide, *Creating Reality* (New York: Sage Publications, 1976); James Aronson, *The Press and the Cold War* (Indianapolis: Bobbs-Merrill, 1978); Peter Berger and

Thomas Luckmann, *The Social Construction of Reality* (New York: Doubleday-Anchor, 1967); Murray Edelman, *The Symbolic Use of Politics* (Chicago: University of Illinois Press, 1985); Erving Goffman, *Frame Analysis* (Philadelphia: University of Pennsylvania Press, 1974; Gaye Tuchman, *Making News: A Study in the Construction of Reality* (New York: The Free Press, 1985).

11. Robert Kagan, "Power and Weakness," *Policy Review*, no. 113, June 2002. Available online at: http://www.policyreview.org/JUN02/kagan_print.html. Kagan developed his thesis in a book, *Of Paradise and Power: America vs. Europe the New World Order* (New York: Knopf, 2003).

12. For the results of the latest survey by the Chicago Council on Foreign Relations on European and American attitudes on these and other policy issues, see Craig Kennedy and Marshall Bolton, "The Real Transatlantic Gap," *Foreign Policy*, November-December 2002. Quoted in Tony Judt in "The Way We Live," *New York Review of Books*, March 27, 2003, p. 8. On opinion polls in Europe and the United States on the Middle East, see "Dealing with Iraq: When Squabbling Turns Too Dangerous," *Economist*, February 15, 2003, pp. 23–25.

13. "Fear of America," *Economist*, February 1, 2003, p. 46.

14. Quoted in "Enough, Children," *Economist*, March 1, 2003, p. 34.

15. Victor Davis Hanson, "Goodbye to Europe?" *Commentary*, October 2002, p. 4.

16. See Mark Steyn, "War Between America and Europe," *Spectator*, December 29, 2001

17. "Old America v. New Europe, *Economist*, February 22, 2003, p. 32.

18. See "Half a Billion Americans?" *Economist*, August 22, 2002, pp. 20–22; and George W. Will, "Europe's Decline," *Washington Post*, March 11, 2002.

19. "American Values: Living with a Superpower," *Economist*, January 2, 2003. Available online at: http://economist.com/PrinterFriendly.cfm?Story_ID=1511812.

20. Richard Bernstein, "Germans Balk at the Price of Economic Change," *New York Times*, March 19, 2003.

21. Timothy Garton Ash, "Anti-European in America," *New York Review of Books*, February 13, 2003. Available online at: http://www.nybooks.com/articles/16059.

22. Goldberg is quoted in Paul Gottfried, "Cheese-eating Surrender Monkeys," *Spectator*, June 1, 2002.

23. See Tony Judt, "Anti-Americans Abroad," *New York Review of Books*, May 1, 2003.

24. "Old America v. New Europe," *Economist*.

25. Victor David Hanson, "Geriatric Teenagers," *National Review Online*, May 2, 2003. Available online at: http://www.nationalreview.com/hanson/hanson050203.asp.

26. Emmanuel Todd, *After the Empire: The Breakdown of the American Order* (New York: Columbia University Press, 2003).

27. George Will, "'Final Solution,' Phase 2," *Washington Post*, May 2, 2002.

28. Christopher Caldwell, "Liberte, Egalite, Judeophbia," *Weekly Standard*," March 6, 2002, p. 25.

29. Charles Krauthammer, "Europe and 'Those People,'" *Washington Post*, April 26, 2002.

30. David Brooks, "Among the Bourgeoisophobes," *Weekly Standard*, March 15, 2002. Available online at: http://www.weeklystandard.com/Content/Public/Articles/000/000/001/102gwtnf.asp.

31. Quoted in John Lloyd, "Sign of Life from the Past," *FTWeekend, Financial Times*, November 16, 2002.

32. Tony Judt in "The Way We Live," *New York Review of Books*, p.8.

33. See "Anti-Semitism: Europe and the Jews," *Economist*, May 4, 2002, pp. 12–13.

34. Polls are available in "Anti-Semitism in Europe: Is It Really Rising?" *Economist*, May 4, 2002, pp. 47–48.

35. Judt in "The Way We Live" refers to "L'image des juifs en France" at www.sofres.com/etudes/pol/130600_imagejuifs.htm and compares it with "Anti-Semitism and Prejudice in America: Highlights from an ADL Survey, November 1998."

36. "Germany and its Jews," *Economist*, June 15, 2002, p. 54.

37. Judt, "The Way We Live," *New York Review of Books*, p. 8.

38. See Robin Shepherd, "In Europe, Is It a Matter of Fear or Loathing?" *Washington Post*, January 25, 2004.

39. See Nadav Safran, *Israel: The Embattled Ally*, (Cambridge: Harvard University Press, 1978), pp. 359–81; and Avner Cohen, *Israel and the Bomb* (New York: Columbia University Press, 1998).

40. See Leon T. Hadar, "The United States, Europe, and the Middle East: Hegemony or Partnership," *World Policy Journal*, VIII, no. 3, Spring 1991.

41. See Stepping on Israeli Toes: Britain Acting for the European Union Has offended the Israeli Government," *Economist*, March 19, 1998.

42. See "Palestinians and the EU: European Attitudes Have Shifted With The Change of Israeli Prime Minister," *Economist*, April 20, 2000.

43. "A Grudge Match: Why the Israelis and Europeans Getting on so Badly," *Economist*, January 11, 2003.

44. See Robert Kagan, "Resisting Superpowerful Temptations," *Washington Post*, April 9, 2003; and Max Boot, "America Must Not be Tied by Lilliputians," *Financial Times*, March 10, 2003.

45. See Anne Applebaum, "Here Comes the New Europe," *Washington Post*, January 28, 2003; and Amity Shlaes, "Rumsfeld Is Right about Fearful Europe," *Financial Times*, January 28, 2003.

46. James C. Bennett, "An Anglosphere Primer," presented to the *Foreign Policy Research Institute*. Available online at: htttp://www.pattern.com//bennettj-anglosphereprimer.html.

47. See Paul Johnson, "Au Revoir, Petite France," *Wall Street Journal*, March 18, 2003.

48. Doug Struck, "Australian Leader Reaps Political Benefits of War, *Washington Post*, May 18, 2003.

49. Glenn Frankel, "Blair's Policies Driven by International Vision," *Washington Post*, April 3, 2003.

50. See Amity Shlaes, "New Europe, New Divide," *Financial Times*, February 22/23, 2003.

51. "Central Europe and the United States: We Still Rather Like the Americans," *Economist*, February 1, 2003, pp. 43–44

52. "America Values: Living with a Superpower," *Economist*, January 2, 2003,

53. Andrew Higgins, "'New Europe' Wary of U.S., Too," *Wall Street Journal*, March 18, 2003.

54. Figures in the *New York Times*, January 24, 2003, quoted in Judt, "The Way We Live," *New York Review of Books*, p.8.

55. See James Blitz, "European and the US Must Unite, Says Blair," *Financial Times*, March 3, 2003; and Quentin Peel, "An Understanding Lost in Translation," *Financial Times*, March 3, 2003.

56. See Robert Graham, "Chirac Vents Ire Over Behavior of EU Candidates," *Financial Times*, February 19, 2003.

57. In "European Rift," a *News Hour with Jim Lehrer* transcript, January 30, 2003. Available online at: http://www.pbs.org/newshour/bb/middle_east/jan-june03/iraq_1–30.html.

58. See Quentin Peel, "Paris and Berlin Remember What Links Them," *Financial Times,* January 21, 2003; and Christopher Rohads, "French Word, German Accent: Rapprochement," *Wall Street Journal,* March 25, 2003.

59. See Robert Graham, "No One Dares Put a Price on the Cost of Breaking So Sharply with the U.S. Over a Major Issue," *Financial Times,* March 12, 2003.

60. See "Why Gerhard Schroder has Gone Out on a Limb," *Economist,* September 14, 2002, pp. 51–52; and Huge Williamson, "War Berlin Takes Tough Line Against Waging War, *Financial Times,* January 1, 2003.

61. See Michael Gonzalez, "Lest We Forget," *Wall Street Journal,* April 10, 2003.

62. Pamela Rolf, "For Spanish Leader, War Is A Gamble," *The Washington Post,* March 20, 2003.

63. Gerard Baker, "Why Blair is in with the Bad Guys," *Financial Times,* February 6, 2004.

64. See "The European Union: Menage a Trois," *Economist,* February 21, 2004.

65. See "Three's a Crowd," *Economist,* January 31, 2004.

66. Baker, "Why Blair is In with the Bad Guys," *Financial Times,* February 6, 2004.

67. Olivier Roy, "Europe Won't be Fooled Again," *New York Times,* May 13, 2003.

68. "Behind the U.S., Rift With Europeans: Slights and Politics," *Wall Street Journal,* March 27, 2003, p. 1.

69. Roy, "Europe Won't be Fooled Again."

70. See Martin Sieff, "Making the Middle East Safe for Bin Laden," *American Conservative,* May 19, 2003.

71. See Philip Stephens, "If America is to Remodel the World, it Must Start in Israel," *Financial Times,* January 1, 2003.

72. For a comprehensive analysis of European involvement in the region, see Leon T. Hadar, *Quagmire: America in the Middle East,* and especially chapter 6, "Between American Hegemony and European Free Riding: Confronting the Gulf War Rift," and chapter 7, "The Coming American-European Struggle Over the Middle East," (Washington, D.C.: Cato Institute, 1992); Leon T. Hadar, "Meddling in the Middle East: Europe Challenges U.S. Hegemony in the Region," *Mediterranean Quarterly,* Vol. 7, No. 4, Fall 1996.

73. See Donald Neff, *Warriors at Suez: Eisenhower Takes America into the Middle East* (Simon & Schuster, 1981).

74. Kissinger, "The Atlantic Alliance in its Gravest Crisis," *Tribune Media Services International.*

75. Quoted in Kissinger, "The Atlantic Alliance in its Gravest Crisis," *Tribune Media Services International.*

76. David Newsome, "America Engulfed," *Foreign Policy* Vol. 43, Summer 1981, p. 26.

77. See Raymond Cohen, "Twice Bitter? The European Community's 1987 Middle East Initiative," *Middle East Review* 20, no. 3, Spring 1988.

78. Cohen, "Twice Bitten? The European Community 1987 Middle East Initiative." *Middle East Review.*

79. See President Jimmy Carter's State of the Union Address 1980, January 21, 1980. Available online at: http://www.jimmycarterlibrary.org/documents/speeches/su80jec.phtml.

80. See Ellen Laipson, "Europe's Role in the Middle East: Enduring Ties, Emerging Opportunities," *Middle East Journal* 44 (Winter 1990).

81. This argument is developed in Leon T. Hadar, "The Persian Gulf: Iraq and the Post–Cold War Order," in M. E. Ahrari and James H. Noyes, *The Persian Gulf After the Cold War* (Wesport; Connecticut: Praeger, 1993).

82. Kevin Phillips, *American Dynasty: Aristocracy, Fortune, and the Politics of Deceit in the House of Bush* (New York: Viking, 2004). See chapters 5, 8 and 9.

83. Klare quoted in Robert Dreyfuss, "The Thirty-Year Itch," *Mother Jones*, March-April 2003, p. 41.

84. Ellen Laipson, "Europe's Role in the Middle East: Enduring Ties, Emerging Opportunities," *Middle East Journal* 44 (Winter 1990), p. 16.

85. *Crisis in the Persian Gulf Region: U.S. Policy Options and Implications.* Hearings before the Committee on Armed Services, U.S. Senate (Washington, D.C.: U.S. Government Printing Office, 1990), p. 278.

86. See Charles Krauthammer, "Bless Our Pax Americana," *Washington Post*, March 22, 1991; and Joshua Muravchik, "At Last, Pax Americana," *New York Times*, March 24, 1991.

87. Josef Joffe, "In the Gulf, Allies Are Doing Their Part," *New York Times*, October 9, 1991.

88. Quoted in David Border, "The Thatcher View: America Must Leader," *Washington Post*, March 13, 1991.

89. *Le Monde*, December 6, 1991, as quoted in Tominlav Sunic, "The Gulf War in Europe," *Chronicles*, May 1991, p. 49.

90. Quoted in Alan Riding, "French Maneuvering: Taking the Lead for Europe," *New York Times*, January 6, 1991.

91. Quoted in Flora Lewis, "A Shabby French Sulk," *New York Times*, February 29, 1991.

92. See Nicholas Henderson, "The Special Relationship," *Spectator*, January 19, 1991.

93. Quoted in Tominlav Sunic, "The Gulf War in Europe," *Chronicles*, May 1991, p. 49.

94. See Sabri Sayari, "Turkey: The Changing European Security Environment and the Gulf States," *Middle East Journal*, Winter 1992, p. 14.

95. Quoted in "The Second Trojan's Empire," *Economist*, September 29, 1990.

96. See Ian Buruma, "The Pan Axis from Germany to Japan," *New York Review of Books*, April 25, 1991.

97. Quoted in Shada Islam, "European Community: Let US in, Or Else," *Middle East International*, April 19, 1991, p. 14.

98. See Charles Krauthammer, "Bless Our Pax Americana," *Washington Post*, March 22, 1991.

99. Quoted in Walter S. Mossberg, Urban C. Lehrer, and Fredrick Kempe, "Some in U.S. Ask Why Germany, Japan Bear So Little of Gulf War," *Wall Street Journal*, January, 11, 1992.

100. Quoted in Hella Pick, "Europe left out of Gulf Decisions," *Guardian*, December 14, 1990.

101. Patrick E. Tyler, "U.S. Strategy Plans Calls for Insuring No Rivals Develop," *New York Times*, March 7, 1992.

102. Quoted in Theo Sommer, "A World beyond Order and Control," *Guardian Weekly* 28, 1991, p. 10.

103. See Leon Hadar, "Covering the New World Disorder: The Press Rushes In Where Clinton Fears to Tread," *Columbia Journalism Review*, July/August 1994.

104. Quoted in William Drozdiak, "French Peace Plan Draws Lebanese, Syrian Backing," *Washington Post*, April 23, 1996.

105. Quoted in William Drozdiak, "U.S.-French Dispute Said to Continue Despite Lebanon Cease-Fire," *Washington Post*, April 30, 1996. See also David Buchan, "France's Mideast Initiative Rebuffed," *Financial Times*, April 17, 1996 and "France Pressed Peace Role in Middle East," *Financial Times*, May 1, 1996.

106. Quoted in Dominique Moisi, "The Allure of Gaullism," *Financial Times*, April 19, 1996. See also, "Jacques Chirac and France's Middle East Policy," *JIME Review* (Japanese Institute of Middle Eastern Economics) Summer 1995, pp. 5–22.

107. See Stephanie Nall," "D'Amato Confident His Iran-Ban Will Pass," *Journal of Commerce*, March 17, 1995; and David E. Sanger, "Congress Curbs Iran Investment from Overseas," *New York Times*, June 20, 1996.

108. See Robert S. Greenberger and Laurie Lande, "Progress of Iran-Sanctions Measure in Congress Signals Comeback of Pro-Israeli Lobbying Group," *Wall Street Journal*, June 18, 1996.

109. Quoted in Robert Swann, "Self-Interest Wins Out," *Middle East International*, December 20, 1991, p. 13.

CHAPTER 5

1. See Scott C. McDonald, "European-Middle Eastern Relations: What Looms on the Horizon," *Middle East Insight* 8, July-August 1991, p. 4.

2. Brian Beedham, "A Survey of Defense and Democracies: A New Flag," *Economist*, September 1, 1990.

3. Srdja Trifkovic, "NATO in Afghanistan," *Chronicles* magazine online, August 20, 2003. Available online at: http://www.chroniclesmagazine.org/News/Trifkovic/NewsST082003.html.

4. Patrick E. Tyler, "U.S. Strategy Plan Calls for Insuring No Rivals Develop," *New York Times*, March 7, 1992.

5. *The National Security Strategy of the United States of America*, issued by the White House, September 2002.

6. See Michael Moran, "France Plays the "Eisenhower Card," *MSNBC News*, March 6, 2002. Available online at: http://stacks.msnbc.com/news/881591.asp>

7. Barry Rubin, "1956 Suez Conflict Present Striking Parallels to Iraq," *Jewish Bulletin of Northern California*, February 21, 2003. Available online at: http://www.jewishsf.com/bk030221/comm2.shtml.

8. *Intelligence Online*, No. 447, February 2, 2003. Available online at: http://www.intelligenceonline.com/

9. Stephen Cohen, "Euro Shield," *Wall Street Journal*," March 29, 2003.

10. For a detailed discussion of this policy, see Diane B. Kuntz, *The Economic Diplomacy of the Suez Crisis* (Chapel Hill: University of North Carolina Press, 1991).

11. See Joseph Nye, "Europe is Too Powerful to be Ignored," *Financial Times*, March 11, 2003.

12. Niall Ferguson, "True Cost of Hegemony: Huge Debt," *New York Times*, April 20, 2003.

13. F. William Engdahl, "A New American Century? Iraq and the Hidden Euro-Dollar Wars," *Current Concerns*, No. 4, 2003. Available online at: http://www.current-concerns.ch/archive/contents04_03.php.

14. Ibid.

15. For the most detailed and comprehensive history of U.S. oil policies in the Middle East, see Daniel Yergin, *The Prize: The Epic Quest for Oil, Money and Power* (New

York: Simon & Schuster, 1991), especially part 2, "The Global Struggle." See also Leonard P. Liggio, "Oil and American Foreign Policy," *Libertarian Review*, July/August 1979, pp. 62–69.

16. Yergin, *The Prize*, p. 644.

17. Ibid., p. 634.

18. Engdahl, "A New American Century? Iraq and the Hidden Euro-Dollar Wars."

19. See Paul Kennedy, *The Rise and Fall of Great Powers* (New York: Random House, December, 1987).

20. Srdja Trifkovic, "Dollar, Achilles Hill of Empire," *Chronicles* magazine website, April 30, 2003. Available online at: http://chroniclesmagazine.org/News/Trifkovic/NewsST43003.html.

21. Melvyn Krauss, "The Euro Also Rises," *Wall Street Journal*, April 15, 2003.

22. See Youssef I. Ibrahim, "U.S.-Mideast Oil Ties Undergo Rapid Change," *Daily Star* Online (Beirut), January 22, 2004. Available online at: http://www.dailystar.com.lb/

23. See Robert McCartney, "French Businesses Say U.S. Boycott Is Hurting Them," *Washington Post*, March 6, 2003.

24. According to figures supplied by the Center for Defense Information and quoted in Gregg Easterbrook, "American Power Moves Beyond Mere Super," *New York Times*, March 7, 2003.

25. See Brandon Mitchener, "Europe Hears a Call for Arms," *Wall Street Journal*, April 29, 2003.

26. Judy Dempsey, "Europe Needs Its Own Security Strategy," *Financial Times*, March 9, 2003.

27. Barry Posen, "Europe Cannot Advance On Two Fronts," *Financial Times*, March 25, 2003.

28. George Parker, Daniel Dombey and Judy Dempsey, "Belgian Plan is a Sign of Multi-Speed Europe," *Financial Times*, March 26, 2003.

29. Robert J. McCartney, "4 European Leaders Form Pact to Boost Defense Cooperation, *Washington Post*, April 30, 2003; and Elaine Sciolino, "4-Nation Plan for Defense of Europe," *New York Times*, April 30, 2003.

30. Guy Dinmore, "NATO is the 'Glue' Holding Together the Transatlantic Relationship, Says Powell," *Financial Times*, April 30, 2003.

31. See Joe Stork, "New Enemies for a New World Order: From the Arc of Crisis to Global Intifadah," *Middle East Report* 176, May/June 1992.

32. Anthony De Jassey, "Lesson from the Gulf War," *National Review*, May 27, 1991.

33. See William Drozdiak, "France, Germany Unveil Crops as Step Toward European Defense," *Washington Post*, May 23, 1992.

34. For a discussion of these and related issues, see Judy Dempsey, "Words of War: European's First Security Doctrine Backs Away From American Style Pre-Emptive Military Intervention," *Financial Times*, December 5, 2003.

35. See Pepe Escobar, "(Dis)united Europe: Part 2—Ever Changing Alliances," *Asia Times*, February 7, 2004. Available online at: http://www.atimes.com/atimes/Front_Page/FB07Aa02.html

36. Charles Grant, "Europe Can Sell Its Defence Plan to Washington," *Financial Times*, December 12, 2003.

37. Judy Dempsey, "German Soldiers to Join Anglo-French Rapid Deployment "Battle Groups," *Financial Times*, February 11, 2003.

38. Marc Champion, "Balkan Balm for Fractured Ties," *Wall Street Journal*, April 15, 2003.

39. Bradley Graham, "NATO Weighs Wider Operations," *Washington Post,* December 2, 2003.

40. See Marc Champion, "U.S., Europe Seek to Mend Split," *Wall Street Journal,* January 26, 2004.

41. Mike Allen, "Allies Rancor Over Iraq Is 'Over' Bush Contends," *Washington Post,* June 27, 2004.

42. Elizabeth Bumiller, "Amid Protests, Bush Sees Thaw in Europe over Iraq," *New York Times,* June 27, 2004.

43. Elaine Sciolino, "Drifting NATO Finds New Purpose with Afghanistan and Iraq," *New York Times,* February 23, 2003.

44. See Roula Khalaf and Guy Dinmore, "Bush Seeks Backing for 'Greater Mideast' Plan, *Financial Times,* February 5, 2004. See also R. Nicholas Burns, "The New NATO and the Greater Middle East," Remarks at Conference on NAO and the Greater Middle East, Prague, Czech Republic, October 19, 2003. *US Department of State* Available online at: http://www.state.gov/p/eur/rls/rm/2003/25602pf.htm, and "U.S. Plans Middle East Pact," *AlJazeera.Net Available* online at: http://english. aljazeera.net/NR/exeres/554FAF3A-B267–427A-B9EC–54881BDE0A2E.htm.

45. See Eric Schmitt and Mark Landler, "Cheney Calls for More Unity In Fight Against Terrorism," *New York Times,* January 25, 2004; and Dick Cheney, "The Greater Middle East—the Bush Administration's Perspective," *theglobalist*.com Available online at: htttp://www.theglobalist.com/DBWWeb/printStoryID/ aspx?StoryID=3754.

46. Quoted in Escobar, "(Dis)united Europe."

47. See William Pfaff, "Washington Makes Nice," *International Herald Tribune,* January 29, 2004.

48. See Carla Anne Robbins, "Iraq-Contract Feud Reopens Wound," *Wall Street Journal,* December 11, 2003.

49. Quentin Peel, "A Big Idea that Europe Won't Buy," *Financial Times,* February 5, 2004.

50. Quoted in Alan Cowell, "Europe is Back Playing Its Flute to America's Trumpet," *New York Times,* February 22, 2004.

51. See Roula Khalaf, "Iran Still Under Pressure to Give Arms Assurance," and Guy Dinmore, "U.S. Backs Europeans Efforts With Misgivings," *Financial Times,* October 22, 2003; and Glenn Frankel, "Iran Vows to Curb Nuclear Activities," *Washington Post,* October 22, 2003.

52. Patrick E. Tyler and James Risen, "Secret Diplomacy Won Libya Pledge on Arms," *New York Times,* December 21, 2003.

53. Quoted in Cowell, "Europe is Back Playing Its Flute to America's Trumpet," *New York Times,* February 22, 2004.

54. See Steven Weisman, "U.S. Allies in New Effort to Get Along," New York Times, February 11, 2004; and Alain Dieckhoff, "The Israeli-Palestinian New War of Attrition: A European Perspective." Prepared for the IISS/CEPS European Security Forum, Brussels, March 11, 2002. Available online at: http://www.iiss.org. eusec/diecjhoff/htm.

55. Quoted in Quentin Peel, "A Big Idea that Europe Won't Buy," *Financial Times,* February 5, 2004.

56. See Marc Champion and Philip Shishkin, "U.S. Seeks Help on Mideast Project," *Wall Street Journal,* February 9, 2004: Bradley Graham, "NATO to Expand Force in Afghanistan, *Washington Post,* February 7, 2004.

57. See Glenn Kessler and Robin Wright, "Arabs and Europeans Questions 'Greater Middle East' Plan," *Washington Post*, February 22, 2004.
58. Glen Kessler and Robin Wright, "G–8 Poised to Back U.S. Plan for Mideast Democracy," *Washington Post*, June 8, 2004.
59. Mike Allen, "NATO Partners Agree to Train Iraqi Troops," *Washington Post*, June 28, 2004.
60. Robert Graham, "French President Spells Out Limits on Iraq Support," *Financial Times*, June 11, 2004.
61. A French analyst quoted in Philip Shishkin and Marc Champion, "NATO Splits on Afghanistan Mission," *Wall Street Journal*, June 30, 2004.
62. Raphael Minder and Guy de Jonquieres, "Barroso Criticizes 'Arrogant' America," *Financial Times*, June 14, 2004.
63. See Leon Hadar, "John Kerry—the European Candidate," *the globalist.com*, August 27, 2004. Available online at: http://www.theglobalist.com/DBWeb/StoryId.aspx?StoryId=4074.
64. See Richard Bernstein, "To Europeans, Rice Brings Mitigated Hope of Harmony, *New York Times*, November 20, 2004
65. Richard Phillips, "Why Europe Needs—and Wants—Bush to Win," *theglobalist.com*, October 13, 2004. Available online at: http://www.theglobalist.com/DBWeb/StoryId.aspx?StoryId=4208>

CHAPTER 6

1. See Romano Prodi and Chris Patten, "Europe's Commitment To Iraq," *Washington Post*, June 26, 2004.
2. Robert Kagan "Can NATO Patrol Palestine?" *Washington Post*, April 18, 2003.
3. Robert S. Greenberger and Karby Leggett, "President's Dream; Changing Not Just Regime but a Region," *Wall Street Journal*, March 21, 2003.
4. Christina Balis and Simon Serfaty, "Trading Battles: Europe's New Economic Crusade in the Middle East," *Euro-Focus* (Center for Strategic and International Studies) 9, no. 5 (May 22, 2003): 1.
5. Dominique Moisi, "The Allure of Gaullism," *Financial Times*, April 19, 1996.
6. See "De Michelis Urges 'Helsinki' Talks On War's Aftermath," *International Herald Tribune*, February 18, 1991.
7. Tom Burns, "EU Turns Attention to Southern Flank," *Financial Times*, November 27, 1996.
8. David Gardner and David White, "Clashed Delay Launch of 'Euro-Med' Pact," *Financial Times*, November 28, 2003.
9. See figures in Balis and Serfaty, p. 2.
10. See Roula Khalaf, "EU and US Clash over Mideast Bank," *Financial Times*, October 2, 1995.
11. See Tom Burns, "EU Turns Attention to Southern Flank," *Financial Times*, November 27, 1995.
12. I first broached the subject of Israel's accession to the EU in an op-ed published in May 2003; see Leon Hadar, "Iraq and Israel in the EU: Peace through Accession?" *inthenationalinterest.com*, May 21, 2003, Available online at: www.inthenationalinterest.com/Articles/ Vol2Issue 19/vol2issue19hadar.html. That same week, Israel's Foreign Minister Silvan Shalom informed an EU delegation that his country was considering applying for membership in the body; see Martin

Walker, "Analysis: Israel Weighing EU Membership," *United Press International,* May 21, 2003. Italian President Silvio Berlusconi, who assumed the six-month rotating presidency of the EU in July 2003, likewise indicated an interest in an expanded EU that would include Israel. See Zia Iqbal Shahid, "Israel Wants Full EU Membership," *News International* (Pakistan), July 7, 2003. Available online at: www.jang.com.pk/thenews/jul2003-daily/07- 07–2003/main/main 17.htm.

13.   Quoted in Safa Haeri, "Concocting a 'Greater Middle East' Brew,' *Asia Times,* March 4, 2004. Available online at: http://www.atimes.com/atimes/Middle_ East/FC04Ak06.html.

14.   See Howard W. French, "China Moves toward Another West: Central Asia," *New York Times,* April 23, 2004.

15.   See James Harding, "Bush Tries to Embrace Challenge of Emerging Superpower Competitor," *Financial Times,* November 22, 2003.

16.   In Andrew Higgins, "As China Surges, It Also Proves a Buttress to American Strength," *Wall Street Journal,* January 30, 2004.

17.   See Peter Wonacott, Jeane Whalen, and Bhushan Bahree, "China's Growing Thirst for Oil Remakes the World Market," *Wall Street Journal,* December 3, 2003.

18.   See David Pilling, "A Grown-Up Nation? The Hostage Crisis in Iraq Sharpens Debate Over Japan's Proper Role On the International Stage," *Financial Times,* April 14, 2004; and Anthony Faiola, "Japan's Military Sculpts a New Image in Iraqi Sand," *Washington Post,* February 10, 2004.

19.   Quotes and figures in Wonacott, Whalen and Bahree, "China's Growing Thirst for Oil Remakes the World Market," *Wall Street Journal.*

20.   Kennedy's conclusions and estimates mentioned in Lionel Barber, "The Power Paradox: The US Moves towards Selective Alliances and Away from 'Mindless Multilateralism,'" *Financial Times,* December 19, 2003.

21.   Quoted in Lionel Barber, "The Power Paradox," *Financial Times.*

22.   William Pfaff, "Against the World," *The American Conservative,* May 24, 2004.

23.   Leon T. Hadar, "What Green Peril?" *Foreign Affairs,* Vol. 72, No. 2, Spring 1993.

24.   See Leon T. Hadar, "Israel in the Post-Zionist Age: Being Normal and Loving It," *World Policy Journal,* XVI, no. 1, Spring 1999.

25.   That kind of approach was outlined in the report *A Clean Break: A New Strategy for Securing the Realm* prepared in 1996, submitted to then Israeli Prime minister Benjamin Netanyahu—long before the Second Intifadah and 9/11—by the Institute for Advanced Strategic and Political Studies (IASPS) in Jerusalem and was signed by such American neoconservative and pro-Likud figures such as Richard Perle, Douglas Feith, and David Wurmser. It called for developing a very ambitious long-term U.S.-Israel strategy to contain threats in the Middle East, providing Israel with the kind if security margin that would make it unnecessary for it to make territorial concessions to the Palestinians and Syria. For the complete report see the IASPS: website http://www/israeleconomy.org/strat1.htm.

26.   Hannah Arendt, *Anti-Semitism: Part I of The Origins of Totalitarianism* (New York: Harvest Books, 1968).

27.   Greg Jaffe, "At the Pentagon, Quirky PowerPoint Carries Big Punch," *Wall Street Journal,* May, 11, 2004.

Index

Iraq, 1–5, 12, 14–36, 40, 42–63, 69–75,
    87–100, 104–108, 112–118,
    120–127, 139–151, 154, 158–160,
    164–169, 171–173, 178, 180
    invasion of, 30, 32, 42, 51, 62, 72, 75,
        88, 98, 150, 169
    and nation building, 49–52
    and "no-fly zones," 15, 35
    post-Saddam, 26–28, 53–55, 165
Iraq-Iran War, 30
Islam, 7–8, 10–11, 31–32, 52–54, 57–59,
    71, 108–109, 117, 125–126, 168–179
    radical elements of, 3, 28–29, 40–41,
        73, 86, 130, 139, 178–179
Israel
    alliances with, 86, 95, 104, 111–112
    Jewish settlements, 57, 78, 81–82, 88,
        100, 120, 164
    Jewish state, 8, 12, 16, 37, 58, 60, 65,
        67–69, 77–78, 86, 99, 102, 130, 153,
        159, 164, 174, 178–179
    policy, 58, 64, 78, 89, 101–102, 130,
        159, 176–177
    problems facing, 173–179
    see also Gaza; West Bank
Israeli-Palestinian, 2, 16–17, 36, 61, 81,
    83–84, 92–93, 108, 119, 123–124,
    131, 150, 159–160, 162–163, 165

Japan, 5, 7, 75–76, 103–104, 112–113,
    123, 135–137, 140, 144, 153, 156,
    158, 167–169
Jordan, 26, 31, 33, 54, 68, 159, 161–163,
    165, 172–173
Judt, Tony, 100

Kagan, Robert, 87, 95–97, 103, 159
kaleidoscope model of Middle East, 13,
    25, 32–35, 41–42, 51–52, 54–56, 61,
    153, 180
Kennedy, John F., 36, 102
Kennedy, Paul, 138, 169
Kerry, John, 151
Kissinger, Henry, 92, 94, 109, 114–115,
    121, 137
Kohl, Helmut, 118
Kuhn, Thomas S., 6, 10, 18
Kurds, 15, 27–31, 33, 35, 44, 51–56, 60,
    63, 79, 120, 165, 170–172

Kuwait, 3, 14–15, 30, 52, 70–71, 112,
    114–117, 120–121, 129, 142
Kyoto Treaty, 93

Labor party (Britain), 105
Labor party (Israel), 102, 127
bin Ladin, Osama, 16, 30–32, 42, 57, 72,
    86, 96, 130–131
Lawrence of Arabia, 55
Le Pen, Jean-Marie, 101
Leadership Project, 95
Lebanon, 12, 27, 29–30, 34, 36, 52–53, 77,
    83, 109–110, 112, 125, 130, 162,
    165, 172–174, 178–179
Lebanon War, 29, 69, 119, 179
liberal internationalism, 14, 19, 42, 56,
    122, 155–157
Libya, 70, 112, 126, 149
Likud, 87, 102, 120, 127, 130, 175, 177,
    179

Mackinder, Halford J., 6–7
Madison, Angus, 169
Madrid Peace Conference, 16, 26, 29, 78,
    88, 112, 117, 120, 123
Maronite, 34–35, 174
Mars, 28, 95–98, 103, 107, 160, 178
Marshall, George, 178
Maud, F.S., 55
Mexico, 73–74, 165
Middle East, 1–23, 25–33, 35–40, 42–46,
    48, 50–51, 53–80, 82–89, 91–92,
    94–95, 99–100, 102–104, 106–126,
    129–143, 145–151, 153–180
    post–Cold War, 78–79, 106, 112
    tribal influences in, 13, 28–29, 33, 41,
        45, 51–52, 54–56, 79, 159, 170–172
Middle East Paradigm (MEP), 5–6, 9,
    11–12, 14–21, 23, 35, 40, 42–43, 56,
    59, 61, 64, 66–68, 71, 73–74, 76,
    84–88, 95, 103, 113, 124, 130, 132,
    138, 153–159
    American bureaucracy and, 66–69
    costs of, 12–13, 69–70, 73–76
    need for a new MEP, 21–23
military power, 46–48, 52, 64, 75, 87–89,
    93–96, 98, 103, 110–114, 122,
    133–145, 148–149, 156–158, 164,
    167, 171, 177